TWELVE CRIMES
THAT SHOCKED THE NATION

For Tom Sharp—
Vietnam veteran,
former Sydney detective and family man—
who found me my first job in 1980

TWELVE CRIMES
THAT SHOCKED THE NATION

ALAN J. WHITICKER

NEW HOLLAND

First published in Australia in 2005 by
New Holland Publishers (Australia) Pty Ltd
Sydney • Auckland • London • Cape Town

14 Aquatic Drive Frenchs Forest NSW 2086 Australia
218 Lake Road Northcote Auckland New Zealand
86 Edgware Road London W2 2EA United Kingdom
80 McKenzie Street Cape Town 8001 South Africa

10 9 8 7 6 5 4 3 2 1

National Library of Australia Cataloguing-in-Publication Data:

Whiticker, Alan.
Twelve crimes that shocked the nation.

Includes index.
ISBN 1 74110 110 7.

1. Crime - Australia - History. I. Title.

364.994

Publisher: Fiona Schultz
Managing Editor: Angela Handley
Editor: Glenda Downing
Designer: Karl Roper
Production: Linda Bottari
Printer: Griffin Press, Adelaide

This book was typeset in 11 pt Bembo

All photos are courtesy of News Ltd unless otherwise stated.

Contents

Acknowledgments

There are many people whom we would like to thank for their help in the writing and publishing of this book:

Fiona Schultz, Monica Ban, Angela Handley and Karl Roper at New Holland; Cheryl Yates at News Ltd; Mick McDonald, Russell Oxford, and my family and friends for their on-going support.

Introduction

Some crimes shock an entire nation, and in doing so define that nation forever. The 12 infamous crimes detailed in this book have become part of Australia's cultural landscape — among them Gatton, Pyjama Girl, Shark Arm, Brown-Out, Backpacker and Port Arthur — and each are now synonymous with our own criminal history. And when normal police methods fail to produce results, as in the Bogle and Chandler mystery, the Wanda Beach murders, the disappearance of the Beaumont children and, more recently, the Norfolk Island murder case, the crimes become part of our urban mythology, where fact and fiction are sometimes difficult to separate. But a deeper question needs to be asked: How do the recurring themes of the beach, the bush, our colonial past, social aspirations and the role of mass media reinforce the unique nature and context of these crimes?

The murders of Michael Murphy and his two sisters, Nora and Ellen, on the outskirts of the southwest Queensland township of Gatton on the night of 26 December 1898, shocked Brisbane, greater Queensland and then all of Australia. On that Boxing Day night, three members of the Murphy family were raped, shot and battered to death as they returned home in their horse and buggy from a dance that had been cancelled due to lack of numbers. The investigation into the murders was plagued by police incompetence, small-town prejudice and malicious gossip. The person or persons responsible for the Gatton murders were never brought to justice and the crime has since become part of Australian bush folklore.

Few more gruesome crimes have been played out under the gaze of the public eye than that of the Pyjama Girl, real name Linda Agostini. In 1934 the body of a young woman — badly burnt, viciously battered about the head and wearing only pyjamas — was found in a road culvert near the township of Albury. The case remained open for another 10 years, with Sydney detectives taking the extraordinary step of preserving the unidentified body in a lead-lined formalin bath. During that decade tens of thousands of people viewed the woman's ghastly remains at Sydney University, and later Sydney Police Headquarters, before the man responsible — the husband of the victim, Italian immigrant Tony Agostini — was brought to justice. Thus ended one of the most macabre murder investigations this country has seen.

While the remains of the Pyjama Girl were resting in a formalin bath, a bizarre event occurred on Anzac Day 1935, when a shark on display at the Coogee Palace Aquarium south of Sydney disgorged a human arm. After a series of sensational newspaper articles, and some clever forensic work from investigating detectives, the identity of the victim was revealed as that of small-time Sydney criminal James Smith. One of Smith's associates, forger Patrick Brady, was charged with the crime, but the subsequent murder of informant Reginald Holmes on the eve of the coronial inquest into Smith's death saw the investigation collapse. No-one was charged with the murders of Smith and Holmes — now known as the Shark Arm murders — a case that included the unlikely elements of a captured shark, a severed arm, Sydney's criminal underworld and smuggling on Sydney Harbour during the Depression.

In May 1942, the murder of three Melbourne women by an American soldier shocked the country at the height of the Second World War. The crimes were dubbed the 'Brown-Out' murders because they were committed at night when Melbourne was in the grip of strict regulations that required all windows to be covered and street and car lights dimmed. Although there was enough evidence to suggest that the murderer, 24-year-old Private Edward Joseph Leonski, was insane and should never have stood trial, the US Military took charge of the case and dealt with it expediently. For the first and only time in Australian criminal history a military tribunal was conducted by a foreign power on Australian soil. Leonski was never charged under Australian law for the offences he committed against Australian citizens and was executed at Melbourne's Pentridge Prison in November 1942.

It is interesting to note that many of these crimes involved immigrants in search of the 'Australian' dream — the Murphys were the offspring of proud Irish farmers; the Agostinis were Italian and English immigrants in search of a new life; James Smith was an Englishman who came to Australia to pursue his dream of becoming a world-class boxer. Another common thread was that many of these crimes were committed on public holidays — 'Gatton' on Boxing Day, 'Shark Arm' on Anzac Day, 'Bogle-Chandler' on New Year's Day and the 'Beaumont' disappearance on Australia Day — while most of the country was enjoying the hedonistic, easy-going lifestyle that has attracted millions of immigrants to these shores.

However, the 1960 kidnapping and murder of eight-year-old Graeme Thorne from his Bondi home was seen as an attack on Australia's very way of life. That the innocent boy's parents had recently won a £100 000 lottery only made the kidnapping even more offensive to the Australian public. The capture and subsequent trial of Stephen Bradley (a Hungarian immigrant, born Istavan Baranyay) was played out in the national media and fired up deep-seated xenophobia in conservative Australia. But the fundamental basis for community hatred was the fact that Bradley chose kidnapping and murder as his way to gain a foothold on the 'Australian dream' at the expense of the Thornes' good luck — resulting in the death of a little boy.

The deaths of Gilbert Bogle and Margaret Chandler on New Year's Day in 1963 have continued to fascinate and shock Australia for the past four decades. The fact that the deaths of Dr Bogle, a world-renowned New

Zealand physicist, and Margaret Chandler, the wife of one of Bogle's work colleagues, could not be explained using forensic technology at the time only fuelled speculation about likely scenarios, possible motives and potential suspects. At the very heart of the Bogle and Chandler case were the relaxed sexual mores of the victims and their associates in the context of conservative Australian society in the early 1960s. Investigators used every means to find the cause of their deaths — the FBI also maintained a file on the case — before advances in DNA technology began unlocking the secrets to their true fates.

The beach has always been an important part of the Australian identity, especially the explosion of youth culture in the 1960s. Two events involving Australian beaches, barely a year apart, have permanently scarred the national psyche. The 1965 rape and murder of West Ryde schoolgirls Christine Sharrock and Marianne Schmidt on a southern Sydney beach called Wanda sparked a media feeding frenzy. The abduction and probable murder of three South Australian children — Jane, Arnna and Grant Beaumont — from Glenelg Beach on Australia Day in 1966 has haunted Australia for almost 40 years. For as long as the Wanda Beach murders and the disappearance of the Beaumont children remain unsolved, the victims will always occupy a mythical place in Australian culture. For that alone, these crimes deserve to be solved.

The abduction, pack-rape and murder of Anita Cobby in February 1986 has been described as one of Australia's most shocking murders. Almost two decades after the body of the 26-year-old Sydney nurse was found in a paddock in Prospect, in western Sydney, the appalling details of the young woman's final hours continue to resonate in the wider Sydney community. The subsequent capture and trial of the five men responsible for Anita's death generated both fear and loathing within the community and led to the demonising of the perpetrators and calls for the return of the death penalty. But where such crimes at first impact negatively on a community, the murder of Anita Cobby and the subsequent example of her parents, Garry and Grace Lynch, have continued to shape community attitudes and behaviours that reconcile, empower and inspire the families of murder victims.

Introduction

Those of us who have grown up reading the poetry of 'Banjo' Paterson and singing colonial songs in primary school could be excused for having a romantic notion of life in 'the bush'. The cold reality is that life in the bush was traditionally harsh, often brutal and with the capacity to strip whole communities of people of their dignity. The bush has also been the scene of some of Australia's most vicious murders — many of them unsolved to this day. The abduction and murder of seven backpackers in the early 1990s and the subsequent discovery of their bodies in the Belanglo State Forest, 140 kilometres southwest of Sydney, made international headlines. Australia had been seen as a safe haven for domestic and overseas travellers — especially young people journeying away from home for the first time — but the crimes of Ivan Milat have changed that perception forever.

And as if we can't escape our convict heritage, the final two crimes in this book provide echoes from a time long since gone. The Port Arthur massacre of April 1996 may well go down in history as one of the world's worst peacetime atrocities. That this single act of madness by a lone gunman took place at a former penal settlement where brutality was once a daily way of life should not be lost on us as a nation. It is as if we are somehow still shackled to our past by invisible chains, never to be released. The as yet unsolved murder of mainlander Janelle Patton on Norfolk Island on Easter Sunday 2002 was committed in a tightly knit island community, again with convict origins. The public innuendo generated by the failure to bring the murderer or murderers to justice — and the dissection of Ms Patton's private life in the media — shows that in the hundred-odd years since the Gatton murders we have not come all that far.

Twelve Crimes That Shocked the Nation explores how certain crimes have become part of the Australian cultural landscape. These 12 crimes in particular have left an indelible mark on Australian society. More than that, our fascination and curiosity about them reveal a great deal more about us as a nation than we may care to know.

Chapter 1
The Gatton Murders (1898)

In the final days of 1898 Australian newspapers carried the story of 'one of the most horrible outrages ever reported in this colony'[1] carried out on a moonlit Boxing Day night in the small southern Queensland township of Gatton. The murders of Michael Murphy and his younger sisters, Ellen and Norah — three children of farmers Daniel and Mary Murphy of Blackfellow's Creek, Tenthill — polarised the Gatton community and ultimately shocked an entire nation. The failure to bring those responsible to justice has not only seen the 'Gatton Murders' become one of Australia's oldest and most intriguing unsolved crimes, it has become an integral part of bush folklore.

On 26 December 1898 most of the population of Gatton, 90 kilometres west of Brisbane and 25 kilometres east of Toowoomba, visited the Boxing Day horserace meeting at nearby Mount Sylvia. That night the annual 'Bannerman's Dance' had been organised in Gatton, but there was talk at the races that it was on the verge of being cancelled because of a lack of numbers. Most of the Murphy clan had been at the races that day and had been invited to the dance that night. After returning home for supper, Michael, aged 29, rigged up a two-wheel buggy belonging to his brother-in-law, Bill McNeil, and drove his two sisters into Gatton at around 8 pm in clear moonlight. They arrived in town to learn the dance was cancelled, and, without stopping to talk to anyone, turned their buggy around and headed back to Tenthill shortly after 9 pm.

When the Murphys did not return home that night, Bill McNeil rode into Gatton the next morning to inquire after them on behalf of his concerned in-laws. About 2 kilometres along the Tenthill Road into Gatton he noticed wheel tracks turning off across the road and into a paddock belonging to a neighbour. Although the sliprails bordering the paddock were secured in place, McNeil saw that the wheel tracks belonged to his buggy — the left wheel did not run straight and made a distinctive wobbly pattern. McNeil lowered the rails, thinking that at the end of the old timber track he would find a homestead where the Murphys may have stayed due to some unforeseen circumstance. Instead, following the tracks of his buggy through thick scrub to a clearing near a culvert, he discovered the bodies of his three in-laws, with their horse lying dead beside his trap.

On the way into Gatton to raise the alarm McNeil encountered a local man, Charles Gilbert, who later told police that McNeil was in a very excited state. Gilbert said that McNeil quickly volunteered that 'the three Murphys are lying dead out in a paddock. There must have been an accident as the horse is dead too.'[2]

While the Murphys' brother-in-law continued his journey into Gatton, Charles Gilbert yoked his horse to a buggy and started out for where McNeil had said the bodies lay. When McNeil told the local sergeant Bill Arrell what he had found, Arrell immediately recalled seeing the Murphys on the road into Gatton the previous night. Arrell had also been to the Mount Sylvia races and was riding the track into Gatton with a friend when they encountered a man on horseback talking to three others in a sulky. It was another sibling, Patrick 'Paddy' Murphy, on horseback and the sergeant assumed that the three people in the buggy must have been the victims, just hours before meeting their fate.

'Do you think the horse bolted and smashed them up?' the sergeant asked. No, McNeil didn't think so. The horse was a quiet, old horse.

By the time Sergeant Arrell and McNeil arrived at the place in the road known as Moran's Sliprails, Charles Gilbert was waiting there and had been joined by a number of other locals. The sliprails across the entrance to the paddock were lying on the ground and it was clear that a buggy had driven over the rails on entering the paddock. When Arrell and McNeil led their horses on foot down the circular track they were once again heading back up towards the roadway. Once over the culvert, the wheel tracks veered off the course to the right — making a track where there was no track, Arrell would later say — and down a ridge to a clearing just as McNeil had described.

McNeil identified the three bodies lying on the ground as Michael, Ellen and Norah Murphy. Norah's body was lying on its right side on a rug, which was neatly spread out, some 10 metres away from the other bodies and partly concealed behind a tree trunk. Sergeant Arrell could see a large wound on the left side of her head 'about 4 inches [10 centimetres] long and about 3 inches [7 centimetres] wide', he later wrote, 'and of a concave shape.'[3] Her head and face were lying in a pool of blood, and a hat that had been fastened to her hair with a hatpin was lying nearby on the ground. The girl's hands were tied behind her back with a white handkerchief. Her white blouse, which was fastened at the band around her waist, was torn and pulled up around her neck. Arrell also noticed a leather strap fastened tightly around her neck. A black corset she was wearing was unloosened at the back and the black skirt she had on was pulled up 'a good way on her body at the back'. Her black and red petticoat was down on her knees.

Arrell saw that Norah was wearing black stockings and leather shoes and that her left leg was thrown across her right one. When the police sergeant lifted up her clothing and examined her undergarments he noticed there were a 'great many scratch marks on the inside of each thigh as if done by fingernails'. He also saw that the elder of the two girls still had on her drawers but because they were large and loose they could easily have been pushed up. Arrell did not see any blood on her underclothing but noted that the drawers were 'quite damp' and that there was a stain on them 'like a thick starch fluid'.

Sergeant Arrell then went to the body of the youngest victim, Ellen, lying on her side some 10 metres away from Norah with her back to her brother Michael, whose body was about 30 centimetres away from her. While Ellen's clothing did not immediately appear to be disarranged, Arrell could see that her light-coloured blouse and black shirt were pulled up slightly above her knees. He could see without touching her that Ellen's hands were also tied behind her back, her hat was lying nearby and she had a similar head wound to that of her sister, on the left side of her head. When Arrell examined the girl's undergarments of white cotton petticoat, white cotton drawers and white chemise he found dark red bloodstains on all three garments. As he lifted Ellen's petticoat he could see a 'thick, starchy fluid' inside the legs of the drawers near the top. As was the case with her sister, there were scratch marks on the inside of both of Ellen's thighs 'right up to her private parts'. It was later determined after discussions with the Murphy family that Ellen was menstruating at the time but Norah was not.

Michael Murphy's body was lying almost parallel to that of Ellen. While Arrell examined the bodies of the two girls, Gilbert and the other men had walked all around the crime scene — Arrell had forgotten to tell the others to stay away. There was a large leather breeching strap lying on the ground nearby but Arrell could not determine if it had been moved or not. The strap had more than likely been used to tie Michael's hands behind his back, although his hands were no longer tied.

Arrell saw a large wound on the right side of Michael's head — concave, 10 centimetres by 7 centimetres — the same as the two sisters. A soft felt hat was lying about 60 centimetres away with dark bloodstains on it. Michael's hands, which were bent backwards at the palms, held an open purse with nothing in it. Arrell noticed some dead timber lying near Michael's head with spots of blood on it. Less than a metre from Norah's head he noticed a mark on the ground as if a piece of timber, about a metre long, had been lying there for some time. It was now missing.

The buggy belonging to McNeil was standing 6 metres from where the bodies of Ellen and Michael lay. The horse was lying on its right side on top of the right buggy shaft, which had been broken by the weight of the dead animal falling on it. There was a wound on the horse's forehead — a small round hole made by a bullet — and a pool of blood. The reins were neatly curled round the horse's bit but the breeching strap was missing.

Arrell formed the opinion that the three Murphy children had been murdered where they lay — it was as if their heads had been violently driven into the ground by the blows that had killed them. From the evidence of bark and branches broken off by the wheels of the buggy, it was clear that the trio were brought into the paddock against their will — and in some haste — probably at gunpoint. The Gatton sergeant told the group of bystanders that he would wire the commissioner in Brisbane to inform him of what had happened and ask him to send blacktrackers. Arrell would also have to send for a doctor to examine the bodies. He asked two locals — Messrs Wilson (a magistrate for the colony of Queensland) and Devitt — to guard the scene while he returned to town.

When Sergeant Arrell returned to the murder scene later that morning he found between 30 and 40 people milling around the bodies, including the parents of the victims. Bill McNeil, who had not stayed longer than five minutes at the crime scene with Arrell, had returned with them and Reverend Father Walsh. Mrs Murphy was praying at the head of the body of her daughter Norah while Messrs Wilson and Devitt kept the others at a distance of 10 metres. Mrs Murphy pleaded with Sergeant Arrell to allow the bodies to be moved out of the sun and away from the ants now crawling over them but he told them that he was waiting for the doctor to arrive. When other locals also asked for the bodies to be removed, Arrell finally relented — against his better judgment — and had the bodies taken to Gatton.

That afternoon Dr W. Stury von Lossberghger arrived from Ipswich at 4 o'clock and was taken to the Brian Boru Hotel, where the bodies of the victims were being stored. During the post-mortem examinations, Arrell saw that the strap around Norah's neck was in fact the 36 centimetre hames strap that was missing from the dead horse's harness 'placed on with one turn drawn tightly through the buckle and fastened with a half hitch', he noted. In his official report Von Lossbergher stated that:

> The body of Michael Murphy: compound comminuted [sic] fracture of the frontal, parietal and occipital bones, likewise fracture base of the scull [sic]. A thick paste of dark blood on the right side of the throat and neck, after cleaning it found a small wound behind the lower part of the right ear, in which I could introduce my finger in a channel 3 inches [7 centimetres] long. I considered it a course of a bullet, but could not find it. The scull [sic] was completely smashed ... I believe he was killed first of the three.[4]

However, the autopsies were abruptly ended when Lossbergher injured his finger in searching for the bullet in the wound behind Michael's ear. A newspaper report in the *Darling Downs Gazette* the following January reported that 'Dr W.V. Lossberg' [sic] recollected that '[Ellen] was in an erect position when struck'.[5] He concluded from the examination that 'the girl [Ellen] was a virgin ... Norah showed symptoms inwardly such as Ellen of being outraged ...with regard to Michael Murphy ... stated positively that the bullet was in the head but had no exit ... the fracture of the skull of Michael Murphy took place after death, because there was no blood there.'

When Sergeant Arrell returned to the scene of the murders a local man handed him a piece of wood, weather-beaten on one side as if exposed to the elements for a long time and about 1 metre in length. At the knotty end of the stick there was blood and hair, and when Arrell placed it in the indentation near where Norah lay, it fit perfectly. He concluded that it was the murder weapon. The throat lash of the bridle of the harness was later found in a paddock about 800 metres from the scene of the murder by Supernumerary Constable Portley. The animal's carcass was later boiled and a bullet retrieved with the same .38 calibre as a cartridge case found near the horse's body.

Mysteriously, a newspaper clipping was also found at the scene. It was of an obituary of Mary Cooke, a friend of Ellen's who had died of blood poisoning the previous year. Detectives assumed that the year-old clipping was a keepsake of Ellen's in memoriam of her friend. And one other odd piece of the puzzle — Michael Murphy had left home with a horsewhip but none was found at the crime scene. The whip had been a Christmas gift to Norah from her brother-in-law Bill McNeil. Where was it?

Some of the locals who used the road between Tenthill and Gatton that night told of seeing the silhouette of a man standing beside the sliprails. Although nearly all the residents of Gatton knew each other, no-one at first could identify who it was. Local man Thomas Drew informed police that the mystery man 'was about five feet eight or nine inches [about 154 centimetres] ... he was thickset'.[6] Margaret Carroll saw the man pass the Murphys while they were on their way into Gatton and watched as he turned and looked in the direction that they were going. At the bottom of her police statement Carroll wrote, 'P.S. The man I saw had something in his hand.'[7] Albert Murray, like Sergeant Arrell, said that he had seen Paddy Murphy talking to his brother and sisters that night. It was about 9.30 and Paddy was on his way into Gatton as the other Murphys were returning home to Tenthill.

The subsequent murder investigation was headed by Sub-Inspector Fred Urquhart of the Brisbane Criminal Investigation Branch. The Brisbane CIB had just been set up and was more suited to handling horse theft and cattle duffing, while Urquhart's career before becoming a detective was mainly as a 'native' policeman in the Queensland bush. Urquhart later lamented that 'tracks and traces of the murders had all been obliterated at the scene of the murder by crowds of people who had passed all over the ground'.[8]

By the last day of 1898, police concluded that the 'post mortem examination of the bodies had been unsatisfactory' and the possibility of exhuming the freshly interned bodies was discussed. (The bodies of the three Murphys had been hastily buried on 27 December — the day after their discovery — because of rapid decomposition in the Queensland summer heat.) On 3 January a £1000 reward was posted in the Brisbane *Telegraph*. The following day the bodies of the victims were exhumed and the 'superficiality of the first post mortem' was quickly demonstrated. A .38 calibre bullet was extracted from the head of Michael Murphy, and, to stem the flow of careless talk, it was reiterated that the girls were not pregnant.

The two initial suspects of the crime were Bill McNeil, who had found the bodies, and Thomas Joseph Ryan, who was described as a 'drover of somewhat drunken and disreputable habits'. Thomas Ryan was known to be a disappointed suitor of Polly Murphy, the wife of Bill McNeil. However, there was nothing to link Ryan with the murders. Of McNeil, Sub-Inspector Urquhart later hastily concluded, 'it is now clear that if he is connected with the crime it must be with the knowledge of at least the senior members of the Murphy family who must be shielding him'. McNeil aroused suspicion because he displayed 'considerable activity' in advertising the fact that he was scouring the countryside looking for clues. McNeil, who had been visiting his in-laws that Christmas with his wife Polly, who was recovering from a stroke after giving birth to her second child, had not been seen after 9 pm on the night the Murphys drove into Gatton.

There was obvious tension between Urquhart, an Englishman, and the Murphys, who were Irish. 'What I did not foresee and could not have believed existed had I not seen them,' Urquhart declared at the subsequent magisterial inquiry, 'were the nerveless apathy and wooden indifference not only of the people of the district generally but of the grown up male members of the Murphy family in particular.'

At the time of the murders the humble Murphy homestead was home to parents Daniel Snr and Mary, Bill, aged 31, Michael (29), Norah (27), Jeremiah (20), Ellen (18), John (15) and Katie (13). Bill McNeil was married to the eldest sister of the deceased, Polly (32), while two other children, Paddy (Patrick) and Daniel, lived away from home. Paddy had returned home for Christmas but when Daniel Murphy was contacted where he worked as a police constable in Roma he remarked, 'Oh it must have been some member of the family that done it.'[9]

Public infighting among the family did not present the Murphys in the best of lights. On one occasion in Toowoomba the mother accused her daughter Polly of being 'a whore'. 'You streetwalker; you lay in the dirt with McNeil before he married you ... The McNeils are worse than Chinamen,' she was quoted as saying. Other avenues for the police to investigate included disputes with the neighbouring Moran family regarding the price of building a fence, and even 'old scores' settled from way back in the family history in Ireland from 40 years before.

There was no evidence to suggest that these motives had any basis in fact. The police took great pains to state that these assumptions were 'a monstrous attack on the unblemished characters of a Catholic family who had lived in the district their whole lives'.[10] The public perceptions of the case were founded on 'strained inferences drawn from circumstances of which the more natural explanations have to be ignored in order to concoct a hideous tangle of incest, fratricide and unnatural barbarity by the light of common sense is sufficient to destroy ...'

Several of the colonies, especially New South Wales and Queensland, were going through a depression in the 1890s and country roads were inundated with 'swagmen' — itinerant workers and the homeless walking the roads looking for work — and quickly, their caste came under suspicion. Richard Burgess, who was discharged from Brisbane prison on 30 November after serving a six-month sentence for indecent assault of an old woman at Leyburn, was described as 'born to be hanged'[11] and was known to police as a petty thief and assaulter of women. On 6 January, Burgess was arrested in Dalby and was charged with 'complicity' in the Gatton murders.

Although his whereabouts could not be confirmed during the period of 10 to 26 December, the linking of Burgess to another murder in Oxley on 10 December (both Oxley and Gatton were on the swagman's route from Brisbane) was enough to implicate him. A 15-year-old boy, Alfred Hill, was murdered in a paddock, sexually assaulted and his horse shot with a .38 calibre gun. Hill's body was not found until 6 January 1899, but the similarities with the Gatton murders were obvious. Although Burgess could not say where he was on Boxing Day, there was nothing to link him to the Gatton crime and he was sent back to Toowoomba, charged with vagrancy and jailed for two months.

It was later determined that Burgess was in Greenmount on 26 and 27 December — some four hours away by horse. It was pointed out that a bushman of Burgess's experience could have made the journey to Gatton on horseback — it may have even explained the absence of Murphy's whip from the murder scene. Burgess, it was argued, could have used it on the return leg of his journey. But Burgess was in his forties at the time; only 167 centimetres tall and of a thickset build. The shadowy figure seen by locals standing near the sliprails could have been as tall as 'a full five feet ten inches' (178 centimetres) and 'a young, overgrown feller'. Who was that man?

It was surmised by police that a man standing beside the sliprails on the left-hand side of the Tenthill Road on the top of a sandy ridge could command a view, backwards and forwards, of about a kilometre each way in the clear moonlight. He would have even had the sliprails down already as he waited for his victims. More than likely the murderer had bailed up the Murphys as the old horse struggled up the ridge and walking alongside them, instructed Michael to turn off into the paddock, ostensibly to rob them. After tying the girls' hands with handkerchiefs, and Michael's hands with the breeching strap, he separated Norah from the others to rape her. He may have shot the horse first to warn the victims that there was no easy getaway. The murderer laid out the Murphys' rug from the buggy on the ground before assaulting Norah and would have taken the hame strap with him in anticipation of her screaming out. Maybe she did.

Louisa Thauerkauf, a local girl working at Clarke's nearby property testified to hearing screams just after 10 pm that night. And maybe it alerted Michael to loosen the strap around his hands before the murderer came over and shot him too. Perhaps the original intention was just to rape Norah and leave the three of them tied up in the paddock. But Norah's screams were silenced by a blow to her head and Michael's struggle was stopped by a single gunshot, before the double murderer turned his attention to Ellen, who was menstruating. Her fate would be the same as the others.

After killing the three siblings, the murderer rearranged the bodies for his own satisfaction — curiously, the legs of the victims were crossed over each other so they pointed to the west. On closer 'microscopic' examination by Dr A.W. Orr, it was found that an impression made in the bloodstain on Ellen Murphy's petticoat was a pattern of moleskin or corduroy material. Maybe a match could be made with a piece of clothing from Burgess, McNeil, or even the Murphys for that matter. Orr made one more startling discovery — Michael Murphy had a semen stain on the fly of his trousers.

This in itself was enough to set tongues wagging. Was Michael Murphy having intimate relationships with his sisters? Had the murderer, a sexual pervert, ordered the male member of the Murphy family to perpetrate one last sexual act on one of his sisters with a gun held to his head before he was shot? Like the poor lad found dead in a paddock in Oxley just two weeks before, was Michael also sexually assaulted? One possible explanation should have been obvious to the country folk of Gatton — even dumb animals have been known to involuntarily ejaculate after they have been bludgeoned to death.

The matter of incest, however, was even raised by the judge and Daniel Murphy was forced to deny the allegation at the magisterial inquiry. But it must be remembered that a gunman was in control of the situation from the beginning, not Michael Murphy. The 29-year-old was a special constable, and said to be one of the smartest men in the Gatton Mounted Infantry. No, the Murphys must have been decoyed into the paddock, or just bailed up at the end of a gun. But the murder weapon, a .38 calibre pistol, was never found nor linked to any suspect. That in itself is not surprising — these were colonial times and there was a lot of uncharted country in which to hide a gun.

While the magisterial inquiry failed to name the murderer, at the subsequent Royal Commission into the crime Acting Sergeant Toomey identified the man at the sliprails as Thomas Day, a swagman who had obtained a position with the local butcher, John Clarke, on 15 December. It was the son of a local family who identified the man behind the shadowy silhouette standing by the sliprails on that Boxing Day night as 'Clarke's man'. Mr Burnett, the local fruiterer, told police that on two occasions between 15 and 26 December he had met Thomas Day on the road near Moran's Sliprails. Clarke also told investigating police that Day had the peculiar habit of sleeping fully dressed with his boots on, and that is how police found him when they visited Day as he rested in a skillion room adjoining Clarke's stables on 30 December.

When questioned by Toomey, the 21-year-old Thomas Day stated that he was in bed on the night of the murders. Despite the fact that Clarke had a fireworks show on that Boxing Day night between 8 and 9 pm, Day was not seen by any other person that night. Toomey found bloodstains on one of Day's jumpers, but the suspect told him that it was from his job as a butcher. Although Toomey failed to place Day 'on the road' that night, he and his colleagues continued to watch Day during the following week. Although told not to by Toomey and Clarke, Thomas Day scrubbed the jumper clean and washed it the day after he was questioned.

On 10 January, Day left Clarke's employment after an argument in which it was alleged that the young man threatened to kill Clarke. When questioned by police shortly before his departure, Day informed them that he was 'going up the line looking for work'.[12] Incredibly, police gave Day a rail ticket to Toowoomba and asked him if he could identify Burgess and place him anywhere between Brisbane and Gatton at the time of the murder. Day later reported to police that he could not and by the time Burgess was cleared as a suspect it was too late — Day had vanished into the Queensland bush. Day did not give evidence at either the magisterial inquiry or the Royal Commission and investigating detectives heard that he had joined the military, enlisted in the Boer War and had been killed. Day was never heard of again.

The naming of Thomas Day as a major suspect might never have happened. Acting Sergeant Toomey and Sergeant Arrell stated at the Royal Commission that they were under enormous pressure from Inspector Urquhart not to name Day — 'a mere boy', their superior maintained — as the murderer. The two sergeants could not even appeal to the commissioner in Brisbane about their concerns — it had to go through Urquhart. The inspector was known to be a proud, obstinate man, and had Burgess pencilled in as the identity of the 'mystery man' from the outset. Urquhart's reputation was at stake and no acting sergeant was going to upstage him.

In the end, no suspect was ever committed to trial. The Gatton task force was disbanded after five months and the police reassigned to other cases in Brisbane. A Royal Commission into the Gatton Murders was later critical of the police investigation. 'Sufficiently exhaustive investigations were not made,' it concluded.[13]

The Gatton murders became the subject of urban myth, passed down and enhanced by swagmen and travellers, and fuelled by pub talk over the generations. 'Old man Murphy' caught the son 'rooting' the two sisters, the story went. The Boxing Day dance had been cancelled and the lad steered the trap off into a paddock outside Gatton on purpose. But the father knew what was going on and had followed them, murdered the three of them and shot the sulky horse to draw attention away from him.

Since the early twentieth century the story of the Gatton murders has been told and retold in country gazettes and national newspapers. In 1907 Arthur Davies — better known as 'Steele Rudd', the author of the 'Dad and Dave' series — published *For Life*, a fictional account based on the unsolved Gatton crime. Davies had been a reporter on the original investigation before coming to Sydney and making his reputation. Queensland barristers James and Desmond Gibney published *The Gatton Mystery* — a clinical, forensic account of the crime and the subsequent police investigation. Recently, Queensland writer Stephanie Bennett wrote *The Gatton Murders*, a social history of the crime in which the murders are linked to revenge killings for gang rapes of which Michael Murphy was allegedly involved. But Bennett did not explore the most obvious suspect — Thomas Day.

Blue Mountains writer Merv Lilley in his book *Gatton Man* wrote that the 'thoroughness and neatness of the killings bespoke a powerful mind, if not a sane one — a mind too good for the local constabulary — a mind trained in orderliness ... a chameleon of a man in action — brutish, fast, self-protective, a machine of speed and some peculiar madness'.[14] Although the Gatton murders took place 21 years before Lilley's birth in 1919, he has no doubt that the murderer was his father, William John Lilley, who was born in Dorset in 1857.

Described as a sexual pervert and sadist by his son, Merv Lilley states that his father was 'Clarke's man', Thomas Day. The pseudonym William Lilley had chosen as a 21-year-old was a combination of his father's name, Thomas, and the surname of a well-known horse trainer in Dorset in the mid-1850s. Another name Lilley was known to use in his wanderings in southwest Queensland at the beginning of the last century, 'Thomas Wilson', was the name of the major landowner in Dorset when Day immigrated with his family to Australia in the late 1880s.

According to the Lilley family, William Lilley served in the Queensland Imperial Bushmen during the Boer War and stayed in South Africa for

10 years after the war 'hunting blacks for the government'.[15] Lilley Snr returned to Australia, raised a family — terrorising and assaulting them — and revealed only snippets of his past that could link him to the Gatton murders. His wife and eldest daughter carried the secret under threat of death until Lilley died in the late 1950s and it was finally left to his son, Merv, to write his father's epitaph.

On a gravestone in a Gatton cemetery there is a fading reminder of the long-forgotten crime:

In Memory
of
Michael, Aged 29 years
Norah, Aged 27 years
Ellen, Aged 18 years
The dearly beloved children of
DANIEL and MARY MURPHY
of Tenthill,
who were the victims of a horrible
tragedy perpetrated near Gatton
on December 26th, 1898
REQUIESCAT IN PACE

The final irony of a vicious, unsolved crime that had provided so much public fodder in the early years of last century is the inscription at the base of the obelisk, faded and tarnished by the decades that have passed since their deaths:

This Monument has been erected by public
subscription to the memory of the
above innocent victims.

Chapter 2

The Pyjama Girl Murder (1934)

In 1934 the body of a young woman — badly burnt, viciously battered about the head and wearing only pyjamas — was found in a road culvert in the township of Albury on the New South Wales–Victoria border. Thus commenced one of the most macabre murder investigations this country has seen. The case remained open for another 10 years until the man responsible was brought to trial, but the fate of the unknown girl was never far from public consciousness. Sydney police reconstructed the dead woman's features and made composite drawings of what she may have looked like in life, but also took the extraordinary step of preserving the body in a lead-lined formalin bath. During the next decade, tens of thousands of people viewed the ghastly remains at Sydney University, and later at Sydney Police Headquarters, before it was positively identified as English immigrant Linda Agostini (nee Platt).

On the morning of Saturday, 1 September 1934 — the first day of the southern hemisphere's spring — Charles Griffiths was travelling into

Albury along Howlong Road. Griffiths had left his stud property, *Delaware*, some 9 kilometres outside the tiny township, in his motor vehicle with his 23-year-old son Tom, to pick up a young shorthorn bull that had won a prize at the Holbrook Show. The plan was to meet the man bringing the bull back from the showgrounds at the halfway mark and for Tom Griffiths to walk the bull back the 5 kilometres to the property. Griffiths senior, who was also the manager of the Dalgety & Co Ltd's stock and station agency in Albury, took charge of the bull at about 8 am and the younger Griffiths started the journey home in brisk sunshine with the road washed clean by overnight rain.

To save wear on the animal's feet on the hard road, Tom Griffiths allowed the bull to stroll on the grassy edge on the north side of the road. Seven kilometres out from Albury, and about 2 kilometres from his property, he noticed something protruding from a brick drain that ran under the gravel road that at first appeared to be a bag of rags. As he approached the culvert he caught the putrid odour of burnt flesh and petrol. Although there was a cloth bag fitted over the head and shoulders, Griffiths could see that it was the body of a woman wearing pyjamas curled up in a foetal position. She was lying on her right side with her feet still in the culvert.

So shocked was Griffiths by the discovery that he immediately tied the bull to a fence post, commandeered a bicycle ridden by a young boy, and rode the remainder of the way back to his family's property. There he phoned the police in Albury and then returned to the culvert, where he was met by his father. Three officers from Albury arrived at the scene in their Morris Cowley tourer, with Inspector Goodsell in charge. The Griffiths, who knew the three police officers well, showed them where the body lay. Before they examined the body the police decided to photograph the scene and send for the local coroner.

Some time later Constable William Kelly returned with Mr C.W. Swiney, the district's police magistrate and coroner, and Albury GP Dr Leslie Woods, who was quickly seconded to act as the government medical officer. While in Albury, Kelly arranged for an ambulance to go to the scene and obtained a camera. After taking several pictures of the woman's body *in situ*, Mr Swiney and Dr Woods briefly examined it before Kelly lifted it into the back of the ambulance, where it was driven to the mortuary at Albury District Hospital.

The police could see from the smoke stains inside the drainpipe that the fire had been lit after the body was placed in the culvert. Water was trickling through the drain after the recent rain and oil stains had formed in a puddle of water 20 metres away in the adjoining paddock, which, ironically, was part of the Griffiths' property. A solitary tyre mark was found in the grass on the northern side of the road, but the wet conditions did not allow a plaster cast to be made from it.

Dr Woods conducted his first examination of the body later that day at Albury District Hospital. The sack placed over the head of the body was typical of the type used for bagging fruit in the Riverina area. He removed the remains of the burned sack from the upper torso to reveal the head wrapped in a white towel. Although the towel had protected the head from fire damage, when it was removed the full extent of the woman's shocking head injuries was revealed. There were eight lineal cuts on the left side of the head and the temple area had a gaping wound that exposed the skull and brain tissue. The woman's facial features, including her pronounced dental features, were swollen and misshapen from the effects of her skull being shattered. There was also a small puncture wound under the right eye that the doctor believed could have been caused by a bullet.

The Albury GP then cut away the burnt remains of the pyjamas from the woman's body. The pyjamas were made from a material known as 'Canton crepe'; the coat was canary yellow and the pants were white with yellow edges. A silk oriental design was worked into the material on the front of the coat. The body was in a state of rigor mortis with the knees bent up towards the chin and the arms wrapped up around the head. While the surface of the woman's entire torso and the limbs were scorched and covered in blisters, the left arm, buttocks and the soles of the feet were the areas most severely consumed by the fire.

Dr Woods stated that the woman was aged between 25 and 30 years. Her hair was dark blonde and in a bobbed style and the eyebrows pencilled in, as was the fashion of those times. Her eyes were wrongly described as blue or grey (they were in fact hazel), her teeth were prominent and her ears were of an unusual shape — they had no lobes and there was an indentation on the top rim of each ear. The woman also had exceptionally large hands and her short legs were out of proportion to the rest of her body.

A hurried telephone conference between NSW Police Commissioner Bill Childs and head of the Sydney CIB, Detective Inspector Prior, resulted in two Sydney detectives, Detective Sergeant Frank Allmond and Detective Constable McDermott, being sent to Albury on Sunday morning to take over the murder investigation. Dr Woods then performed a more thorough post-mortem examination of the body. Local inquiries ruled out that the person came from Albury (a man even came to the morgue late on Saturday night to see if it was his sister-in-law) and the primary focus of the Sydney detectives remained to determine who she was.

The autopsy, which was conducted in the presence of the Sydney officers, revealed an extensive brain injury underneath the large wound on the forehead. The skull was also fractured on the left side of the head under the lacerations but it was not until two days later that Dr Woods located the bullet with the use of X-ray. The .25 calibre bullet was lodged in the left side of the neck about 2 centimetres below the skull. Dr Woods was of the opinion that cause of death was most likely due to the skull fracture and laceration to the brain rather than the gunshot wound (the fact that the woman had been shot was not revealed to the public until the inquest in 1938). Because rigor mortis had already set in, the time of death was put between one and four days before the body was found on 1 September.

News of the grisly find swept Albury and then reached all the way to Sydney and Melbourne. Tom Griffiths later recalled that 35 newspapers contacted him for an interview on the day the body was found but the following day his father kept reporters at bay until his son returned from working the property and held a press conference on the front lawn of the family house.

By Sunday evening the Melbourne *Herald* and the Sydney *Sun* newspapers reached Albury with news of the grisly find. From the first day the story broke it was referred to as 'The Pyjama Girl' murder. *The Sun* led its Sunday, 2 September, headline with:

Pyjama Girl: Body Charred in Culvert
Albury Murder Mystery Revealed
Battered then Soaked in Oil
Head Wrapped in Towel
Tell-tale Car Marks

> [Her] forehead cruelly battered in, legs and lower part of the abdomen charred to a black mass, but clothed in white and yellow pyjamas, the body of a pretty girl of about 20 was found yesterday in a culvert on the Howlong Road about four miles [6 kilometres] from Albury.[1]

But identifying the woman — at a time when, at the height of the Depression, many young women were looking for work or attached themselves to men who were displaced and travelling interstate — was not going to be easy. The Albury newspaper, *The Border Morning Mail*, published the following description of her:

> Between twenty and thirty years of age; five feet two or three inches [about 159 centimetres] in height; slim to medium build; blue grey eyes; plucked eyebrows; light brown hair darker at the roots (may have been peroxided or bleached): fingernails manicured to a point and lacquered pink; two teeth missing from the right lower jaw, and the back tooth of the lower jaw gold filled — rest of the teeth natural and in good condition.[2]

The reference to the woman's teeth proved crucial to solving the case. On Monday, 3 September, and the following Wednesday, 5 September, local dentist Dr F.H. Jackson extracted six teeth from the dead woman's mouth at the Albury morgue. The lower right second molar and upper second molar were filled with gold inlay, which was unusual for the times (the other four were filled with amalgam). A plaster model of the dead woman's mouth was made and the extracted teeth then placed in the model so they could be photographed in the hope that this dental work could be used to discover her identity.

Police learned that at 2.30 am on Tuesday, 29 August, Mr Bern Miley was returning in his car from a dance at Brocklesby when he saw a fire burning in the culvert where the body was found four days later. Heavy rain that night prevented the body being consumed by the flames. Police surmised that whoever hid the body in the culvert did so quickly because the pipe was big enough to conceal the whole corpse but only the back half was inserted. The openness of the drain, situated on a public road as it was, also suggested that whoever hid the body had no local knowledge of the area.

Rumours swept Albury that the murder was linked to the underworld (a St Kilda woman, Jean McKenzie, had recently been battered to death in Melbourne), but there were no fingerprint records for the woman on file in Albury, or in Sydney or Melbourne for that matter. Rumours began to overwhelm the case: a local man was about to be arrested for the crime, locals said; another man was convinced that it was his wife, who had recently run off with another man, and even identified the body until police located his estranged wife and her new lover living in a nearby town; poison pen letters pointed the finger at the Griffiths — Tom in particular — forcing the family to demand a public inquest. The inquest would be a long time coming.

The woman's body was packed in ice and kept on display at Albury Hospital. On 13 September, with the body now over two weeks old, police sent for embalmers from Kinsella & Son Funeral Homes and took the unusual step of embalming the body so that it could be kept on show until identified. However, when a woman viewing the body fainted at the sight of it, police decided to have newspaper sketch artists reconstruct her features and publish a likeness in the newspaper. The sketched image originally published in *The Sun* on Tuesday, 2 September, bore little resemblance to the then unknown woman's real identity but the painting completed at the end of the week captured the woman's mouth features perfectly. Later, police made a cast of the woman's face (covering up the gash in her forehead with plaster) and applied make-up to it to make it more lifelike. But still there was no breakthrough.

At the end of the first week, Detective Sergeant T.W. McRae was sent to join the investigation from Wagga Wagga and Detective Sergeant H. Carey, from Melbourne's CIB in Russell Street, was restationed in Albury's sister town, Wodonga, to assist in the investigation. Police assumed that, because the woman was wearing pyjamas, she may have been murdered in her sleep and if the sighting on Wednesday night was correct, that she could have been transported during the night by car from as far as 80 to 110 kilometres away — the distance from Melbourne. Sydney, which was 10 hours away by car at the time, was ruled out as being too far for concealment, considering that it would have required travel in daylight hours.

By 13 September, 350 women in Sydney, Melbourne and the Albury area who matched the general description of the woman were identified as 'missing'. By the end of the month copies of the woman's sketched image, as well as the post-mortem photo of the woman's face, were sent all over Australia and ultimately New Zealand. Inquiries made of hundreds of dental surgeries in Melbourne and Sydney failed to provide any information about the woman's unique dental work or her identity. A movie 'short' of the investigation was later shot and shown in local cinemas. The dead woman's description was also circulated on all commercial ships that frequented Australian ports during the 1930s. Not even the investigation of the origins of the towel found wrapped around the woman's head — with its distinctive red borders — could reveal any clues to her identity.

On 12 October, the Pyjama Girl's body was transported to Sydney University, where it was put on display and studied by anatomical experts to see if the academic community could provide the key that unlocked her identity. Morbid images of the woman, submerged in her formalin bath *post-mortem*, were ultimately sent to 87 police organisations in some 80 countries, including England's famous Scotland Yard. Within six months of the investigation police had reportedly conducted 'five thousand separate inquiries'.[3] But still the question remained: Who was she?

The first public 'naming' of the victim's possible identity occurred when Lydia Bagley of the Sydney suburb of Newtown informed police that the woman could be 'Beryl Cashmere'. The previous July the two Sydney women had gone to Albury looking for work but Beryl Cashmere had taken off with a man in Wangaratta (77 kilometres south of Albury). Bagley said that the photos looked very much like her friend and when police investigated the whereabouts of Cashmere, the trail went cold two days before the body was found. It was later discovered that Cashmere had split with the man and her failure to come forward during the Pyjama Girl investigation was put down to the fact that she did not want to reveal her whereabouts.

But once the body was displayed in Sydney a number of people, including a Kings Cross police sergeant and his wife, informed police that the woman looked like the English-born wife of former Italian immigrant Tony Agostini. The Agostinis had moved to Melbourne in 1934 and on 25 July the following year Senior Detective Frank Unwin Simpson from Melbourne CIB visited the Italian immigrant at his home in Carlton. Simpson asked Agostini if he had married a woman named Linda Platt. He had, Agostini told the detective, but in about the middle of last August the pair had some 'domestic differences' and she had left him. Linda had gone back to her job as a hairdresser on one of the boats of the Union Steamship Company, Agostini maintained, and he hadn't heard from her for some time.

Had she left him before, the Melbourne detective asked? Yes, she frequently left him, Agostini said. He then gave the detective some details about his wife's dental work and the address of Linda's mother in Littlehampton, England. Simpson then showed Agostini photographs of the Pyjama Girl and asked him if it was his wife. Nine years later, when Agostini was finally brought to trial for the murder of his wife, he admitted that 'my heart was beating so hard I wondered that [Simpson] didn't see it under my shirt. If he had asked a few more questions I would have confessed.'[4]

But Agostini's simple answer of 'no' was enough to convince the detective at the time. Simpson asked Agostini to report to Russell Street the following day to make a formal statement but when the suspect did, Simpson wasn't there and nobody at the police station knew anything about him being there. Agostini did not call back a second time. The police had missed their first chance to get their man.

Antonio Agostini was born in the north of Italy on 29 May 1903. Although he came from a good family, Agostini was jailed briefly in 1923 in Noale, in the province of Treviso, for assault. In 1927 the handsome, dark-haired young man decided to start a new life in Australia and arrived in Sydney on the *Regina d'Italia*. Among his meagre possessions when he arrived was a .25 calibre pistol. Tony Agostini made many friends in his adopted country; the genial, polite Italian secured the lease on the cloakroom at one of Sydney's best-known nightclubs, Romano's in Kings Cross. By all accounts, Agostini was a man of 'ambition and energy'[5] but his quiet demeanour harboured the vicious temper that had seen him jailed in his homeland.

One of the many single girls living near Agostini's address at 88a Darlinghurst Road, Kings Cross, was English girl Florence Linda Platt. Born in the London suburb of Forest Hills in 1905, Platt had left her middle-class family in 1926 after a failed romance and sailed for New Zealand. Settling in Sydney she secured a job as an usherette at the Hoyts Theatre (and later the Strand in Pitt Street) in the city while she completed a course in hairdressing at the glamorously named Hollywood School of Hairdressing. Some time later the woman was employed as a hairdresser on the ship *Aorangi*.

Linda Platt was a small (at slightly over 152 centimetres), vivacious woman with hazel eyes and irregular-shaped ears. She joked that a monkey had once taken a bite out of her but she was self-conscious enough to wear a bobbed hairstyle that hid her ears from view. Linda was attractive, in an unusual sort of way, but also had 'a bright personality' and a 'flair for designing clothes'.[6] She also had three moles on her left shoulder, which should have been more than enough to identify her as the Pyjama Girl, but because of a bizarre set of circumstances involving her dental charts, it didn't.

Linda attracted the attention of Tony Agostini and after what was described as a 'conventional courtship'[7] for that time, Agostini asked her to marry him. Instead of an engagement ring, Tony paid for Linda to return home to England to visit her mother who was living in Littlehampton. After three months abroad, Linda returned to Australia and married Tony at the Sydney Registry Office on 22 April 1930. The couple lived in Kellett Street, Darlinghurst, and for a while the marriage was a happy one. But Linda's social drinking soon developed into acute alcoholism. Under the influence of alcohol Linda Agostini turned from a happy-go-lucky person to a jealous, abusive woman who accused her husband of being unfaithful. Although Linda would apologise to her husband for her behaviour when she sobered, the Agostinis' marriage became a series of running battles sparked by her drinking binges.

In order to save his marriage Tony Agostini took on the position as the Melbourne editor of the English–Italian newspaper *Il Giornale Italiano* in 1933. He hoped that the move to Melbourne would curb his wife's drinking problem, but Linda soon slipped into her old habits. The public behaviour of his wife was the cause of much embarrassment for Tony Agostini, who had quickly become a well-known and respected figure in the Italian community. However, the situation was not helped by the fact that Tony did not earn enough money through subscriptions at the newspaper. The Agostinis moved addresses regularly in order to sever ties with Linda's drinking associates and the pair spent regular periods apart.

The Agostinis reconciled one last time and lived at 589 Swanston Street, Carlton, where Tony ran his newspaper in a room below their upstairs apartment. They secured a Fiat Topolino car on hire purchase, which Tony used for business purposes and weekend trips to the country. But Linda's behaviour had become so erratic (she pulled a gun on her husband when he brought a client home from the Club Cavour one night) that it began to affect their livelihood. Police later found out that, in August 1934, Linda Agostini intended to write to her mother in England, detailing her 'nervous collapse' over her husband's poor handling of their finances, but the letter was never sent. On the other side of the world, Linda's mother had no inkling of her daughter's unhappiness. She was not to hear from her daughter again. Linda Agostini disappeared one last time in late August 1934. Tony Agostini told associates that his wife had left him for good.

In 1937, Tony Agostini ran into Mrs Gertrude Crawford when he returned to Sydney to manage the English–Italian newspaper. A friend of the couple, Mrs Crawford had been to Sydney University to view the body of the Pyjama Girl and thought it looked a little like Linda. Agostini told her that he not seen his wife since they went to Melbourne four years before and that he thought she was in Adelaide. Mrs Gertrude pressed Agostini to go and see the body at Sydney University and when she met Agostini on a later occasion, he told her that he had been to see the body in the formalin bath and that it wasn't that of his wife. When other acquaintances of the couple (including NSW Police Sergeant Victor King) also remarked to Agostini of the Pyjama Girl's resemblance to his wife, the Italian immigrant was always a 'thorough gentleman' about it.[8] It was not his wife, he said.

In January 1938, District Coroner Mr C.W. Swiney conducted an inquest at Albury Courthouse into the death and identity of the Pyjama Girl — more than three years after the body had been found in the Howlong Road culvert. The first sensation in the inquest was the revelation of the presence of a .25 calibre bullet in the skull of the victim. The second was the public clearing of the Griffiths family of having any involvement in the woman's death. Dr Woods determined that although she had been shot, the injuries to the woman's head, which were caused by a heavy, blunt instrument such as a tyre lever, resulted in her death. But Detective Thomas McRae, who had been with the investigation from the beginning, informed the inquest that he had not been able to determine the woman's identity. The coroner ultimately brought down an open finding on the identity of the Pyjama Girl, the reasons for her death and the identity of the person or persons responsible.

On 6 May 1938, an Italian grocer named Luigi Castellano went to the Melbourne Police and informed a young constable that he knew the identity of the Pyjama Girl and that a man had confessed to him of her murder. In his statement to police Castellano said that in 1933 he occupied a shop at 599 Swanston Street, Carlton, and had worked there for about two years. In this time he and his wife had become acquainted with Tony Agostini and his wife Linda, and the foursome often socialised together. On 28 August 1933, Tony had come into Castellano's shop with a long scratch on his face and told him that Linda had left him again. A couple of days later Agostini came into the shop and asked Castellano to go with him for a drive. On the way to Mordialloc in Agostini's car, Agostini told the grocer that the woman's body found recently in Albury was indeed Linda's and that he had been responsible for killing her.

It seemed incongruous that Castellano could keep this secret for almost four years without coming forward but he told police that he had been a sick man and when he saw police questioning Agostini near his Carlton shop in 1935, he felt sure the Italian newspaper owner was cooperating with them. Inquiries among Agostini's friends in Melbourne and Sydney confirmed that Linda's appearance matched the essential elements of the Pyjama Girl, except for the vital dental work. Linda Agostini had eight fillings, as opposed to the victim's six. Detective Alex White of Melbourne CIB wrote in a confidential report that:

> ... it would appear that, if the records of Mr O'Brien, dentist in Sydney, are correct, the body of the victim of the Albury murder could not be that of Mrs Agostini ... I am of the opinion that this information supplied by Castellano is in the form of vengeance against Agostini to cause him some inconvenience ...[9]

In late 1939, the involvement of Dr Thomas Alexander Palmer Benbow, a Sydney physician and amateur criminologist who was obsessed with the Pyjama Girl case, took the focus of the murder investigation further away from the Agostinis. Benbow's own investigations led him to believe that the Pyjama Girl was Anna Philomena Morgan. Ms Morgan was the missing, illegitimate daughter of a Mrs Jeanette Routledge of Bomaderry on the south coast of New South Wales. Despite the fact that Mrs Routledge had viewed the body of the Pyjama Girl at Sydney University and was adamant it wasn't her daughter, Dr Benbow was able to convince her that it was Anna Morgan — even to the extent of telling reporters that there were 'seventeen points of anatomical comparison'[10] between Morgan and the Pyjama Girl. But when Mrs Routledge presented a writ against the Justice Department for the release of the Pyjama Girl's body for burial and then made a claim on her daughter's estate (which was valued at about £75), the court ruled against her and declined to reopen the inquest. Dr Benbow's bizarre allegations concerning the 'murder' of Ms Morgan, which he maintained occurred in a shack in Albury, were even tabled in the NSW state parliament. They were later found to have no basis in fact.

In September 1939, when Australia entered the Second World War, thousands of German and Italian nationals living in Australia were interned as 'enemy aliens'. As the proprietor of an Italian newspaper with decidedly fascist leanings, Tony Agostini was interned at Tatura in Victoria before being moved to Hay, in southwestern New South Wales. From there he was again moved to Loveday, South Australia, where he spent the remainder of his time — a world away from the Pyjama Girl case. When Italy surrendered to the Allies in 1944, the Italian internees were released and Agostini was re-employed at Romano's, where he had first worked when he came to Australia. Only now Agostini was a waiter and one of his regular customers was Bill McKay, the NSW Commissioner of Police.

'Big Bill' McKay hated unfinished business. At the beginning of 1944 he put two new officers, Detective Inspector H.W. Latrobe and Detective Sergeant Joe Rasmus, with the assistance of young Constable First Class R. Stackpool, on the unsolved Pyjama Girl case. In reviewing all the available evidence the detectives decided to have another look at the dental similarities between Linda Agostini and the Pyjama Girl. They arranged for Agostini's dentist, Dr William O'Brien, and two other dentists to inspect the Pyjama Girl's body in its formalin bath. When the body was examined they found that two porcelain fillings had fallen out, leaving cavities in the woman's back teeth. The porcelain fillings were still in the mouth and had not been noticed by the original Albury dentist who examined the body nor detected by X-ray. O'Brien recognised the porcelain work as belonging to his former patient Linda Agostini, and the identity of the Pyjama Girl was finally solved.

When Bill McKay was informed of the identity of the Pyjama Girl he was shocked to find that the chief suspect was his regular waiter at his favourite lunchtime restaurant. On Saturday, 4 March 1944, he sent for Tony Agostini to come to the CIB's Sydney Headquarters. When McKay asked Agostini why he looked so worried, the Italian immigrant quickly confessed to the killing of his wife. 'I have been through hell for the last ten years,' Agostini told McKay, '...but I am very pleased to be here now and I'll tell you what my trouble is and get it off my mind.'[11]

In Agostini's official statement he wrote:

> On the Sunday night referred to we were living in Swanston Street ... [Linda] used to make it impossible for me to go to sleep. I set the alarm clock for seven o'clock next morning. I had a restless nights sleep, but towards break of day I fell into a sound sleep and awakened with a start ... I realised it was a gun she was holding against my head, and I quickly turned my head on the cushion and, grasping her hand in my hand, I commenced a struggle with her for possession of the revolver, intending to disarm her. In doing so we rolled over on the bed. She struggled bitterly and was very determined ... the next thing I heard was a shot going off. She gave a long gasp and ceased to struggle.
>
> The realisation that she was dead gave me a terrible shock and unbalanced my mentality ... I started to see what would happen to my friends, my relations and the firm with whom I was employed, when the big headlines would come out in the paper about the shooting. In the work I was doing I had made a lot of friends in the Italian and Australian communities in Melbourne and I felt I was highly regarded by them all. The thought of what they would think of me swayed my better judgment of going and telling the police straight away ...
>
> At 8 pm on the day of the accident to my wife at 7 am I left Melbourne with the body and took the highway to Albury. I had no plans. I was just running. I continued on, and I realised by the lights I saw that I was nearing Albury, because it was a large town, so I took the first branch road I met and, after travelling some time, I stopped the car at a quiet part of the road where there was a little bridge or culvert. I had taken some extra petrol in a tin because it was late at night and I might have difficulty in waking anyone up at a garage to get a fresh supply. So I poured some of the petrol from the tin onto a bag in which the body was enclosed and placed the body under the bridge and set fire to it ...

> I think I should now tell you what happened in regard to Mr Castellano. In 1938 a court case was brought against the firm I was connected with, and behind the case was a very rich person who had a particular reason for destroying the firm I was working for, and tried to make it an excuse to break the firm. I was called as a witness, and I only realised that Castellano had befriended me previously so that he could, when the opportunity arose, hold me in his clutches ... I was threatened by Castellano that if I would appear in court he would denounce me for the accident that has been raised before and which he had prevented me from telling the police about.[12]

At his trial in Melbourne on 19 June 1944, Agostini's lawyers challenged the 'voluntariness' of his official statement and defended the charge of murder. If found guilty, Agostini would have hanged for the crime but he ultimately took the stand and was able to convince the jury that the crime was not premeditated and that he had panicked after his wife was accidentally shot during the struggle for the gun. Agostini even maintained that for 10 years he thought the Pyjama Girl was *not* Linda. Despite the fact that his wife's head injuries (the real cause of death) were put down to his dropping her body down the stairs (he denied the Crown's assertion that he had used their domestic iron to bludgeon her to death), Agostini was found guilty of the manslaughter of his wife. In sentencing Agostini to six years' hard labour on 30 June 1944, Justice Charles Lowe stated that in his opinion 'the jury was merciful' considering that 'the more probable cause of death [was] caused by an assault committed by you. The weapon you used must have been a heavy one, and must have been used with great violence. Such conduct constitutes a serious crime.'[13]

Antonio Agostini served three years and nine months for the manslaughter of his wife Linda. On his release from prison in 1947, it was determined that he would be deported back to Italy because he had never become an Australian citizen. Agostini was secretly deported on 21 August 1947 aboard the ship *Strathnaver* and returned to the place of his birth. In January 1950 he moved to the island of Sardinia and two years later married Guiseppina Gasoni, a widow with a young daughter. Agostini went into the clothing industry and opened a shop in the city of Caligari in 1952. The man who committed one of the most bizarre murders in Australian criminal history lived a quiet life in Sardinia until his death in 1969. He is buried in the cemetery of San Michele.

And what of the Pyjama Girl? The peculiar fate of the woman in the formalin bath — the subject of countless books and newspaper articles — was buried in relative anonymity on 13 July 1944, in grave number 8341 at Melbourne's Preston Cemetery. The case was later the inspiration for a 1978 Italian film made by Gino Millozza and starring Academy Award-winning actor Ray Milland. But in the decades after the Pyjama Girl's identity was finally revealed, the case was never far from the Australian public's eye. Each year at the Official Police Exhibit Pavilion at the Royal Easter Show, tens of thousands of people — mostly children, this author being just one of them — gazed in awe at the photos of the Pyjama Girl, her image forever preserved in our memory.

Chapter 3
The Shark Arm Murder (1935)

On 25 April 1935, a tiger shark on display at Coogee Aquarium, south of Sydney, disgorged a human arm in full view of a curious crowd that had gathered there that Anzac Day. A medical examination of the arm — which had the tattooed image of two boxers on the forearm — revealed that it had been cut from a man's body with a knife. The 'shark arm' was later discovered to have belonged to James Smith, a former boxer with criminal links to Sydney's underworld. The subsequent murder investigation sparked a media feeding-frenzy and remains one of the most bizarre cases in Australian criminal history.

In the weeks that straddled February and March 1935, three young men, including one from popular Austinmer Beach on NSW's picturesque south coast, were taken by sharks from separate beaches. As a direct result of these deaths bounty hunters were employed to rid beaches of the menace of shark attack. In April 1935, a fisherman named Bert Hobson set a shark line baited with mackerel 3 kilometres off Sydney's Coogee Beach.

When Hobson returned to the spot the next morning, he found a 3.5 metre tiger shark entangled on the line. The head and part of the body of a smaller shark was also on the line and Hobson quickly surmised that the bigger shark had snapped off the body of the smaller shark and then become entwined in the line.

Showing a quick entrepreneurial spirit, Hobson decided to tow the live shark to shore and exhibit it in his brother's aquarium at the southern end of Coogee Beach. The Coogee Palace, which included public baths and an aquarium, was once one of Sydney's best-known landmarks. Opened in December 1887 and built in the style of traditional English seaside resorts, the Coogee Palace was one of the city's most popular entertainment venues. It had a steel dome measuring 17 metres in diameter and an interior decor of blue and gold with silver stars and a rising sun and moon. But by the 1930s the palace was falling into disarray and was a poor shadow of its former glory. However, the Hobson brothers thought that displaying the captured tiger shark would bring the crowds flocking back to Coogee.

While the glass portals on the side of the aquarium's main pool allowed the paying public an unprecedented view of nature's supreme killing machine, the tiger shark proved a major disappointment. Despite its immense size, the shark swam slowly and seemed lethargic in its unfamiliar surroundings. But a week after its capture, the 14 people who had paid their money that April afternoon saw the shark thresh about in the water, bump itself against the walls of the aquarium and dart towards the shallow end of the pool. In clear view of the small crowd, the shark vomited the contents of its stomach and the air was filled with a 'frightful smell'.[1] An oil-like scum covered the water and the rotting carcasses of rats, birds and other shark flesh floated to the surface. When the water cleared, a human left forearm was also floating in the pool.

The local police were informed and Detective Sergeant Bob Young of Randwick Police Station sent two plainclothes detectives to investigate the incredible discovery of a human arm floating in a shark pool. The retrieval of the arm was an amazing stroke of luck — if the shark had not been captured then the fate of the unfortunate victim would never have been known. Detective Constable Frank Head retrieved the floating arm from the shallow end of the pool. Grabbing it by the rope attached to the wrist in a half-hitch knot, he was immediately struck by two things.

Although the skin on the palm of the hand had become detached, the arm had not yet decomposed. It also had an easily identifiable tattoo on it — two boxers shaping up to each other; one in blue trunks and the other in red. Although there were some bite marks on the arm, it was clear from the wound at the point of dissection above the elbow that it had been cut from the body with a knife — not bitten off by a shark. But one thing was certain: the police had a murder investigation on their hands.

By the following day the story had captured the public's imagination. One of the spectators at the aquarium that afternoon, Leo Young, was a journalist for the *Sydney Morning Herald*. Morning newspapers in Sydney, the *Daily Telegraph* and the *Sydney Morning Herald*, each carried erroneous reports that the arm belonged to a suicide victim and that police were appealing for help from Sydneysiders searching for missing loved ones. Police originally thought that it might have been placed there as a joke by medical students from nearby Sydney University but the fact that the aquarium was locked at night ruled this out. Seasoned fishermen never did accept the story that the shark swallowed the arm in the wild; many believed that the arm was intentionally placed in the aquarium to be digested by the shark. But by whom?

The arm was transferred to the morgue and examined by government medical officer Dr Aubrey Palmer, who quickly confirmed that it had not been surgically removed but crudely cut from the body with a sharp knife. There was no evidence of chemical preservation of the arm, as would be the case if it was a medical exhibit, but it was still in a remarkably preserved state. Sharks are cold-blooded creatures and their digestive system is very slow, more so in the cold waters of a Sydney autumn. Palmer explained that the arm could have been in the shark's body for some time. And if the arm had been swallowed by the smaller shark, as Bert Hobson maintained, and in turn swallowed by the tiger shark, the digestion of the arm would have been even slower. It was therefore going to be extremely difficult to establish when the arm had been separated from the victim's body.

Three days after the tiger shark gave up its grisly discovery and became the talking point of all of Australia, the Hobson brothers cut their losses and killed the shark — thus jeopardising the entire police investigation. By the time Sydney CIB heard about the fate of the shark, the body had been gutted and the animal's valuable oil extracted from its liver by an 'expert' who sold it for medicinal purposes and then left the carcass on a rubbish tip. When eventually questioned by police, Bert Hobson said there was shark backbone, mackerel parts and small fish in the shark's stomach but hadn't noticed any other evidence of human flesh, bone or clothing that could identify the victim.

Detectives wanted to retrieve fingerprints from the hand of the arm but because of the increasingly unstable condition of the skin on the hand, traditional fingerprinting methods would not have produced identifiable prints. Detective Constable John Lindsay of the Police Fingerprint Department showed remarkable skill by removing the skin from the fingers to construct a 'human glove'. The skin was then backed with padding, the fingers inked and a set of prints recorded.

Detectives then started the enormous task of matching the fingerprints to police records, while an artist's illustration of the tattoo was published in *The Truth* newspaper. Even then Edwin 'Ted' Smith agonised over the decision of whether to come forward and identify the arm — he had seen only one other tattoo like it and it belonged to his brother James, who had gone missing on 7 April. Police confirmed several points of similarity with fingerprints on file belonging to James Smith, who had been fingerprinted in September 1932 for illegal gambling. The day before this confirmation, the missing man's wife positively identified the arm as belonging to her husband.

James Smith was born in England in 1895 and immigrated to Australia at the age of twenty. Smith had high hopes of becoming a leading boxer in Sydney but despite some success he never had the ability to make the 'big time'. After his boxing career ended he worked in the billiard room at the City Tattersalls Club before buying a 'billiard saloon' in Western

Road, Rozelle. The club was most likely a front for illegal SP (starting price) gambling on horseracing, which was a way of life for most Australians during the Depression. With no off-course betting in that pre-TAB era, millions of pounds were exchanged between illegal bookmakers and suburban punters — for both big and small amounts of money.

Smith lived in Gladesville in Sydney's inner west and was married with a young son but his aspirations — both personal and criminal — were much higher. He drifted into the periphery of Sydney's criminal underworld and was known as a 'snappy dresser' for the times, but it was all a front. The former boxer rented his fine clothes and jewellery to maintain an outward impression, at least, that he had money to invest. The ploy worked. Smith went into business with Reginald William Lloyd Holmes, a wealthy 43-year-old boat-builder from McMahons Point. The pair planned to build 14 flats on a vacant lot near Holmes's speedboat business, with Smith selling his billiards saloon to finance his new career as building materials supplier.

Holmes may have had the veneer of a respectable businessman with his boat-building enterprise on Sydney's Lavender Bay, but he also used his speedboats to smuggle contraband on the harbour — liquor, cigarettes and narcotics. After the flats were built, Smith went into bankruptcy with £8000 worth of debts owed for the costs of building products. The ex-boxer, who knew nothing of the building trade, may have been the unwitting participant in an elaborate fraud by Holmes to cheat creditors of their money. Holmes gave Smith £300 to buy another billiard room (which later became the Rozelle Athletic Club) and employed him as a launch captain on the harbour to shut him up. When Smith was charged with illegal SP gambling, he lost his billiards licence and threatened to blackmail Holmes over another failed insurance scam.

In 1933 Holmes bought a powerful, sea-going yacht named *Pathfinder* for £11 000 but insured it for much more than that amount and sold it to one of his associates. In April 1934, the *Pathfinder* was deliberately sunk off a landmark known as The Skillion, at Terrigal, north of Sydney. James Smith was the only person on board the yacht and earned some unwanted publicity when he declined rescue from a passing collier and rowed ashore. Questioned by police, Smith let slip that Holmes was the original owner. When the insurance claim was presented, the insurance questioned the valuation of the yacht ($150 000 in today's money) and refused to pay. Smith, who was heavily in debt, had risked his life for the scam and wanted his cut of the insurance money whether the claim was paid or not. Holmes began to crack.

In June 1934, Smith rang Holmes with his own 'business' proposition. Smith had given Holmes's signature to a forger named Patrick Brady who had cleverly reproduced it on a £20 cheque. Smith asked Holmes not to challenge the signature when the bank rang about the cheque, thus legitimising the forgery that would be kept on file by bank officials. The bank did ring Holmes, who verified the forged signature as his, and thus Smith had provided a banking loophole that he, the forger and Holmes, could exploit in the future. Smith convinced Holmes to provide the signatures of some of his wealthy friends and clients that the forger could copy onto cheques. To draw suspicion away from Holmes, it was suggested that the wealthy boat-builder travel interstate 'on business' when the cheques were circulated. Smith was quickly becoming a liability to Holmes's legitimate business interests.

On 7 April 1935, Smith's wife and 14-year-old son went away for a short visit to relatives. Smith told her that he would be going fishing for a few days with a man 'of independent means'[2] from interstate. It was not uncommon for Smith to disappear for days on end in his line of business and when the 'few days' turned into more than two weeks, Mrs Smith was still not concerned enough to report his disappearance to police — even though the discovery of the tattooed 'shark arm' was widely reported.

The murder investigation came under the direction of Sydney CIB Superintendent William Prior, who assembled a formidable homicide team of detectives. Detective Sergeant Frank Allmond, who was involved in the still-unsolved investigation into the Pyjama Girl murder, was part of a team of six detectives. Detective Sergeant Frank Matthews, who had recently returned to office duty after recovering from an operation, was brought into the investigation when it was found that the detective knew of Smith's criminal past and many of his associates. Interestingly, police learned that Smith's one-time business partner, Reginald Holmes, had left for Melbourne the day after the tattooed arm had been disgorged in Coogee Aquarium.

Smith's associates in the Sydney underworld would not talk to police about the ex-boxer's final movements, however. 'Ted' Smith told the detectives that his brother had spoken of a fishing trip to Cronulla, south of Coogee. This was confirmed by several other people, but with no starting point in the Sutherland Shire, which takes in the suburb of Cronulla, investigating police conducted around-the-clock checks of local hotels and businesses over the ensuing weeks. Finally, a barman at the Cecil Hotel in the heart of Cronulla identified Smith from a photo the police were circulating, as a man he served on 7 April. Two patrons who remembered playing cards with Smith and another man on the same day told police that the pair said they were staying at a local cottage named *Cored Joy* in Talloumbi Street, on the shores of Gunnamatta Bay, close to Port Hacking.

Police theorised that Smith had been murdered in the district and his body disposed of in Port Hacking, but this was going to be hard to prove without a body. While they tried to identify the man Smith was staying with at *Cored Joy*, detectives questioned Reginald Holmes when he returned from Melbourne. Holmes was less than helpful in providing a motive for Smith's death or identifying the people responsible, but the detectives noted a growing uneasiness in Holmes's demeanour over several weeks of questioning. The wealthy boat-builder, who was clearly a suspect in the case, was increasingly nervous, defensive and mentally unstable.

With the murder investigation threatening to stall, police decided to search an area of Port Hacking closest to Cronulla. The RAAF put a plane and an observer at the disposal of the Sydney CIB while the navy provided a launch and a diver. But the task proved insurmountable and Smith's body was never recovered. The police still had a number of leads to exhaust, however, notably the continued interrogation of Reginald Holmes.

Then, just as the investigation appeared set to make an important breakthrough, a letter was received by Smith's 14-year-old son. Dated 3 May, the crudely constructed letter stated:

> Son, keep your mother quiet. I am in a jam. I plead its OK call the cops off tell your mum I will have plenty soon and will be alright. They want me something in town never mind be a man for me.
>
> Your loving father 'Jim Smith'

There was a postscript: 'Destroy This'.[3]

The letter was an obvious forgery, designed to throw police off the trail and to give the impression that Smith was still alive and 'hiding out' somewhere. But on 16 May, following a concerted investigation, detectives Allmond, McDermott and Matthews went to a flat in North Sydney and arrested Patrick Brady, the man Jim Smith was staying with at *Cored Joy*, and charged him with Smith's murder.

Although Brady denied that he had anything to do with Smith's death there was strong circumstantial evidence linking him to the fateful 'fishing trip' to Port Hacking. Brady was a long-time associate of Smith and drinkers at the Cecil Hotel identified him as the man playing cards with the former boxer on the last day he was seen alive. Brady had rented the cottage at Gunnamatta Bay and had earned the ire of the landlord after he left the premises earlier than expected. A trunk and blanket had been replaced, the rowboat in the cottage's shed had been used without permission and the metal rowlocks and kellick were missing. Suspicious, the landlord also reported to police that the walls and floors of the cottage had been scrubbed clean.

Professor Alex Castles, who was first afforded a look at police files on the Shark Arm case in 1955 and later wrote a book on the case, stated in a radio broadcast in 2002 that:

> A key link for the police in their investigations was information they got from a cab driver who was located at Cronulla. On the morning after Jim Smith was seen for the last time, [Patrick] Brady turned up at the cab driver's home, and wanted a ride into Sydney. He was dishevelled; he had a hand in a pocket and wouldn't take it out. He got in the cab, and they drove through Sydney, and as the cab driver was able to give evidence on later, it was clear that Brady was frightened. He kept looking out the back window, fearful that somebody was following him. And

> then, finally, he came to North Sydney, and he got the cab driver to pull up outside of the home of Reginald Lloyd Holmes.[4]

Brady's taxi ride to Holmes's residence directly linked the pair to James Smith at the time of his disappearance. Police hoped that charging Brady would apply pressure on Holmes, but the wealthy businessman denied knowing Brady and the case against him was purely circumstantial. The police needed a confession.

On 20 May, the case took an extraordinary turn when police were informed that Reginald Holmes had attempted to commit suicide with his revolver and was currently racing madly around Sydney Harbour in a speedboat. In a bizarre series of events that rivalled the 'shark arm' discovery the previous month, Holmes went to his boatshed, pulled out a pistol and shot himself in the forehead. The nickel-jacketed bullet splayed inside his forehead and stunned him. Holmes fell into the harbour but a rope he was holding to steady himself twisted round his wrist as he fell — a faint echo of the rope with a half-hitch knot used to retrieve the tattooed arm in Coogee Aquarium. Falling into the water revived Holmes, and he crawled back into the boat and headed towards Circular Quay.

Detective Sergeant Jim Dunnett of Phillip Street Police Station chased Holmes out on the harbour in the police launch *Nemesis*. Detective Sergeant Matthews and Holmes's brother set out in a smaller launch but neither boat was a match for Holmes, an expert boatman, or his speedboat. Every time the police got close to Holmes (the blood clearly evident on his forehead and face from the attempted suicide), he would turn his speedboat in a tight circle and speed away.

The police chase continued for several hours until Holmes stopped his boat just outside Sydney Heads. The larger, more cumbersome police launch approached the smaller, faster vessel but there was a stand-off as the police waited for Holmes to make his next move. As the boats sat idle outside the harbour some distance apart, Detective Sergeant Matthews steered his smaller vessel alongside Holmes's speedboat. When Holmes recognised Matthews he became agitated and stood up and shouted at the Sydney detective.

'Why didn't you come to me?' Holmes shouted. 'If you give me until twelve o'clock tonight, I will finish the other bastard. Jimmy Smith is dead. I am nearly dead and there is only another left. If you leave me until tonight I will finish him.'[5]

As Matthew's launch came alongside the powerful speedboat, Holmes's brother quietly stepped aboard and grabbed him. There was a struggle, but the badly injured Holmes was quickly subdued and taken onto the police launch. The bullet wound in the middle of his forehead was ringed by a powder burn and his hair was singed. Police found a near-empty bottle of brandy on board his boat and the liquor could be easily smelt on Holmes, who was known not to be a heavy drinker. Holmes was near hysterical now, imploring Matthews to let him go so that he could 'fix' the 'other man'.

When Holmes was taken to hospital it was discovered that the .32 calibre bullet had impacted and flattened against the thick bone at the front of his skull and that he would survive his suicide attempt. He was kept under police guard until he could be questioned, but despite his willingness to tell the police all that he knew, he was now under psychiatric care and police knew that it would be pointless to question him in his current state of mind because nothing of what he said would be admissible in court if Holmes was branded insane.

As soon as Holmes was well enough he went to the Sydney CIB and made a statement. But he kept the police at arm's length and didn't tell everything he knew about Smith's death. On 11 June, Holmes expanded upon his statement for Detective Sergeant Matthews but still did not commit everything he knew to paper. When he had finished, Holmes asked to see Matthews alone and the pair went to the roof of the Sydney CIB, where Holmes supplied Matthews with additional information but refused to put it in writing.

Holmes told Matthews that he had played no part in Smith's murder, nor had he wanted him dead. Smith had been killed over another matter. His body had been dismembered and dumped in a trunk that now sat on the bottom of an unknown part of Port Hacking. Holmes directly implicated Patrick Brady in Smith's murder and the disposal of his body. Once the tattooed arm had been cut from Smith's body, a rope had been tied around its wrist and it was placed in a Gladstone bag to take back to Sydney as proof that the gruesome task had been done. Brady had arrived at Holmes's home and unsolicited, dangled the arm before Holmes at the end of a rope and had allegedly challenged the businessman to 'cut him in' or he'd end up like Smith.[6]

Brady knew enough of Holmes's 'business dealings' to ruin him, and at the very least Holmes was now implicated as an accessory to murder after the fact. All that was required for the crime never to be discovered was the disposal of the arm — it was almost the perfect crime. What were the odds, then, of the recovery of Smith's telltale tattooed arm from the belly of a tiger shark?

Holmes assured the Sydney detective that he would tell the full story of Smith's murder when called as a Crown witness at the coroner's inquiry, which was being held the following day. Matthews had no option but to believe Holmes. One of the main suspects in the death of James Smith, Holmes asked the Sydney detective not to place a guard on him that night and to trust him that, after seeing his barrister, he would go straight home. Holmes promised to call Matthews if he needed to leave his residence that night and Matthews was concerned that if he put further pressure on Holmes he would not tell everything he knew at the inquest the following day. But Holmes had no intention of speaking at the inquest.

On the afternoon of 11 June, Holmes withdrew £500 from his bank account and, after meeting with his barrister, visited friends. Holmes told his friend Bernard Cahill that he was afraid that he, his wife or children were 'going to be bumped off'.[7] Returning home, Holmes complained of a headache, had a whisky and then excused himself and lay down. He was woken by a telephone call and instructed his wife to wake him again at 8 pm as he had to go out that night and 'see a fellow. It's important.'[8] When Mrs Holmes woke her husband at 7.45 pm, she questioned him about the wisdom of leaving the house without informing the police. Holmes assured his wife that he was meeting friends and that there was no reason to tell the police. He would be home at 9.30 pm, he told her.

At about 8.45 pm that night, Jack Thomas was looking out his bedroom window in Lower Fort Street at Dawes Point, which overlooked the southern pylon of the Sydney Harbour Bridge in Hickson Road. Thomas saw a car with its headlights on and a man standing beside the near side door, which was open. The man seemed to be speaking to someone inside the car when Thomas heard three sharp shots. The man stepped back from the car door, walked to the front of the car and examined the headlights and then calmly walked away. The man was never identified. Other locals also heard gunshot noises about the time Jack Thomas had stated but none had thought to contact the police — it was just another night in Sydney.

Just before midnight, and with Reginald Holmes not yet returned, Mrs Holmes contacted the police. At 1.20 am the following morning, the body of Reginald Holmes was found sitting in the front seat of his car by two constables patrolling Hickson Road. Holmes was in an upright position, facing the near side passenger door, and at first the constables thought that he was asleep. When they shone their torches inside the car, they saw the man was sitting in a pool of his own blood with three bullet holes in his left side below the heart. Three spent .32 calibre cartridge shells were on the floor of the car. It was clear that Holmes could not have shot himself and detectives agreed that he had been killed instantly by a gunshots fired at a distance of just 30 centimetres.

The following day, 12 June 1935, Coroner Oram began an inquiry into the death of James Smith. Mr Clive Evatt, the famed jurist and a future leader of the federal Labor Party in Opposition to Prime Minister Robert Menzies, acted on behalf of Patrick Brady. Evatt successfully applied to the Supreme Court for an injunction restraining the coroner from conducting the inquest on the grounds that there was no body — just an arm. Although the Crown applied for a magisterial inquiry and Brady was eventually committed for trial, Chief Justice Jordan dismissed the case at Central Criminal Court without calling for any evidence to be tabled.

Subsequently, the Shark Arm case against Patrick Brady collapsed and no-one was ever charged with either murder. Brady died in old age, but the spectre of his involvement in one of the most bizarre murder investigations in Australian criminal history hung over him for the remainder of his life.

When Patrick Brady, then in his seventies, was interviewed by Sydney writer Vince Kelly for his 1963 book *The Shark Arm Case*, it sounded like he was talking in metaphors of James Smith's ultimate fate. 'The newspapers drag it up every year or so and serve up a few bits and pieces, mostly disjointed and distorted.' An American TV movie about the case, shown in Australia in the 1960s, only succeeded in keeping the murders in the public's mindset. 'I don't like it,' Brady maintained. 'My relatives don't like it. I tried to stop it being put out to the world on millions of TV sets [but] the court held I wasn't sufficiently identified with [the case] to be granted [the injunction] prohibiting the TV show in Australia. Can you beat that?'[9]

Holmes's killer was never discovered, although police formed the opinion that his death was probably a case of 'suicide by proxy'. Knowing that he could be charged with being an accessory to murder, and the fact that being a Crown witness would not protect him, Holmes may have arranged his own murder; having failed in one attempt to take his own life, Holmes had placed a 'contract' on his own life. In his fragile state of mind, Holmes kept his appointment with fate in Hickson Road to spare himself and his family the public disgrace of being sent to jail. Holmes left an estate worth £50 000 at probate and had life insurance worth £15 800.

It was later revealed in Alex Castles' book *The Shark Arm Murders* (1995) that James Smith was actually murdered by a criminal named Eddie Weyman after the former boxer had become a 'fizzer' — a police informer. As a result of information Smith had given to police, Weyman, one of the most dangerous criminals in Sydney in the 1930s, and an accomplice were caught in the act of conducting a bank robbery. It is most likely that Weyman contracted Brady to murder Smith; Weyman, in turn, was shot dead 10 years later by notorious Sydney gunman 'Chow' Hayes during a gangland quarrel.

The Shark Arm murders belong to an era long past. The Coogee Aquarium became run down after the Second World War and the pools were replaced by a motel. The original building later housed a garage on the ground floor with some flats, and was saved from demolition when the

Heritage Council placed a Permanent Conservation Order on the structure in 1982. Although the rusted dome collapsed during a storm in 1984, it was sold the following year for $1.62 million. An ambitious $5 million restoration program was planned but it was not until a decade later that the site was redeveloped. It is now the home of the Beach Palace Hotel.

Sharks have become an iconic part of Australian culture and folklore. As writer Noel Sanders observed, the shark has continued to provide us with almost 'totemistic proof'[10] of the worst attributes of human nature ... violence, criminal threat, vindictive justice, used car salesmen. Stories of shark attacks have both terrorised and mesmerised the public in the decades since and probably reached its zenith in the mid-1970s with the making of the Steven Spielberg film *Jaws*.

In April 2001, four recreational fishermen captured a tiger shark off the coast of Newcastle, in New South Wales. When they opened up the shark to check the contents of its stomach, the first thing that was found was some whalebone. Curious to find out what else the shark had eaten Bob van Leuwick, the skipper of the boat, searched further and discovered a human skull. Police checked missing person files to try to identify the remains, and because the skull was well preserved with a full set of teeth, police were able to determine the identity of the victim. The discovery of a human skull inside a tiger shark immediately brought comparisons with the Shark Arm murder.

In 2002, Brisbane-based director David Barker optioned Alex Castles' book with a view to making a feature film about the story that has mesmerised Australians for 70 years. The Shark Arm murder was always regarded as being stranger than fiction, and a proposed film about sharks, a severed arm, the murder of a Crown witness on the eve of a coronial inquest and smuggling on Sydney Harbour in the 1930s, would make a remarkable movie indeed. Sometimes truth is stranger than fiction.

Chapter 4

The Brown-Out Murders (1942)

On 7 December 1941, the United States of America was thrust into the Second World War when Japanese bombers launched an unprovoked attack on the American naval base in Pearl Harbor, Hawaii. The United States looked towards Australia, which had been at war with Germany for over two years, as not only an important ally but also as a strategic Pacific base for training and resting its troops. But in May 1942, the murder of three Melbourne women by an American soldier fully tested the bonds that exist between the two countries. The crimes were dubbed the 'Brown-Out' murders because they were committed at night while the city was in the grip of strict regulations that required all windows to be covered and street and car lights dimmed.

Although there was enough evidence at the time to suggest that the murderer, 24-year-old Private Edward Joseph Leonski, was insane and should never have stood trial, the US Military, with the backing of President Franklin D. Roosevelt and Pacific Commander General Douglas

MacArthur, took charge of the case and dealt with it expediently. Leonski was never charged under Australian law for the offences he committed against Australian citizens — for the first and only time in Australian criminal history a military tribunal was conducted by a foreign power on Australian soil — and was executed at Melbourne's Pentridge Prison in November 1942.

On 21 December 1941, just two weeks after the Japanese bombing of Pearl Harbor, the first American ships sailed up Brisbane River to prepare for the defence of Manila. In February 1942, Task Force 6814 arrived in Melbourne in a convoy of ships. The American troops were stationed in army camps in Ballarat, Bendigo, Royal Park in Melbourne (Camp Pell) and the Melbourne Cricket Ground (Camp Murphy). Camp Pell, which was located in the suburb of Parkville in Melbourne, was named after Major Floyd Pell of the 33rd Pursuit Squadron USAAC. On 10 April 1942, an operating platoon (of 45 men) of the 121st Signal Radio Intelligence Company arrived in Melbourne and set up camp at Camp Pell where they trained in 'intercept and direction finding' operations. By the winter of 1942 the 'browned-out' Melbourne streets were crowded with American servicemen intent on spending their money. The city was also packed with young girls — and some not so young — who had obtained work during the war. The presence of so many foreigners, and able-bodied ones at that, caused tension with the local men and led to the popular lament, first expressed in Britain, that the Americans were 'oversexed, overpaid and over here'.

One of the men who disembarked from the *Mariposa* with the 52nd Signal Battalion was Private Eddie Leonski (No. 32 007 434). Born in 1918 in New Jersey, Leonski later moved to Brooklyn, New York, with his mother and stepfather. Leonski's mother was mentally unstable and fought depression and had numerous nervous breakdowns during her son's childhood, while both his father and stepfather were alcoholics. The 24-year-old serviceman was something of a 'gentle giant', but his personality changed when under the influence of alcohol.

Three months after joining the army Leonski was charged with trying to strangle a girl in San Antonio, Texas, but he was not prosecuted.

Arriving in Melbourne, Leonski at first shunned alcohol and spent his time playing chequers with local volunteers in a canteen set up in a church hall in Gatehouse Street, Parkville. Leonski was well liked; he was blond and had 'an open, boyish face'[1] with a wide, friendly smile. But once he became familiar with the many hotels in Melbourne, Leonski's behaviour became increasingly erratic. He started spending his leave binge-drinking in local pubs and would often try to impress drinkers by walking on his hands after becoming intoxicated — and he would drink anything. One of his favourite tricks was to fill a large glass (called a 'pot' in Victoria) with different types of spirits and drink the lot in one go.

In the early hours of Sunday, 3 May 1942, part-time barman Henry Billings found the body of 40-year-old Ivy Violet McLeod strangled in Victoria Avenue, Albert Park. She was partially naked and she had been badly beaten by her attacker. Robbery did not appear to be the motive for the crime as her purse contained about £1 worth of small change. Billings recalled seeing an American soldier stooping in the doorway of a shop next to his hotel at about 3 am that morning. The soldier left the doorway and headed off up Beaconsfield Road at a brisk walk just before Billings came across a crumpled body in the recessed doorway of a dry cleaning shop. He struck a match and saw that it was the body of a woman. 'The clothes had been ripped from her body and her legs folded back,' Billings later said.[2] The barman went back to the hotel and roused the publican to ring police.

The post-mortem examination revealed that death had occurred sometime between 3 am and 6 am. The fleshy parts of the victim's body had been torn at by hand, her arm had been broken and parts of raw scalp were showing where clumps of hair had been pulled out. There was also a shocking injury to her throat, as if the killer had tried to rip out the woman's larynx. Ivy McLeod, who was separated from her husband, had bought six bottles of beer from a nearby hotel and had spent the evening with a male friend at his apartment. She had left the man's apartment just before 3 am and mingled with the late-night revellers returning home from their Saturday night out on the town.

Although hotels in Melbourne were supposed to shut at 6 pm, most publicans took advantage of the overflow of cashed-up American personnel and stayed open 'after hours'. Eddie Leonski had been at the Bleak House Hotel until about 1 am, when he borrowed money from another American, Private Spencer Neil Smith, to continue drinking. Although Leonski disappeared later that night and told friends at Camp Pell that he couldn't remember where he had got to, he still made it back to barracks in time for mess call at 6 am.

Six days later, on 9 May, the body of a second victim was found. A 31-year-old Bendigo woman, Pauline Thompson, known to everyone as Coral, was a stenographer by day and switchboard operator at a local radio station by night. The mother of two was also heavily involved in charity work, which included hosting groups of visiting American servicemen. Thompson told her husband, a local policeman, that she was going to a dance at the Music Lover's Club in Melbourne with a number of her girlfriends, but she had secretly planned to meet a young American, Private Justin Jones from Camp Pell, at the American Hospitality Club before going on to the dance at 7 pm. Private Jones was 30 minutes late, however, and Thompson gave up waiting for him. It was a wet and miserable night and the Bendigo woman was later seen leaving the Astoria Hotel with another American soldier at 11.15 pm.

Pauline Thompson's body was found at about 4 am by nightwatchman Henry McGowan on the bluestone steps of the Morningside House boarding house in Spring Street. McGowan recalled:

> I had been patrolling the vicinity of Spring Street from about 3 am. It was raining and visibility was bad. At 4 am the rain had stopped and the moon was shining. I was searching in a lane at the rear of Spring Street. Something caught my eye and I shone my flashlight on it. It was a black handbag with its contents scattered nearby. I gathered them up and stuffed them back in the bag.
>
> There is an all-night garage in Exhibition Street that I use as a kind of base headquarters ... There was no paper money, only a small amount of silver and some coppers. An identity card gave the name of Mrs Pauline Thompson. There was a ration book, some cosmetics, Aspro, chewing gum, comb, hairpins, and a few other odds and ends.

> At 5 am I was at the corner of Spring Street and Railway Parade, opposite the Exhibition Gardens. It had started to rain again and the wind was icy. I turned into Spring Street towards a two-storey residential with long, narrow steps. There was something dark sprawling near the bottom step. I half ran towards the residential, fumbling for my flashlight. When I got it working I said, 'Oh my God'. It was the body of a woman. One leg was twisted back, and her arms were underneath her body as if she might have tried to protect her head. When I got close up I saw that her clothes had been ripped, also her body.[3]

Despite the fact that Thompson had a pre-existing arm injury that meant that she wouldn't be able to ward off her attacker, the bruising on her neck suggested the attacker was a man with massive hands and immense strength.

Melbourne was a city gripped by fear ... there was a maniac on the loose, possibly an American soldier. With the Japanese threatening to invade Australia from the north, the presence of a crazed murderer within the local community added to Melbourne's growing sense of paranoia. Newspapers referred to the murders as the work of a 'brown-out' strangler and police issued warnings to women not to travel alone after dark. The panic that the murders caused resulted in many women moving out of the city to stay in country areas. Some businesses even let their female employees leave work early so they would not have to travel home after dusk.

Detective Sergeant Sidney Harold McGuffie, who was in charge of the 'Brown-Out' case, was something of a celebrity in Melbourne. It was said that the snappily dressed head of homicide wore a blood red rose in his lapel to signify that he was investigating a murder case. McGuffie was also known to wear down suspects during interrogation sessions with long pauses in which he took deep puffs of his pipe. Investigating detectives entertained the theory that the murderer may have been a local man dressed as an American GI to distract attention, but several other women came forward and said that they, too, had been attacked by an American soldier but had managed to escape.

In one incident, a soldier tried to force a woman into her house but was confronted by the woman's uncle who chased the offender away. In another attack, the soldier entered a woman's flat and attempted to assault her but noise from the outside hallway distracted the attacker and the woman was able to scream for help. The stranger ran from the scene but left behind an American GI singlet with the initials 'EJL' on it.

Incredibly, it was later revealed that Eddie Leonski admitted to fellow soldiers that he had murdered the two women. Private Timothy Gallo Ledena first met Leonski in November 1941 and the pair was stationed together at Camp Pell. On the night of 11 May, Ledena encountered Leonski outside a tent at about 7 pm. Leonski appeared to be drunk and Ledena advised him that he would be better off if he went to bed. Leonksi was mumbling to himself, 'I killed, I killed,' and seemed unhappy and maudlin. It didn't register with Ledena at the time that Leonski was talking about the murder of the second Melbourne woman and Ledena didn't question his friend about it any more. However, Leonski insisted that his friend buy a newspaper.

'We bought a paper and went to the canteen,' Ledena explained. 'He read it and said, "Doorway — doorway — that's the one." The waitress brought us coffee but he didn't touch it. He just kept reading the paper.'[4] Ledena wouldn't believe the gentle giant at first, but Leonski told him that he was the only person he could trust. Leonski wondered aloud why he would attack women older than him.

'Have you heard of Jekyll and Hyde?' Leonski asked. When Leonski told Ledena that he might have two personalities, Ledena suggested that he give himself up. 'I said to him, "You could say you were temporarily insane."'[5] But Leonski couldn't do it. Leonski also told the private that he had 'done these murders. It may be one or two ... I guess ... I strangled them.' But when the pair spoke about the murders again, Leonski showed his darker side. Ledena pointed out to his friend a newspaper article that suggested the murderer was an American soldier. 'So what?' Leonski said. 'There are plenty of US soldiers so there is nothing to worry about.' When Leonski put his massive arms around Ledena's shoulders that night, the private was genuinely scared of his friend for the first time.

On 14 May, Melbourne detectives conducted a line-up of the 15 000 servicemen at Camp Pell. All leave was cancelled and the soldiers were confined to base. American MPs and Melbourne detectives brought the young woman who had been attacked in her doorway to the camp to see if she could identify her attacker. Before the line-up Leonski remarked to Tim Ledena, 'Well this looks like the end of the trail.'[6] But when Leonski failed to be identified by the witness, Ledena assumed that his friend had been 'kidding around' about the murders. That was until four days later.

On 18 May, Eddie Leonski spent the afternoon at the Parkville Hotel. Barman Herbert Everett said Leonski consumed 25 beers up until 5.30 pm and then drank six whiskies. Leonski also walked around on his hands and bragged to others in the bar: 'Aussie soldiers are not tough, just bitter. Most US soldiers have got buddies, but my buddy is *bad*.'[7] Leonski giggled and rolled his tongue around in a suggestive manner. Another drinker at the hotel, Australian Robert Burns, later said that when Leonski drank too much he went pale and the vein on his forehead started to swell. Leonksi continually muttered to himself and his voice seemed to change, becoming more high-pitched as he became drunker.

That night 40-year-old Gladys Hosking became the strangler's third victim. It was raining when, at about 6 pm, Hosking left the chemistry department of Melbourne University with her friend Dorothy Pettigrew. The woman lived within walking distance of the university but, after saying goodbye to her friend, Hosking was seen sharing an umbrella with an American serviceman. Private Nick Vitale was coming out of a milk bar when he saw a fellow soldier holding an umbrella over a woman. Vitale asked the soldier if he knew where there was a hotdog stand. The soldier answered him with what seemed to be a slight foreign accent, but as the couple passed under a dim light, Vitale could see that the man was a tall American GI with a broad nose and a dark complexion. The petite woman, whom Vitale later identified as Gladys Hosking, did not appear to be in any apparent danger.

At 9 pm Australian soldier Private Noel Seymour, who was guarding a number of army vehicles positioned just outside Camp Pell, saw a soldier covered in yellow mud stumbling through Royal Park. Private Seymour asked the serviceman what had happened and he replied that he had fallen in the wet conditions while coming through the park. The serviceman appeared to be drunk. 'My girl is nice,' the American soldier giggled. 'I thought I could drink but she drank me under the table.' The American indicated that he was stationed in Area One of Camp Pell in the street near the zoo and asked Seymour which tram he had to catch to get home.

In the early hours of the following morning, butcher Albert Whiteway was driving his meat lorry along Gatehouse Street when he noticed a woman's hat lying on the ground on the side of the road. He then saw what appeared to be a body lying on some earth that had been excavated from a defence trench. Whiteway approached Australian Private Donald Wallace, who was on duty at the time, and asked if it was a body. 'The soldier took a glance', Whiteway recounted, 'and replied, "It's a body alright." We ran up to the body. The soldier said, "She's been dug out of the trench. She's all cut up." I replied, "Not on your life! They don't dig them up with their clothes on like that."'[8] The woman's umbrella was found nearby.

Detective Sergeant McGuffie arrived at the crime scene at about 7 am. The body of Gladys Hosking was lying face down in the yellow slush; her stockings and shoes were still on but her garments were torn and disarranged and her overcoat was lying near her body. There was no doubt in McGuffie's mind that the murder was related to the other two. The fact that the woman's body was discovered so close to Camp Pell appeared to support the theory that an American soldier was involved and the positive sighting by Private Seymour appeared to confirm it.

Back at Camp Pell, US Private Peter Briscoe saw Eddie Leonski covered in yellowish mud in the early hours of 19 May. Briscoe told Leonski to wash the mud off before it dried, but Leonski said that he was tired and was going to bed. There was no blood on his clothes nor was he trying to hide from anyone, but he did appear drunk. Leonski spoke slowly and seemed to be in a daze. When Tim Ledena entered the tent and saw Leonski asleep in his bed, he remarked how pale his friend was.

Later that day more witnesses were brought to Camp Pell. This time Eddie Leonski was identified by the uncle of one of the soldier's intended victims as the American GI walked towards the camp oval. Leonksi was arrested for the murder of Gladys Hosking and handcuffed to a bed in the camp stockade. He was then positively identified by Private Seymour, the young Australian soldier on guard duty who had seen him covered in mud outside Camp Pell on the previous night. The serviceman's 'reign of terror' had finally ended after 16 days. Leonski's platoon was quickly redesignated and became the First Operating Platoon, 126th Signal Radio Intelligence Company. The platoon moved to Mount Macedon in Victoria on 6 June 1942.

The United States won the right through the courts to establish a military tribunal under which to try Eddie Leonski. The *Melbourne Truth* wrote of the move, 'It was the first time that any person has ever been tried in this country by a military tribunal for a crime which violated civilian law.'[9] However, it was clear that Leonski's crimes had the potential to harm US–Australian wartime relationships and that the military authorities wanted the matter quickly dealt with. When Leonski's court martial finally got under way in August, a Colonel Drumwarring told the military tribunal:

> It would be unreal to deny that amongst certain sections of the Australian armed forces there is a feeling of rivalry and hostility towards us. On no account can we allow this feeling to worsen or the situation to get out of hand. I need hardly remind you, Colonel, that Australia as a base is absolutely essential for our defence of the Pacific and our return to Manila. It is not difficult to imagine the explosive potentiality of a situation when an American soldier is held responsible for the brutal murders of three Australian women.[10]

Australian authorities tried to fight this complete disregard of its legal sovereignty but the federal government did not want to further inflame the situation. On the morning of Thursday, 13 August 1942, in Russell Street in the heart of Melbourne, Leonski's trial commenced in an upstairs hall that had been converted into an impromptu court. However, the court martial was convened without the presence of civilian lawyers.

Colonel Matt Frost of Dallas, Texas, president of the military board, opened the trial by asking for a report from Major Edwin Gristner concerning the accused's mental health. Leonski was examined for 'organic mental illnesses' such as growths, inflammation of the brain or venereal disease. All were negative. During July and August, Gristner had visited the accused twice a week. 'My examination took the form of determining whether the accused could differentiate between right and wrong,' Gristner told the hearing. 'The conclusion of the board is that at the time of the examinations and at the time of the alleged offences, Edward Leonski was sane, but under the influence of alcohol.'[11]

Leonksi's defence counsel objected to the tabling of the report because it was 'highly prejudicial' in that it expressed an opinion of not only the defendant's sanity but also whether he committed the crimes. It also commented on the circumstances in which he was alleged to have committed them. Although Colonel Tremayne, the member of the board who advised on points of law and procedure, agreed and recommended that the other board members disregard the report, Leonski declined to change his plea. When he stood to face the bench, Leonski pleaded 'not guilty'. His chance to plead guilty on the grounds of insanity was gone ... his fate was sealed.

During his trial, evidence of Leonski's fragile mind was presented to the military board. US Private Mitchell Ford Kappy told the court that, 'When Leonski gets drunk his voice changes ... [he] talks more like a girl ... giggles. Different to his usual style... [he says] stuff about poltergeists, werewolves, demons. Creepy stuff. Talks to himself a lot ... other times it's like he's talking to someone. It's scary. Once I heard him shouting and swearing like he was having an argument.'

Leonski suffered from a dual personality disorder — his alter ego 'Buddy' committed the crimes. Leonksi identified with older women because of his love-hate relationship with his mother. The death of the victims satisfied the loathing that he had for his mother. Alcohol was the trigger for his psychosis. The injuries to the women's throats were part of Leonski's undiagnosed mental condition; he later explained the strangulations as part of his wanting 'to capture the woman's voices'.[12]

When Leonski's defence team tried to raise the question of sanity Colonel Drumwarring went on the front foot. 'Now I ask you frankly, isn't the last resort of the degenerate, the depraved, the shiftless, and the morally weak, insanity? How many riff raff, after being apprehended for a brutal crime, cry insanity? But Colonel, this is no civil case being tried in the calm atmosphere of peace. This is a time of emergency. We are faced with a dangerous and inflammatory situation. There is only one way to deal with such a situation, that is to act with authority, decision and above all, speed.'[13]

Despite the fact that there was only the sighting of an American serviceman in the doorway of a shop to connect Leonski with the first murder, nothing to connect him with the second and the circumstantial issue of him being found near the body of the third victim, there was never any doubt that Leonski was the killer. Late in the trial, however, Leonski's defence team still clung to the 'not guilty' plea on the grounds of the accused's mental state. His legal team maintained, 'The defence contends there is grave doubt about the defendant's sanity. If he is convicted without full consideration of this issue there is the possibility that a serious miscarriage of justice will have been done.'[14]

On Thursday, 20 August 1942, in accordance with article 52 of the Military Code, Eddie Leonski was found guilty by a majority of the members of the military board, who voted by secret ballot. At 4 pm Leonski rose in his seat and faced the court as Colonel Frost read the verdict to him:

> Edward Joseph Leonski, it is my duty as president of the court to inform you that, in closed session and upon secret and written ballot, three fourths of the members of the court present concurring when the vote was taken, you have been found guilty in all three specifications and charges ... It is the judgement of this court that you shall be taken from here to a place of execution and hanged by the neck until you are dead.[15]

When the verdict was handed down, the prisoner grinned widely and broke out into a high-pitched laugh.

The *Melbourne Truth* commented:

> Leonski was an enigma whose name will be constantly referred to by succeeding generations of psychologists. Seemingly indifferent to his own fate, always polite to his guards and visitors, he nevertheless constantly erupted with grisly humour.
>
> An official who visited Leonski at the city watchhouse where he was being held was greeted with a saucy grin. 'We are planning to hold a party,' he was told. 'Hope you can come along.'
>
> 'Sure,' Leonksi [added], highly amused. 'A necktie party.'
>
> Leonski asked another official if he liked 'swing'. The unsuspecting official, thinking he was talking about big-band music, answered in the affirmative. 'Good,' he was told. 'We've got a real swing session coming up. I've been given top billing.'[16]

Edward Leonski was sentenced to death by hanging without the right of appeal. On 4 November 1942, General Douglas MacArthur confirmed the sentence. The week before his execution, Leonski was visited by Detective Sergeant Syd McGuffie. The serviceman offered to demonstrate how he strangled his victims. Grabbing the detective by the throat for a moment, Leonski showed how easily he could snuff out a life with his massive hands. The doomed man let go of McGuffie's throat before any damage was done, and then laughed heartily as the shocked detective left the watchhouse.

On Monday, 9 November at 6.15 pm, a hearse drove Leonski from the city watchhouse to Melbourne's infamous Pentridge Prison — the same place where 62 years before, almost to the day, Ned Kelly had been hanged by the neck until dead. As Leonski was escorted to the gallows, he was singing to himself; 'It's a lovely day tomorrow, tomorrow is a lovely day.'[17]

The Melbourne *Herald* reported:

> Edward Joseph Leonski, 24 years old, American private and triple murderer, was hanged early this morning. Brought from his cell in the City Watchhouse in a black maria, he was driven non-stop to Pentridge Prison and taken direct to a room adjoining the scaffold in D Division.

> The hangman was waiting on the bridge where the drop is placed. Nearby were two US doctors and a priest. The usual procedure with civil execution was carried out.
>
> Leonski came into the scaffold and a black cap was put over his head, while his legs and hands were shackled. He maintained such an attitude of calm indifference to the end as to leave everyone associated with him aghast and amazed. Certainly no other murderer in the memory of Australian students of criminology was so obviously uninterested in his own fate.[18]

In order to deter the Melbourne public from turning his gravesite into a spectacle, the body of the 'Brown-Out' murderer was buried on three separate occasions in two segregated sites in Springvale Cemetery. In May 1945, Leonksi's remains were recovered and he was buried in a USAF cemetery in Ipswich, west of Brisbane. In 1947, the US military decided that all US servicemen buried in Australia would be relocated to American soil. Leonski's remains were unearthed once again and sent to America, where they stayed in an army mausoleum for six months. They were then transferred to an army distribution centre for another nine months until it could be decided what to do with them. The body of Eddie Leonski was buried in his final resting place on 14 April 1949 in the Schofield Barracks Post Cemetery in Honolulu, Hawaii — plot 9, row B, grave 8.

If authorities hoped that the animosity between US servicemen and Australian military personnel would dissipate, then the issues proved to be much more complex than first appreciated, 'Aussie' males thought that the 'Yanks' were far too forward with the local women and there was anecdotal evidence of African American soldiers being treated with disdain in some cities. Many Australian soldiers had already seen action in Europe and North Africa and felt that, in early 1942, the Americans were still unproven in battle. Deeper than that, it is now well known that General MacArthur was contemptuous of the undisciplined Australian forces while his Australian counterpart, General Sir Thomas Blayney, thought the American soldier 'lazy' and corresponded with Prime Minister John Curtin in this regard.[19]

On 26 November, the traditional American Thanksgiving holiday, a mini riot erupted in Brisbane between Australian soldiers and US Military Police. What started as a friendly drink in a Brisbane 'canteen' erupted into a fight between American and Australian servicemen. US Military Police intervened in a heavy-handed fashion and in the ensuing melee Australian gunner Ed Webster was fatally shot in the chest when he grabbed one of the MP's rifles. For several days afterwards, locals took out their hostility on American military personnel with several soldiers needing to be hospitalised after being beaten.

The Brown-Out murders impacted on Australian servicemen, and particularly the people of Melbourne, who lived through the terror, and the story of Eddie Leonski went on to become part of Australian urban folklore. In 1979, Melbourne author Andrew Mallon published a partially fictionalised account of Leonski's murder spree, *Leonski: The brown-out murders*, and a film was planned in the early 1980s at a time when the Australian film industry was going through something of a renaissance. One news report maintained that former US entertainer and Australian talk-show host Don Lane would take on the role of Major Dannenberg in the production, which would be called 'The Brown-Out Incident'. When the screenplay was finally finished by William Nagle (*The Odd Angry Shot*), it was not until 1986 that the film, now called *Death of a Soldier*, got under way.

Directed by noted Australian filmmaker Phillippe Mora, the film starred Australians Bill Hunter and Maurie Fields as two Melbourne cops, unknown American actor Reb Brown as Leonski, with veteran James Coburn as the major who ultimately defends the accused at his court martial. While the movie was not a great success, the memories of the Brown-Out murders remain. A Melbourne company named White Hat Tours even conducted a detailed tour of the Brown-Out crime scenes — Camp Pell and Pentridge Prison — as part of its Murders and Mysteries Tour.

After the Second World War, the Victorian Housing Commission used the army huts at Camp Pell as transit camps to accommodate families who had been evicted by the commission's slum reclamation program. Once again Camp Pell gained a degree of unwanted notoriety, with some of the newly relocated residents being classed as 'incorrigible'.[20] The original guard shelters at the gate can still be found, but the site is now covered with netball and basketball facilities as well as a new hockey stadium.

Chapter 5

The Graeme Thorne Murder (1960)

Just as the kidnapping and murder of the infant son of world-renowned aviator Charles A. Lindbergh left an indelible stain on the American dream, the 1960 kidnapping and murder of nine-year-old Graeme Thorne similarly affected the whole of Australian society. The Lindbergh case in 1932 reflected the clash between newfound celebrity and vicious opportunism — surely the best and worst characteristics of American life. In Australia, commonly promoted as the 'lucky country' for the thousands of immigrants who came to these shores after the Second World War, the Graeme Thorne kidnapping — and his subsequent murder — came after the boy's family had seemingly secured their future by winning a £100 000 lottery prize.

At 8.30 am on Thursday, 7 July 1960, eight-year-old Graeme Frederick Hilton Thorne left his family's Bondi unit in Edward Street, to meet family friend Phyllis Smith to be driven to school. When Graeme wasn't sitting at the usual meeting place on the corner of Wellington and O'Brien streets, Mrs Smith drove to the Thorne residence to see if the boy was going to school. At first Graeme's mother, Freda, thought that her son may have taken another lift or had walked to school, but when Mrs Smith arrived at Scots College in Bellevue Hill to drop off her own sons and found that the boy had not arrived, the police were notified.

When the kidnapper telephoned the Thorne home at 9.40 am, a Bondi Police sergeant, Larry O'Shea, had already arrived. The call was taken by Mrs Thorne, but when the male voice with a foreign accent asked for Graeme's father, who was away in northwestern New South Wales on business, the local sergeant said that he was the boy's father. The mysterious caller demanded £25 000 before 5 o'clock or 'the boy will be fed to the sharks'.[1] That amount of money was an extraordinary sum for the times, even considering the fact that the Thornes lived in 'the good part'[2] of Bondi and their son attended an exclusive boys' grammar school. At the time, Sergeant O'Shea didn't know that the Thornes had recently won the lottery and instinctively expressed his doubt in being able to raise the money.

'Where would I be able to get that kind of money?' O'Shea asked.

'You've got it, you've got it ... Oh yes you have!' the voice replied.[3]

The kidnapper said that he would ring back at 5 pm with further details but made no mention of where or how the money should be delivered. Police quickly learned that Bazil Thorne had won first prize in the tenth Opera House Lottery — a newly established lottery to fund the then unfinished Sydney Opera House — on 1 June. The Opera House Jackpot Lottery was not for everybody — the £3 ticket cost (which was increased to £5 in August 1960) was at the time equal to a week's wages for many people — and was pitched at middle-class income earners (the £100 000 prize would be valued today at over $5 million). In 1960 the names of lottery winners were not withheld from the public and the Thornes' good fortune in purchasing winning ticket 3932 had been splashed all over the Sydney papers.

The press caught wind of the abduction when Bondi police sealed off Edward Street. Although the police said little, the afternoon papers broke the sketchy details of the boy's disappearance. The kidnapper rang again at 9.47 pm that night, but the call was answered by another police officer.

Whether the caller realised that this was a different voice from the person he spoke to that morning is unclear, but after asking if the money was ready and giving instructions for it to be placed into two paper bags, the caller abruptly hung up. The reality that the police were in charge of the case must surely have occurred to the kidnapper and grave doubts were now cast over the safe return of Graeme Thorne to his family.

The *Sydney Morning Herald* wrote that 'police said that the kidnapping, uncommon in Australia but not overseas, suggests that it might have been masterminded by a New Australian'.[4] That night Detective Inspector George Grey made a direct appeal on television to the kidnappers for Graeme Thorne's safe return. On 37-year-old Bazil Thorne's arrival back in Sydney, the boy's distraught father made his own impassioned appeal: 'If the person who has my son is a father of his own, all I can say is, for God's sake, send him back to me in one piece.'[5]

The Sydney media became intensely involved in the case. The public were briefed about the details of the kidnapping and the progress of the investigation in the daily papers, and then updated by black-and-white news bulletins in the evening news. 'In the streets, hotels, homes, buses, offices, factories, shops and clubs, the talk was of the kidnapping,' wrote one account of the time.[6] The state government offered a £5000 reward, which was equalled by Australian Consolidated Press and then bettered by Fairfax Newspaper Group's £10 000.

Some of the leads were scurrilously opportunistic — a woman held a séance in the Bondi Police Station; a male diviner with 'vibrating bones' offered to lead detectives to the kidnapper; an Anglican priest, acting as a go-between for the family, travelled to the Blue Mountains, west of Sydney, and handed over an envelope with £100 in it to a 'mystery woman' who ultimately eluded the police who were trailing her. Each false lead led to further heartbreak for the Thorne family. Against police wishes, the Thorne's offered all or part of their lottery win for the safe return of their son. They wrote:

> We the mother and father of Graeme Thorne earnestly request you to return our son to us at the earliest possible moment. We plead with you

> to at least let Graeme contact us. We again emphasise we are prepared to pay the sum of £25 000 and wish to do all we can to make that easy.[7]

Almost subconsciously the Sydney public were conscripted into action and provided many of the breakthroughs in the case. The day after the kidnapping, the victim's school case was found behind a stone wall on the Wakehurst Parkway in Frenchs Forest in Sydney's northeast. The school case, with the name 'Graeme Thorne' embossed on it, was found by an elderly man collecting bottles. The man had seen the appeals by police on television and was well aware of the importance of his discovery. Several days later, the missing boy's school cap and the contents of the school case — a lunchbox, raincoat and maths book — were found a kilometre away. A thorough search of the surrounding bushland failed to turn up any sign of Graeme.

In the initial stages of the investigation a peculiar incident that had occurred several weeks before at the Thornes' Bondi unit came to light. On or about 14 June, a stranger with a strong foreign accent had called at the Thorne's ground floor, two-bedroom flat inquiring after a 'Mr Bognor'. The man was seen by Mr and Mrs Thorne and was told by Freda Thorne that they had just moved into the flat and while she knew that the previous tenant's name was Bailey, she did not know of a Mr Bognor. The man read from a small notebook and asked Mrs Thorne, 'Is the telephone here 30 7113?'

The Thornes had applied for the installation of a telephone after moving into the flat but although the number quoted by the man had been allocated to them, the phone had not been installed nor was the number in the directory. When Mrs Thorne asked where the man had obtained their number, he replied that he was a 'private inquiry agent' who was investigating a 'husband and wife affair'.[8] He also facetiously added that 'we have ways and means' of obtaining telephone numbers. (It was later suggested that the number was given out by a staff member of the State Lotteries, but it could just as easily been given by the New Services Branch of the Postmaster-General's Department where it was recorded while awaiting connection.)

Mrs Thorne told the man to ask Mrs Lord, the lady upstairs who had been living at the address for a much longer time. When the stranger spoke to Mrs Lord he inquired about a 'Mr Bailey' but did not mention anyone with the name 'Bognor'. The man's visit was thought to have been a simple case of mistaken identity until Graeme Thorne's disappearance. Now it took on a sinister overtone — was the kidnapper staking out the family of his intended victim? It was equally likely that the Thorne's daughter, Belinda, was the intended victim but the opportunity for the three-year-old's kidnapping did not present itself.

It also seemed as though the Thorne kidnapping had been inspired in part by a similar event unfolding on the other side of the world. In April 1960, the four-year-old grandson of Jean-Pierre Peugeot, the multi-millionaire owner of the French car company, had been kidnapped. A modest ransom was demanded ($A35 000) and paid, and the child was safely returned to his family in Paris. At the time of Graeme Thorne's disappearance, the Paris kidnappers had not been caught (they were subsequently found and sentenced to 20 years' imprisonment) but that was another world away, not Australia. The NSW Crimes Act did not even have a classification for kidnapping. The closest charge was 'abduction', with a maximum penalty of 14 years' imprisonment, but all that was about to change.

The case was so far from the Australian experience that even hardened criminals were affected by the kidnapping. One underworld figure, described as a 'hard man' stated that, 'I'll bet a thousand quid to a peanut it's not an Australian knockabout man responsible for this. I'll be proud to call myself a "copper" if I can help in any way to find the little kid.' Mrs Kate Ryan, a former associate of many of Sydney's crime figures stated that, 'The last thing any one of the Sydney mobsters would do is to terrify or injure a child ... our bad men, no matter what they've been in could never stoop this low.'[9]

Another lead in the case was provided by a man and a woman, who when driving to work at 8.20 am on the morning of the boy's disappearance noticed an iridescent blue 1955 Ford Customline parked at the corner of Francis and Wellington streets. The man, Cecil Denmeade, told police he almost crashed into the double-parked car. The position of the car on the side of the narrow footpath would require pedestrians using Wellington Street to walk around the car. The witnesses were able to supply a general description of the driver but were unable to recall any part of the car's licence plate.

Detectives investigating this lead learned that all 1955 Ford Customline cars had an engine number starting with SQ if the engine was fitted to an imported body, or ASQ if the engine was fitted to an Australian model. Of the 270 000 Fords registered by the Department of Motor Transport, four thousand vehicles had engine numbers with the two prefixes and police began the painstaking task of finding every one of them.

On 16 August 1960, the kidnapping became a murder investigation when Graeme Thorne's body was found hidden in a vacant block of land in Grandview Grove, Seaforth (a few kilometres away from where the boy's belongings had been strewn along the Wakehurst Parkway). Brothers Peter and Phillip McCue casually mentioned to their parents across the dinner table that there was a 'body in the bush' on a vacant block of land that they used as a pretend 'fort'. The boys had known about the body for some time but had not told anyone.

The decomposing body of eight-year-old Graeme Thorne, which was wrapped in a blue tartan rug, was found fully clothed in the uniform that he had left home in six weeks before. The boy's feet were tied together with twine and one of his school shoes was lying nearby. A scarf tied loosely around his neck, with a knot under his jaw, had obviously been used as a gag. The body was hidden under an overhanging shelf of rock and behind some low scrub.

The subsequent autopsy by government medical officers Drs John Laing and Clarence Percy found that there was a wound on the left side of the back of the head, with an underlying fracture to the back of the skull and some bruising of the scalp. There were also abrasions on the right side of the boy's neck. The lungs and upper air passages showed scattered surface haemorrhages. It was determined that Graeme Thorne died from the effects of the head injury or asphyxia, or a combination of both. The very nature of the skull fracture was indicative of the use of considerable force, while the dotted haemorrhaging on the lungs and the upper air passages indicated deliberate obstruction to the boy's air passages, either by throttling or 'mechanical' means.

It was the opinion of the government medical officers that the boy was alive when hit on the head because of the bruising to his scalp (if the heart had stopped pumping there would be no flow of blood to the top of the head to cause bruising). The position of the haemorrhaging in the upper larynx, they argued, was not consistent with asphyxia due to being tied up in a confined space.

A combination of scientific deduction and simple logic determined that the boy's fate was sealed the day that he was kidnapped. The growth of fungi found on the boy's shoes, the contents of the stomach and the general condition of his clothing indicated that Graeme Thorne was killed within 24 hours of his kidnapping and his body had lain where it was found for almost six weeks. The fungi found on the boy's shoes was examined by the School of Agriculture at the University of Sydney and it was determined that it took a minimum of three to six weeks for the fungi to reach that stage of development in consistently humid conditions. (Obviously, if the shoes were still being used the fungi would not have had time to fully develop.) As the stomach was empty it would have taken a minimum of two or three hours for the boy's breakfast to digest. Lastly, Graeme Thorne's necktie was still as his mother had tied it the morning he disappeared; his coat was fully buttoned up with two handkerchiefs still neatly folded and unused as his mother had given him.

The rug in which the boy's body was wrapped yielded a number of significant clues. The tartan pattern was identified as No. 0639, manufactured at the Onkaparinga Mills in South Australia between May 1955 and January 1956. Numerous hairs were found on both sides of the rug, including soft, wavy, animal hairs of reddish colour — identified as being from a Pekinese dog or similar animal. There were three classes of human hairs found — light to medium brown hairs, dyed and to a length of 23 centimetres; undyed dark brown head hairs; and light-coloured blonde or grey hairs dyed with a henna rinse. Several samples of vegetable foliage were also found inside the rug, with the majority of samples present at the top near the opening of the rug.

However, only one type of foliage was found on the vacant lot where the body was discovered. Samples of two plants not found on the block of land where the body was recovered were subsequently identified as *Chamaecyparis pisifara* var. *squarrose* and *Cupressus glabra* — both distinctive forms of cyprus plants. Both shrubs were found separately on other blocks in the street but the combination of both plants was not present on the particular allotment where the body was hidden or any other home in the area. Soil scrapings taken from Graeme Thorne's coat, trousers and shoes — and samples found on the knot in the scarf tied around the boy's neck — showed minute pink and white fragments identified as lime-stock mortar. This meant that the body had been lying on its back under a brick building somewhere other than where it was found.

Taking into account what they knew about the ransom demand made by the man with a foreign accent, and the forensic pieces of the puzzles identified after the discovery of Graeme Thorne's body, detectives were now looking for a building — most likely a domestic dwelling — with high foundations and pink mortar with two identifiable shrubs in the yard. Detectives started a detailed search of neighbouring homes, slowly radiating out from where the boy's body was found. The breakthrough came when a local postman — an amateur botanist with an encyclopaedic knowledge of local plant forms — identified a house in the nearby suburb of Clontarf with the two cyprus plants easily visible in the front of the yard.

Detectives first visited the house in question on 3 October 1960. The red brick building in Moore Street was constructed with pink mortar on high foundations with a garage underneath. The two plants in question bordered the garage on either side of the driveway. At the time of the boy's disappearance the home was rented by a Hungarian immigrant, Stephen Leslie Bradley, his wife Magda and their three children. Bradley had left Australia just a week before, on 26 September, and was en route to the United Kingdom with his family on SS *Himalaya*.

Stephen Bradley was an ambitious man. Born Istavan Baranyay in Budapest in 1926, Bradley immigrated to Australia in 1950. He later claimed that he was an engineer and even a doctor in Italy before coming to Australia, but he was mainly employed in menial jobs after immigrating — first as a labourer, a mechanic and then an electroplater, although he also had stints as a real estate agent and guesthouse proprietor. Anglicising his name and changing it by deed poll, Bradley married Eva Marie Lazlo in Melbourne in 1952, where they lived with their child Helen until Mrs Bradley was killed in a car accident in 1955. In 1958 Bradley married a wealthy divorcee, Magda Wittman, and moved to Sydney with his daughter and her sons, Peter and Robert. After renting the Clontarf home, Bradley made the decision to move his family to a nearby unit in Manly.

On 7 July, the day of Graeme Thorne's disappearance, Stephen Bradley had arranged for removalists to be at his Moore Street home at 11 am. Mrs Bradley left the house at 10 am in a taxi for Kingsford-Smith Airport for a holiday on Queensland's Gold Coast. The doors to the Bradleys' garage beneath the home were locked and at no stage did the removalists go inside it. Bradley moved into a flat in Osborne Road, Manly, on the northern peninsula of Sydney, where the family lived until abruptly deciding to return to Europe.

Former neighbours of the Bradleys in Clontarf had already contacted police to inform them that Stephen Bradley owned a 1955 Ford Customline, registration number AYO 382, matching the car seen in Wellington Street on the morning of Graeme Thorne's disappearance. Bradley was even interviewed by police at his work on 24 August — eight days after the discovery of the boy's body — but police had not thought him a suspect, despite the fact that he had a foreign accent. Unknown to police, Mrs Bradley bought a passage to the United Kingdom on the day after her husband was interviewed, and the family left Australia the following month.

The 1955 Ford once owned by Bradley was later traced to a car saleyard in Granville, some 25 kilometres west of the city, shortly after he had left the country. An examination of the vehicle found a hairbrush with samples of dog hair indistinguishable from the samples found on Graeme Thorne's clothing or the rug in which his body was wrapped. Similar hairs were found on the floor of the car, along with human hairs matching the brown and blonde hairs found on the tartan rug. Investigating police found that Bradley also owned another car — a Goggomobile, registration number BZD 432. Police recovered the Goggomobile from the premises of a finance company in Leichhardt. Hairs of a similar nature, both animal and human, were also found in that car and in the Manly unit in which the Bradleys were living before leaving for overseas.

The forensic evidence started to mount up against Stephen Bradley:

- a brown Pekinese dog was found in a Sydney veterinary clinic where Bradley had left it (the dog later died and police had it stuffed so that it could be kept as an exhibit);
- pieces of twine found in the Bradleys' Clontarf home, his Manly unit and those used to tie furniture pieces retrieved from a second-hand dealer, were matched in weight of unit length and types of fibre to that used to tie Graeme Thorne's ankles together;
- soil samples examined from under the Bradleys' Clontarf home matched the chemical composition of the soil (with similar heavy fragments of sand and pink and white mortar) found on Graeme Thorne's clothing and the scarf used to silence him;
- a pale blue tassel found near the foundation of the Clontarf house corresponded with the tassels on the tartan rug that wrapped the boy's body;
- photographic evidence that the Bradleys owned the tartan rug — a roll of 35mm film negative had been torn up and thrown out of a window into the garden of the Bradleys' Manly flat — was also discovered. Pieces of a black-and-white negative showed an image of one of the Bradley children sitting on the rug with the tartan pattern easily distinguishable. A Melbourne family later proved that they had given the rug as a present to Mrs Bradley in 1955.

Once the police had enough evidence, they showed a number of photos, including one of Stephen Bradley, to the Thornes and their Bondi neighbour, Mrs Lord. Each in turn identified Bradley as the man who had come to the Bondi flat the month before the kidnapping. Their identification of Bradley was supported by the man and woman who had provided police with a description of a man sitting in the car parked in Wellington Street on 7 July. It was then that police learned that Bradley was currently crossing the Indian Ocean en route to Colombo (in Ceylon, now known as Sri Lanka) with his wife and children. A warrant was issued for Bradley's arrest on 8 October.

When the *Himalaya* docked in Colombo on 10 October, Sydney detectives Brian Doyle and Jack Bateman were waiting for Bradley. Australia had no current extradition treaty with the newly independent country, however, and according to Doyle, Colombo police 'refused point blank to pull Bradley off the *Himalaya*, although we said we wanted him for murder'.[10] Bradley was actually arrested by officers from the Ceylon Police Harbour Patrol and was held in custody for six weeks while Doyle and Bateman presented their case to a Ceylonese court patently hostile to any member of the British Empire, their former colonial masters. After Mrs Bradley and the children continued the voyage to London, Stephen Bradley was finally extradited to Sydney on 18 November.

On the flight back to Australia, Bradley opened up to the detectives who were escorting him. He had been responsible for the kidnapping, Bradley told them, but the boy had accidentally suffocated when tied up in the boot of his Ford after it was locked away in the garage of his Clontarf home while the removalists were working.

On 19 November 1960 at 10.15 am, Stephen Bradley handwrote the following confession, which was later presented at his trial. The confession was witnessed by Detective Sergeant Jack Bateman, who informed Bradley that he was not obliged to make any statement unless he wished to, and that any statement he made may be used in evidence against him. In broken English, Bradley wrote a confession chilling in its simplicity:

> I have red in the newspaper that Mr Thorne won the first prize in the Opera House Lottery. I disided that I would kidnap his son. I knew the address from the newspaper and I have got their phone number from the telephone exchange. I went to the house to see them. I have asked

for someone but can not remember what name. Mrs Thorne said that she did not know that name and she told me to enquier in the flat upstairs. I went upstairs and I seen the woman there. I have done this because I thought that the Thornes will check up. I went out and watched the Thorne boy leaving the house and seen him for about three mornings and I have seen where he went. And one morning I have followed him to the school at Bellevue Hill. One or two mornings I have seen a womman pick him up, and taken to the school. On the day we moved from Clontarf I went out to Edward Street. I parked the car in a street I don't know the name of the street it is off Wellington Street. I have got out from the car, and I waited on the corner, untill the boy walked down to the car. I have told the boy that I am to take him to the school. He sed why, where is the lady. I sed she is sick and cannot come today. Then the boy got in the car and I drove him around for a while, and over the harbour bridge. I went to a public phone box near the spit bridge and I rang the Thornes. I talked to Mrs Thorne and to a man who sed he was the boys father. I have asked for £25 000 from the boys mother and father. I told them that if I don't get the moneys I feed him to the sharks, and I have told them I ring later. I took the boy in the car home to Clontarf and I put the car in my garage. I told the boy to get out of the car and to come and see another boy. When he got out of the car I have put a scarf over his mouth, and put him in the boot of the car, and slamed the boot. I went in my house and the Furniture Removalist came, a few minutes after. When it was nearly dark I went to the car and found the boy was dead. That night I tied the boy up with string and put him in my rug. I put the boy in the boot of the fod [Ford] car again, and then I throw his case and toys near Bantry Bay [sic], and I put the boy on a vacant lotmount near the house I went to see with a Estate Agent, to buy it some time before.

S.L. Bradley[11]

But further forensic investigation by police started to unravel Bradley's defence that Graeme Thorne had accidentally suffocated in the boot of the car. An examination of Bradley's car found that, in the closed position, the boot had an air circulation exchange of .55 times per hour. A forensic expert even breathed air through a tube and facemask for a period of seven hours to prove that someone could survive such conditions. While readings showed a slight increase in the levels of carbon monoxide over the first six hours until a state of equilibrium was reached with the oxygen level, it was proved that this could not have caused suffocation. The expert even factored in a degree of activity — as much as a boy walking up a flight of 50 steps for six hours to simulate the possibility that Graeme Thorne may have struggled for his life in the boot of his kidnapper's car — but the findings were the same.

More than likely Bradley tied Graeme Thorne up with the twine and a knotted scarf to silence him and placed him in the boot of the car on the way across the city before striking the boy over the head with a blunt object and manually strangling or smothering him in the garage of the Clontarf house. The boy's body was hidden near the foundations of the garage before Bradley wrapped it in the rug and took it to the vacant allotment in Grandview Grove. Even the possibility that Graeme Thorne may have hit his head on the rim of the spare tire or as the boot slammed down on him would be disproved in court. Stephen Leslie Bradley was eventually arraigned on a charge of murder.

When Bradley's trial commenced on 20 March 1961 at Sydney's Central Criminal Court, the former Hungarian immigrant pleaded not guilty. Bradley took the coward's route, maintaining that his statement was dictated to him by police and that he was coerced into writing it and then signing it under threats against the safety of his family. His wife had been in the Auschwitz concentration camp during the Second World War, he said; he himself had been a prisoner of the Gestapo and was part Jewish. But his alibi for the morning of Graeme Thorne's disappearance was threadbare ... Bradley said that he sat in his car in the garage and read the papers, annoyed that his wife was going to Queensland on holidays and was leaving him to do all the packing for their move. He had never even been to Edward Street, Bondi, he maintained.

But the court was told that on Monday, 21 November 1960, Bradley was placed in a police line-up with 15 other men of similar build and

European nationality. Bazil and Freda Thorne, their neighbour Mrs Lord, and the man and woman who had seen Bradley sitting in his 1955 Ford, each placed him at Bondi. When Mrs Thorne was asked to place her hand on Bradley's shoulder in order to identify him to police, she refused, saying, 'I will not put my hand anywhere near him.'[12] But the police line-up, in itself, was not enough ... Bradley's photo had already been published in the newspapers when arriving back in Australia in handcuffs.

When Magda Bradley returned to Australia and took the stand to give evidence on behalf of her husband, the prosecution under Crown prosecutor W.J. Night went onto the attack. Night suggested that Mrs Bradley was privy to the kidnapping plot from the beginning — she had taken a taxi into the airport because she knew that her husband had the boy in his car. The scarf that was used as a gag was hers; the rug that was wrapped around the boy's body was hers; was it just a coincidence that she bought tickets for Europe the day after the police interviewed her husband on 24 August? It was, Mrs Bradley said. She didn't even know her husband had been interviewed.

The nine-day trial that mesmerised Australia drew packed crowds to Sydney Central Court and attracted national and international media attention. Although much of the evidence was circumstantial, such was the overwhelming body of forensic material linking Stephen Bradley to the crime that he was subsequently found guilty of the kidnapping and murder of eight-year-old Graeme Thorne. Bea Miles, a well-known Bondi identity, echoed Bradley's original threat when she screamed from the public gallery, 'Feed *him* to the sharks!'[13] Sentenced to life imprisonment (the death penalty had been repealed in New South Wales, but if Bradley had committed the crime in Melbourne he would surely have hanged for it), the Full Court of the NSW Supreme Court dismissed his appeal on 22 May 1961.

The existence of a handwritten confession did not sway Justice Herron when he handed down the unanimous decision against Bradley at the subsequent appeal. In 20 years as a judge Herron doubted that he had seen a confession 'more convincing in its truth'. Bradley's public defender, Fred Vizzard, had tried to insinuate that his client was 'verballed' but Detective

Sergeant Brian Doyle, later to be Assistant Commissioner of Police, was unimpeachable under cross-examination. 'You only have to look at the wording and phraseology,' Doyle maintained.[14] The grammatical features and syntax of the confession were as powerful as Bradley's fingerprints on a murder weapon.

In the aftermath of the kidnapping and murder of Graeme Thorne, lottery winners were given the option of having their names withheld. Whether kidnapping was a foreign crime imported into this country by 'New Australians' or not, the Graeme Thorne kidnapping tapped into the most basic of parental fears and even touched upon deep-seated racism. In a statement from the dock Bradley tried to play the 'racism card', maintaining that he was never given a chance because of 'prejudice' and 'powerful emotions'.

The tragedy of the Graeme Thorne case was that Stephen Bradley had many of the same aspirations as the Thornes — he, too, was renting a home near the sea, he had two cars and he wanted the best for his children. But Bradley chose murder as his way to gain a foothold on the 'Australian dream' at the expense of Bazil Thorne's good luck. When Bradley read of Thorne's lottery win, he saw kidnapping as his chance to gain financial respectability in his adopted country. The end result was the death of Graeme Thorne — the innocent victim of a carelessly planned kidnapping.

Although her behaviour did not endear her to the conservative Australian public, Magda Bradley was never implicated in any way in her husband's crime and returned to Europe. After divorcing Bradley in 1965 she lived in anonymity with her children. Bazil and Freda Thorne, with their daughter Belinda, moved to the nearby suburb of Rose Bay, but never got over the death of their son. Bazil Thorne passed away in 1978.

Stephen Leslie Bradley was held in protective custody while in Long Bay Jail to keep him safe from other prisoners. On 6 October 1968, he dropped dead while playing a game of tennis. He was 42.

Chapter 6
The Bogle and Chandler Mystery (1963)

In the early 1960s Australian society was remarkably unaware of the cultural change that was to swamp the country later in the decade. Political unrest, the Vietnam War, the explosion in youth culture and the sexual revolution — these were just some of the issues still to confront Australia as the nation prepared to celebrate New Year's Eve in 1962. Prime Minister Robert Menzies had been in power since 1949 and was preparing to host another royal tour by Queen Elizabeth II. Despite the fact that the rest of the world was involved in a 'cold war' — and had pulled back from the brink of nuclear conflict when US President John Kennedy ordered a blockade of Russian ships delivering missiles to Cuba — Australia was still a conservative stronghold.

Sydneysiders woke on New Year's Day, 1963, hung-over but basking in the city's cosy, suburban affluence. Ritchie Benaud's Australian cricket team was battling to save the Second Test against England, while Rod Laver flew the nation's flag in international tennis and 'Midget' Farrelly was on his way to winning the first professional surfboard championship. By midmorning on 1 January 1963, in the middle of a traditional Australian sporting summer, the temperature was already starting to climb to its predicted maximum of 100 degrees on the old Fahrenheit scale.

Shortly after 10 am, two teenage boys hunting for golf balls in the Lane Cove National Park, northwest of Sydney, found the partly naked body of a man on a dirt track. The body, which had blood and mucus trickling from its nose, was lying face down with its legs fully extended. The man's head was turned and was resting on his left arm, which was bent and tucked under his body. The man's right arm was extended at a right angle to his body. The boys ran to a nearby house and raised the alarm.

When police reached the dirt track 15 minutes later, they noted that the dead man was wearing only socks, shoes, shirt and tie. The man's face was a deep blue colour and his eyes and mouth still open. Someone had placed a piece of brown carpet on his back and then carefully placed the coat and trousers of his blue suit over his naked body. The sleeve of the jacket was carefully arranged to follow the angle of his right arm — it was as if he was wearing the suit. The police then removed the suit and turned over the body before it could be photographed. As rigor mortis had set in and the man was clearly dead, this break in police protocol was inexcusable.

It was then that the body of a woman was found lying in a depression in the ground about 18 metres away. Someone had covered the woman's face and torso with a piece of mouldy cardboard from flattened-out beer cartons so that her body was almost completely obscured in the shallow, 1.5 metre by 60 centimetre ditch. Detectives justified the removal of the cardboard before the woman's body could be photographed because they needed to determine whether the woman was dead or merely unconscious. The woman was lying on her back and her body was also partially naked — her floral frock was hunched around her waist exposing her breasts and her brassiere was resting upside down on her stomach. A pair of men's underpants was between her ankles. There was a slight abrasion, about 1 centimetre long, on the bridge of her nose that had been bleeding. The woman's body was still warm and rigor mortis had not yet set in.

The discovery of two bodies so early on New Year's Day caught police by surprise; because it was a public holiday there was no police photographer available and no doctor on duty at the city morgue. Uniformed police, who were the first to arrive at the Lane Cove National Park, failed to secure the crime scene. When investigating detectives arrived they found police and reporters walking freely between the bodies, which had both been disturbed. The post-mortems of the victims were not carried out until Wednesday, 2 January, and doctors were later forced to defend the extended refrigeration of the bodies at the official inquest, stating that this was not responsible for their subsequent failure to determine the causes of death.

Police retrieved the man's wallet from the trousers of the blue suit and identified him as Dr Gilbert Bogle of Turramurra. The wallet contained £15 — about $300 dollars in today's money — and so murder as the result of robbery seemed most unlikely. Because there were no visible wounds on the victims — and the fact that both had defecated and vomited — police speculated that the pair may have been poisoned. As early as 2 January 1963, newspapers carried that line of reasoning in their reports of the New Year's Day find. *The Sun*'s headline in its evening paper that day was:

DID MYSTERY POISON KILL TWO?
Scientist, woman found dead in bush

Sydney, Tues. — Detectives are convinced that poisoning caused the death of a brilliant scientist and a married woman whose bodies were found in a heavily wooded spot on the Lane Cove River, Sydney, today.

But detectives have not been able to discover what the poison was, how it was administered or by whom.

The dead man was Dr Gilbert S. Bogle, 38, of Turramurra, Sydney. Dr Bogle, a married man with four children, was a specialist in solid-state physics with the Commonwealth Scientific and Industrial

> Research Organisation and was a Rhodes Scholar. His brother, Professor A.G. Bogle of Auckland University, was also a Rhodes Scholar.
>
> The dead woman was Mrs Margaret Chandler, 29, mother of two children, of Croydon, Sydney. She was formally [sic] attached to the CSIRO. Her husband, Dr Geoffrey Chandler, is an experimental officer in the CSIRO Division of Radio Physics.[1]

However, the newspaper story in the conservative early 1960s could only hint at the circumstances that led Dr Bogle and a young married woman to Lane Cove National Park in the early hours of the morning. Although it was later determined that the pair had not had sexual intercourse, they were half-naked and that was clearly their intention.

Gilbert ('Gib') Stanley Bogle was born in New Zealand in 1924. A Rhodes Scholar immediately after the Second World War, he had a master's degree in science and arts, and a doctorate in physics from Oxford University. Bogle earned an international reputation as a scientist specialising in solid-state physics and came to Sydney in 1956 with his wife Vivienne to work for the CSIRO. At the time of his death, Dr Bogle was living in a rented house in Warragal Road, Turramurra, on Sydney's upper north shore with his wife and four children — Janet (aged 11), Christine (nine), Mark (seven) and Anna (four months). He had recently achieved a world breakthrough in the development of MASERs (Microwave Amplification by Stimulated Emission of Radiation), which allowed scientists to listen billions of kilometres into space. In February 1963 the Bogles were due to sail to the United States where Dr Bogle was to take up a two-year research fellowship with Bell Laboratories.

Privately, Gib Bogle did not conform to the generally accepted stereotype of a staid, conservative scientist. It was alleged that Bogle suffered from satyriasis, a condition defined as 'excessive, often uncontrollable sexual desire',[2] more commonly known by its female form — nymphomania. Bogle reportedly conducted as many as five affairs with the wives of associates at the same time, although only three could be corroborated after his death. His trysts were often opportunistic and devoid of romance (his affair with Margaret Fowler, aged 38, was consummated in his tiny

Ford Prefect car outside Turramurra Squash Courts) but his lack of style was more than made up for by his dashing good looks, intellectual ability and, of course, his rampant sexuality. Bogle's wife Vivienne was not aware of his extramarital dalliances.

Bogle was also a member of a group known as 'the Push' — a loose band of artists, intellectuals and libertarians who congregated at the Royal George Hotel in Sydney and discussed everything from art to literature and politics to sex. The members of the Push have been variously described as 'sexist bastards', 'Bohemian loudmouths' and an 'island of excitement in a sea of dullness'.[3] The Push, which grew out of the 'Libertarian' Society of the 1940s — which basically believed that people should be free to do anything they wanted (including, as professional 'ex-pat' Clive James noted, helping themselves to each other's girlfriends) — included Kenneth Buckley, a senior lecturer in economic history at Sydney University and the 1994 biographer of Dr H.V. Evatt, critic Robert Hughes, writer Paddy McGuinness and later *Oz* magazine founder Richard Neville, editor Wendy Bacon and even feminist Germaine Greer as members.

One of Bogle's associates in the Push was CSIRO colleague Geoffrey Arnold Chandler, who was a specialist in solar radiometry. Dr Chandler, then aged 32, had been married to the former Margaret Morphett for six years and they had two children together; boys aged two years and ten months, but his wife was not known to other members in the Push or to most of her husband's colleagues at the CSIRO. Chandler and his wife had an understanding that each could conduct extramarital affairs without hurting their marriage. While Margaret Chandler had allegedly been conducting an affair with another CSIRO scientist, Geoffrey Chandler had been seeing Push member Pamela Logan, a 22-year-old Sydney University secretary, for the last six months of 1962.

On 21 December 1962, the Chandlers attended a CSIRO Christmas party at an outstation at Murraybank. Gib Bogle attended the party alone and met Margaret Chandler for the first time. A man at the party later stated that he 'almost trod' on Gib and Margaret in the bushes at the party.[4] Later that night Bogle, the Chandlers and others went back to the

Chatswood home of another colleague, photographer Kenneth Nash and his wife Ruth, for coffee. Ruth Nash invited Bogle to a New Year's Eve party in 10 days' time — and possibly at Bogle's urging, the Chandlers, who were not usually part of their social circle — and outlined the theme for the night. Each person was asked to bring, for discussion, 'an original art contribution of your own creation in any medium or dimension'.[5]

Geoffrey Chandler later told police that his wife had remarked that the thought of going to bed with Dr Bogle would be an 'interesting experience'.[6] Chandler had not objected about his wife's previous lovers and told her that she should have an affair with his work colleague if she wanted to. Margaret Chandler went shopping for a new frock at Kerr's Ladies Wear in Liverpool Road, Ashfield, and according to the sales assistant who served her, took a lot of interest in her appearance. The same could not be said for her husband. Dr Chandler wore a green-checked shirt, casual slacks and sandals to the party. The Chandlers, who lived in Cromwell Street, Croydon, dropped their children off at the home of Margaret's parents in Granville. Geoffrey Chandler drove his 1924 Vauxhall — distinctive with its aluminium body, folding hood, high wheels, long wheelbase and loud engine — to the Nash residence 40 kilometres across town, arriving there at 9.30 pm.

Ken and Ruth Nash had hosted several New Year's Eve parties since moving into their Waratah Street home in 1956. In most years there was a 'fancy dress' theme to the gatherings but the 1962 New Year's Eve party was designed to be a 'jacket and tie' affair for the approximately 20 guests. The guests included 'a Macquarie Street specialist, a company director, an author, a journalist, photographers, a sculptor and several scientists'.[7] When Geoffrey Chandler walked into the party without a coat, tie or an 'artistic' contribution, his appearance — accentuated by his bushy red beard — drew several wry comments from the guests.

Gib Bogle was the first guest to arrive at the party, just after 9 pm, carrying a box of chocolates, his clarinet and his 'artwork' under his arm. It was a line drawing in pencil and crayon, which he signed 'Beaugualle' (loosely translated as 'beautiful Frenchman'). The drawing was in the style of Picasso; the face of a woman with two mouths, one sticking out from the right side of the head, with a right hand drawn above her face and a left foot underneath it. Bogle was most proud of his drawing and told his hosts that he planned to take it home with him to show his children. He was the life of the party; dancing a mock flamenco to the song *In a Little Spanish Town* and then changing to the twist which drew applause from the other guests.

Ken Nash manned the bar until midnight and later said that he served Margaret Chandler three small glasses of beer. When the group sang *Auld Lang Syne* at midnight, Ken Nash noticed that Geoffrey Chandler was missing. Whether or not he felt out of place or was bored — or the fact that he had another party on his mind — Chandler left the Nash residence at 11:30 pm without telling anyone. Chandler later told detectives that he left the party to buy cigarettes but when he couldn't find any shops open he turned right at Longueville Road and continued on to Balmain. He had been invited to another New Year's Eve party, a bigger affair thrown by the Push's Ken Buckley for 100 guests, which Pamela Logan was also attending.

Geoffrey Chandler arrived at the Buckley party at just about midnight. He later told police that Pamela Logan was 'not feeling well'[8] and because she had only recently received her licence, she asked him to follow her home to her flat in the inner-city suburb of Darlington. Chandler and Logan arrived at the flat between 1 and 1.30 am and drank coffee. He then returned to the Nash party at Chatswood at 2.30 pm after an absence of three hours.

Ken Nash later saw Margaret Chandler and Gil Bogle talking outside, and turned off the outside light 'partly in jest, from a point of puckish humour', which drew the pair back inside.[9] Margaret Chandler had left her handbag and purse in her husband's car and because she could not call a cab, Gib Bogle offered her a lift home. When the Nashes said goodbye to Lester and Francis Cotton at 2.30 am, Ruth Nash noticed that Geoffrey Chandler had returned to the party. Ruth Nash served supper at 3 am and coffee 30 minutes later. Margaret Chandler had some chicken and asparagus but her husband declined anything to eat.

Bogle was drinking coffee with Margaret when Geoffrey Chandler informed them he was again leaving. Chandler told police that it was he who had asked Bogle to take his wife home — Chandler had already made his mind up to go back to Pamela Logan's house for the night and thought that his wife was aware that their Croydon home would be empty. Bogle looked hard at Geoffrey Chandler and said, 'Right',[10] giving the impression to Chandler at least that Bogle had his work colleague's tacit approval of the arrangement. Chandler left the Nash party shortly before 4 am.

Another couple at the party, the Day-Hakkars, told police that they had noticed Bogle and Mrs Chandler sitting together on the couch, talking. Margaret Chandler had a 'glassy' stare and that Gib Bogle 'was stooped over and looked sick'.[11] At 4.15 am Bogle left the party but returned a short time later and asked Ken Nash for his 'artwork'. Five minutes later, the Nashes were saying goodbye to Margaret Beavis, another guest, when they noticed Margaret Chandler standing outside at the foot of the steps. She looked up at them, then slowly walked away. Ken Nash later told the police that there was nothing abnormal about either Bogle's or Chandler's behaviour.

Geoffrey Chandler drove back to Pamela Logan's flat in Darlington Road, Darlington, and woke her up at about 4.30 am. Ms Logan was annoyed but somehow he persuaded her to accompany him to Gladesville to collect his children. Chandler picked up his two children from his in-laws while Pamela Logan waited in Parramatta Road. (A witness later identified Chandler's distinctive vintage car crossing Parramatta and Great North roads at 4.50 am.) The group then drove back to Darlington and had breakfast with one of Ms Logan's friends, a Miss Fullager. Chandler returned to his Croydon home after 10 am and was surprised to discover that his wife was not there — [he assumed] she must have gone somewhere else with Bogle. Chandler was asleep in bed when police woke him later that day with the grim news of his wife's death.

Sunrise was due at 4.46 am that day and it was almost dawn when Gib Bogle drove off in his khaki green Ford Prefect and picked up Margaret Chandler at the bottom of the Nash's driveway. The minimum temperature that night was about 20°C, but no-one could explain what made Bogle choose the Lane Cove River as a suitable spot for a love tryst. On the Pacific Highway, Bogle turned right at Fullers Road and drove 2 kilometres to Fullers Bridge and turned right again into Lady Game Drive. A witness, Kenneth George Challis of Rushcutters Bay, was walking along Lady Game Drive at 4.30 am when he saw Bogle's car stopped halfway off the side of the road. The driver, who Challis later identified as Bogle, covered the woman who was sitting in the car from Challis's view. According to the witness, the man 'looked pale' and he thought he might be 'sick from a New Year's Eve party' as he walked past from a distance of about 3 metres.[12]

Gib Bogle left his car at the side of Millwood Avenue with the windows wound down, the car unlocked and the keys hidden above the sun visor. He, or a third party later that morning, took a piece of brown carpet measuring 90 by 60 centimetres from the boot of the car, which could not be locked. Bogle and Mrs Chandler then set off across Fullers Bridge and entered the O.H. Reid Memorial Park in the Lane Cove National Park and walked down a dirt track towards the Lane Cove River. They were found there dead, five hours later.

The Nash party was in its final stages at 7 am when Vivienne Bogle rang the Chatswood residence inquiring about her husband's whereabouts because he had not yet returned home. Ruth Nash told Mrs Bogle that he had left the party some time ago. Ten minutes later the last guests left and Ken and Ruth Nash went to bed. They had planned to clean up the effects of the New Year's Eve party later that day but were woken by police that afternoon. Yes, Gib Bogle had been at their party the previous night, they told police, but had left with Margaret Chandler. Systematically, police collected the unwashed glasses, cups, plates, ashtrays and liquor bottles, so they could be tested. In 10 hours the 20 guests had drunk 16 bottles of beer, two bottles of scotch, one of gin and one of vodka.

Investigating police considered four scenarios to explain the mysterious deaths of the two victims: a suicide pact, murder-suicide, deliberate double murder by a third party, and accidental poisoning. The casual relationship between the victims ruled out the first two options and focused attention on the latter two. Had Bogle and Chandler been murdered by another person, or had one or both of them inadvertently administered a toxic substance to each other? At the time, without knowing the substance involved, it was difficult to determine the circumstances of their deaths. But another, equally mysterious question, needed to be asked: Who covered the bodies at Lane Cove and why?

When police investigated the crime scene on New Year's morning they found Dr Bogle's green Ford Prefect parked on Millwood Avenue near the track that led down to where the bodies were found. Under the seat they found a case containing Bogle's clarinet and on the back seat, the drawing he had done for the party. When they examined the boot of the car, they found the carpet missing. It measured the same dimensions as the piece of carpet covering Bogle's back and was later identified by Bogle's car mechanic as being one and the same.

But why would Dr Bogle have taken such a small piece of carpet with him? To sit on? To make love on? Surely not. Had Margaret Chandler retrieved the carpet once Bogle became sick? Why had Bogle driven there in the first place? There were better places, even inside the Lane Cove National Park, for a late-night dalliance. Why then did they go down a dirt track? Were they disorientated? Or drugged? If Bogle had been the first to die, why wouldn't Margaret Chandler, a trained nurse, go to one of the houses on the other side of Fullers Bridge for help? And who covered *her* body? At the inquest it was agreed that it was almost impossible for Mrs Chandler to cover herself with the mouldy cardboard.

Dr John Laing, director of NSW Forensic Medicine, examined the bodies of the victims and found that the cause of death was 'acute heart failure, associated with pulmonary oedema and anoxia'.[13] There were no signs of death by violence, hypodermic needle or asphyxia, but toxicology results failed to determine what type of 'poison' caused the couple's deaths.

Ernest 'Sammy' Ogg, the state government analyst, later testified at the May 1963 inquest into the deaths that he had examined the brains, hearts, livers, spleens, kidneys and blood of the victims. Ogg tested hair for arsenic and used ultraviolet and infrared rays and other measuring equipments for evidence of radiation (because Dr Bogle was a CSIRO scientist there was already some speculation that he had been exposed to radiation) and also took samples from the victims' fingernails and muscle tissue. Ogg looked for traces of known poisons such as aconite, atropine, strychnine, carbolic acid, henbane, phenyl, mercury and phosphorus; drugs such as cocaine, opium and even nicotine; and toxins from poisonous snakes, spiders, mushrooms and durata seeds, and even a rare Queensland shellfish *Conus geographus*. All tests proved negative.

City coroner Mr J.J. Loomes stated at the conclusion of the inquest into the deaths of Gilbert Bogle and Margaret Chandler that: 'It gives me no satisfaction to sit here and tell you that all we know about this is that two people died from acute circulatory failure, the cause of which is unknown.'[14] The identity of the person who covered the bodies after their deaths was also never satisfactorily explained. Perhaps a passer-by that morning — a late-night reveller on his way home from a New Year's Eve party — stumbled across the pair and covered them out of some sense of decency. We may never know.

Interestingly, police considered that the deaths might have been the result of a little-known hallucinogenic drug called 'LSD' — lysergic acid diethylamide. In September 1960, the drug's Swiss inventor Dr Albert Hoffmann told a medical conference at the University of Sydney that Australian doctors had already successfully used LSD on psychiatric patients. The recreational use of LSD was a much-discussed topic in Sydney's underground intellectual community and it was alleged that members of Bogle's social group used the drug, which was not yet illegal. LSD is a manufactured drug and scientists at the CSIRO were certainly capable of producing it. It was boasted that 'any school science lab' could make it.[15]

The implications were that the drug could have been ingested voluntarily, or a lethal dose was slipped into Bogle or Chandler's drink as a prank or out of jealousy. In the early 1960s there were no tests available that could detect the presence of LSD in a person's system. In 1966 Dr Geoffrey Oettle discussed the 'LSD theory' with NSW Police Commissioner Norm Allen. Oettle spent three months overseas visiting forensic facilities in the United States, United Kingdom, France, Germany and Austria and discussed the mysterious deaths of Bogle and Chandler with colleagues at international conferences. 'They all thought the deaths were consistent with an overdose of LSD; the mode and circumstances of the deaths certainly supported that view.'[16]

Police also investigated the hosts of the New Year's Eve Party — the Nashes. A hint to their line of inquiry was Kenneth Oswald Nash's admission that he had turned the lights off on an obviously besotted Margaret Chandler and Gib Bogle as they stood outside 'purely in jest, from a point of puckish humour'. Did Ken Nash, knowing that Bogle and Mrs Chandler were going home together, mischievously slip his guests an accidentally lethal dose of LSD as he manned the bar? The Nashes denied any knowledge of LSD being used at the party. They later moved out of their Waratah Street home and lived in another street in Chatswood, but were hounded by the mystery for the rest of their lives.

When it was revealed that Ken Nash had an interest in 'dark mysticism', rumours swept Sydney that Bogle and Chandler had been murdered as part of a weird cult. The *Sunday Telegraph* speculated that the victims were engaged in a black mass ... 'a blasphemous parody of a religious service involving sexual deviations and practices in which sex drugs are sometimes used'.[17] It was all such nonsense. But in a macabre twist, Ruth Nash died on 1 January 1974 from cancer. On New Year's Day 1976, on the thirteenth anniversary of the deaths of Bogle and Chandler and the second anniversary of his wife's death, Ken Nash committed suicide with a .22 calibre rifle.

But still there were other theories. The Hong Kong Police Department's director of Forensic Medicine stated that the couple might have died from an overdose of the aphrodisiac 'yohimbine'. Given Gib Bogle's alleged satyriasis, it would not be unnatural for him to look for stimulation to enhance his sexual performance. Yohimbine is an organic alkaloid found in the bark of the West African evergreen tree. The drug engorges blood vessels in the genitals of both men and women and stimulates the part of the brain controlling sexual responses. However, American researchers agree that yohimbine is 'not a safe herb' — either as a cure for erectile problems or as a recreational drug.[18] The side effects listed include headache, dizziness, nausea, vomiting, elevated blood pressure, increased heart rate, anxiety, psychosis and even death.

In 1993 Bill Jenkins, a veteran Sydney crime reporter wrote in his memoirs, *As Crime Goes By*, that the couple had been poisoned with dog-worming tablets. Margaret Chandler owned several dachshunds and police confirmed that she had bought the worm medicine for her dogs several days before she died. On Saturday, 29 December 1962, Mrs Chandler took her dogs to Mrs Sheridan Pausey's kennels in West Granville. The dogs were described as 'worm-infested'[19] and Mrs Pausey sold Mrs Chandler five Hydarex tablets — they looked just like headache tablets but were extremely dangerous to humans. Two months later, Mrs Pausey again inspected the dogs and found that they still had worms. This would not have been the case if the dogs had been given the medication.

This scenario, which would have cast suspicion on Mrs Chandler's husband, was never proven. For his own part Geoffrey Chandler published his own story in 1970 — the provocatively titled, *So You Think I Did It?* A decade later Chandler was quoted in a Sydney press report as saying that Gib Bogle may have been murdered by the members of MI5 or the CIA and his wife killed as an innocent party. Because of the mysterious nature of the deaths, and the fact that Bogle was a top-ranking scientist, international authorities such as the FBI, Scotland Yard and Interpol became interested in the case. Were Bogle and Chandler poisoned by espionage agents?

In October 1980, *National Times* journalist Brian Toohey reported that the US Consul in Sydney had sent a telegram to the American Embassy in Manila concerned about speculation in the Sydney press about Bogle's alleged involvement in 'international espionage activities' that may have been connected with his death.[20] It was alleged that the FBI had even conducted its own investigation into the case. But while one journalist did obtain declassified state department documents that proved FBI chief J. Edgar Hoover had discussed the case with NSW Police, requests from the Australian *National Times* newspaper and Melbourne's *Sun News-Pictorial* to view the FBI files on the case were denied on the grounds of 'national security' and in the interest of 'national defence'.[21]

In 1989 Dr Godfrey Oettle, the then director of the NSW Health Department's division of Forensic Medicine and who had been involved in the original investigation, stated his belief that the deaths of Bogle and Chandler were most likely due to 'accidental death probably caused by an overdose of LSD'.[22] Although the drug could not have been detected using forensic techniques available in 1963, Oettle argued that 'Today, with modern techniques such as radioimmunoassay, which looks at the body's response to foreign poisons ... LSD could be found.' Oettle's view, which later led to the victims' tissue samples being sent to the United States, potentially vindicated Geoffrey Chandler's claims of innocence.

'There was no evidence of LSD found at the [Nash] party,' Oettle stated in a 1989 article in the *Sydney Morning Herald*. 'But I don't think the police knew what they were looking for. I think it is possible they were experimenting with hallucinogenic drugs and I think they [Bogle and Chandler] went down there [to Lane Cove National Park] so they could experience the dawn of a new year together under the influence of the drug.'[23]

But can LSD kill? The drug is not normally considered 'lethal' in terms of toxic side effects. LSD is usually made in laboratories in the form of barrel-shaped pills of about 10 milligrams; the normal dosage of LSD is one-tenth of a milligram, so doses of 50 to 100 times that amount are obviously dangerous. LSD has two stages of chemical breakdown before it is reduced to normal bodily components but it is the effects of that chemical breakdown that induces hallucinations within five minutes. When the drug is ingested in large doses, it takes a number of hours to 'kick in'. Side effects include 'blood pressure and circulatory system abnormalities, along with malignant hypothermia, a condition in which the body [temperature] can soar to 40°C.'[24] According to authorities, LSD overdose can also cause gastronomic distress — nausea, vomiting and diarrhoea.

If the LSD Bogle took on New Year's Eve was made in a CSIRO laboratory, what is to say that he did not ingest a lethal dose — either by his own hand or by a third party — or that the crudely manufactured pill was not a particularly potent mixture? If the same dosage was given to Margaret Chandler, then their fates were already sealed when they drove off in Bogle's Ford Prefect. However, Bogle's boss at the time, Dr Fred Lehany, told police that he had no knowledge of LSD being used or made by CSIRO scientists. Fred Gardiner, a physicist and colleague of Bogle's, stated that his friend would surely have known the correct dosage, if in fact he even needed LSD as a stimulant. Gardiner said, 'If Gib took LSD in a drink, then someone else put it there.'[25]

Finally, in January 1996 — 33 years after the bodies of Gilbert Bogle and Margaret Chandler were found on New Year's Day — evidence was discovered that the pair had indeed ingested LSD. Forensic toxicologist Dr Fredric Rieders, founder of National Medical Services Inc in Pennsylvania, USA, discovered traces of the drug in the victims' tissue samples sent to him from Australia. However, this explanation could not be proven as the cause of their deaths beyond a reasonable doubt, because the amount of LSD present in the victims' bodies at the time of their death could not be determined from the available samples.[26]

As Australia commenced a new century, Sydney detectives working on unsolved crimes met with the surviving members of the Bogle family — now grown to adulthood in New Zealand, with the mystery of their father's death still surrounding them — and briefed them on the status of the criminal investigation. Geoffrey Chandler entered his seventies still proclaiming his innocence and promoting conspiracy theories. It seems that only time and continued advances in forensic technology will eventually solve the Bogle and Chandler mystery once and for all.

Chapter 7
The Wanda Beach Murders (1965)

On an overcast, windswept summer's day in January 1965, two teenage girls were raped, murdered and partially buried in the sand dunes behind Wanda Beach, 20 kilometres south of Sydney. The discovery of the bodies of 15-year-olds Christine Sharrock and Marianne Schmidt, next-door neighbours in the Sydney suburb of West Ryde, created a public outcry and sparked one of the largest police investigations in Australian history. Despite the media frenzy that has fed off the story for almost four decades, the Wanda Beach Murders remain unsolved.

The Schmidts were just one of thousands of West German families who came to Australia on an 'assisted passage' agreement after the Second World War. Helmut and Elizabeth Schmidt arrived in Melbourne on 13 September 1958 with their six children — 10-year-old Helmut, the eldest, followed by Marianne, Hans, Peter, Trixie and Wolfgang (a seventh child, Norbert, was born in Australia). The family moved to the Unanderra Migrant Hostel on the south coast of New South Wales before settling in the Riverina township of Temora. Helmut Schmidt was a carpenter by trade but in March 1963 the family moved to Sydney when he contracted Hodgkin's disease, a form of cancer that attacks the lymph glands. The Schmidt family secured an ex-war service home in Brush Road, Ryde, as Mr Schmidt fought the illness that would ultimately claim his life in June 1964.

When the Schmidt family moved into Brush Road, Christine Sharrock was living next door with her grandparents, Jim and Jeanette Taig. Following the death of her own father, the teenager chose to live with her grandparents after her mother Beryl remarried and moved to Seven Hills with her new husband. Christine and Marianne, whose birthdays were separated by only several weeks, became inseparable. Each shared a love of pop music, an innocent attraction to boys their age and in their own way, a sheltered upbringing — one raised by her grandparents, the other a 'New Australian'. The girls also shared a special bond in that they had lost fathers at a young age.

In January 1965, Marianne's mother was admitted into King George V Hospital at Camperdown to undergo a major operation. Mrs Schmidt left her eldest son Helmut, aged 16 and an apprentice on the railways, and Marianne in charge of the children while she recovered. On Saturday, 9 January, Marianne and Christine visited Mrs Schmidt in hospital. While they were there, they asked Mrs Schmidt if they could take the younger children to Cronulla Beach, immediately south of Sydney — the only beach directly accessible from the suburbs by train. Cronulla had been a favourite picnic destination for the Schmidts when their father was alive and both girls had celebrated New Year's Day with an outing there. Helmut and Hans Schmidt had taken the family there again the following day (2 January) but this time without Christine, who was feeling the effects of sunburn.

Mrs Schmidt gave her permission for the two girls to take the children to Cronulla on the Sunday if they were careful. 'Watch out for the young ones,' she warned.[1] But it rained on Sunday and the children did not go to the beach. On the following day — Monday, 11 January — Marianne and her friend Christine decided to take the children to the beach while the eldest Schmidt boys stayed home — Helmut to paint the kitchen and Hans to mow the lawn.

As she packed for the day trip with her next-door neighbours, Christine Sharrock remarked to her grandmother that it would be 'fun to walk across the sandhills again'. Christine had walked with her friend across the famous dunes behind Wanda Beach on New Year's Day. The area, known as 'Greenhills' formed a long stretch of undulating sandhills stretching from Wanda Beach in the south all the way to the Kurnell Oil Refinery at the northern end of Bate Bay. The hills had been used to film the Australian classic *Fifty Thousand Horseman* and were named 'Greenhills' because of the washed-out, green hue of the sand.

'Don't go today, love,' Christine's grandmother 'Nan' Taig told her. 'You have got the four [Schmidt] little ones with you ... it's too far.'[2]

Christine Sharrock packed a thermos of cold lime-green cordial inside a white and gold beach bag along with a red and white towel, a plastic purse containing a £1 note, a pair of sunglasses and a transistor radio. Christine did not take any food with her (next door, Marianne was making marmite, tomato and cucumber sandwiches for them to eat, along with some fruit) and did not pack a swimming costume because she was menstruating and didn't intend to swim. Shortly before 8.30 am Christine, Marianne and the four youngest Schmidt children walked down to the bottom of Brush Road to catch the bus to West Ryde railway station. When a bus did not arrive they walked to the station, caught a train to Redfern and changed platforms for the trip to Cronulla.

Cronulla is situated at the southern end of a stretch of uninterrupted beachhead at Bate Bay. Four beaches, namely Cronulla, North Cronulla, Elouera and Wanda, embrace the bay. After Wanda, the farthest of the beaches from Cronulla station, there were 8 kilometres of rolling sandhills leading up to a landmark called Boat Harbour near where the Kurnell Oil Refinery is situated.

The party of six arrived at Cronulla sometime before 11 am. When they walked through the Cronulla Park, past the life-saving club and onto the path that led to the surf beach, they found that Cronulla Beach was closed because of dangerous seas whipped up by the wind conditions. Undeterred, the two girls led the younger children to the southern end of the beach, where they left their belongings on the rocks. Eight-year-old Wolfgang was persistent in his wish for a swim so Marianne took him to a shallow end of the beach away from rocks. After a quick dip in the water, the group shared the sandwiches and fruit before Marianne suggested that they walk to the sandhills past Wanda Beach. The children hid their beach bags behind some rocks and walked along the promenade past North Cronulla Beach and the unpatrolled Elouera Beach.

At about 1 pm, some 200 metres past the Wanda Beach Surf Club, the younger children complained that the wind was whipping up the sand and stinging their legs. Marianne told the children to shelter behind a dune while she and Christine returned to the southern end of the beach and retrieved their belongings for the trip home. The older girls covered the younger children with their towels and left them Christine's transistor radio for company. Inexplicably, the teenage girls then headed off in a northerly direction towards Boat Harbour.

It was the last time Christine Sharrock and Marianne Schmidt were seen alive.

Peter, Trixie, Wolfgang and Norbert Schmidt waited in the sandhills for several hours before walking back to the southern end of Cronulla Beach. They found the beach bags untouched — and the girls' purses and tickets intact — and walked to Cronulla Beach in time to catch the last train to Sydney at 6 pm. They arrived back at home at Brush Road, West Ryde, sometime after 8 pm while Helmut Schmidt was visiting his mother in hospital. It was Hans Schmidt, Marianne's 13-year-old brother, who took Christine Sharrock's belongings into her grandmother next door and informed her that the girls had 'gone missing'.[3]

Nan Taig's immediate thought was that the older girls had simply missed the train and because the other children had brought the bags home with the train tickets inside, the girls were now stranded at Cronulla. Christine's grandmother rang her son, Les Taig, who lived in the nearby suburb of Ermington, and he advised her to ring the police. When two constables visited the Brush Road homes at 11.40, Helmut had returned home from visiting his mother. Could the girls have run off with any boys, or be staying with friends somewhere? No, the girls were not like that, Nan Taig told them. The constables asked Helmut if they could talk to the children who had returned from the beach, but he told the police that his brothers and sister were tired and it would have to wait until the morning.

But Christine and Marianne were already dead — buried beneath the sand in a shallow grave on Wanda Beach.

The following day, NSW central coast teenager Peter Smith, who was staying with his sister in Sydney while he looked for work, took his three young nephews for an early afternoon walk along the sandhills past Cronulla. Their journey took them two and a half kilometres past the Wanda Beach Surf Club before Smith turned around and led the boys back towards Cronulla. Smith carried his youngest nephew in his arms as he walked behind the first row of sandhills, about 150 metres from the water's edge. The other two boys — one aged eight, the other seven — raced ahead of him, running in and out of the dunes as they played.

One of his nephews stopped in the valley between two dunes and Smith saw what appeared to be a store mannequin partially buried in the sand. As he moved closer, he could see feet sticking out of a mound of sand, an elbow and a partially exposed head. Smith slowly scraped away some of the sand around the head and realised it was the body of a young woman. He quickly gathered the three boys and ran towards the nearest building, the Wanda clubhouse. His initial thought was that it was the body of a drowning victim washed up on shore, but that was impossible — it was too far inland and appeared to be deliberately buried. Smith still thought that it was only one body — but Marianne's head and Christine's feet combined to form a grim illusion.

Smith found the surf club manned by lifesaver Barry Ezzy and he excitedly asked to telephone Cronulla Police Station. When local detectives arrived at the clubhouse, Smith led them to the crime scene. The detectives did not want to disturb the sand too much, but soon realised that there were two bodies in the makeshift grave. Because the bodies hadn't been dug into the hollow between the two dunes, but merely covered by sand, the wind had exposed them. When the sand was later removed by two government medical officers, the full extent of the horror that had engulfed the teenage girls was revealed.

Marianne Schmidt was lying on her right side in a semi-foetal position, her left leg bent at the knee at a right angle to her body. Christine Sharrock was lying face down in the sand, her right arm bent at the elbow, with her forearm close to her face as if shielding it. The bodies were in line with other, with Christine's head touching the soles of Marianne's feet. Detectives noted a drag mark — 34 metres long — extending north in the sand and down an incline into a gully between two sand dunes. Blood was found in the sand and on grass stalks along the drag mark and police stated in their notes that it appeared that Christine had been dragged towards the grave. At some point Christine had run away from her killer, as Marianne lay dead or wounded, but had been overtaken and bludgeoned or stabbed to death.

Post-mortem results later showed that Christine's killer had hit her on the back of the head, fracturing her skull, subdued her with a blow to the chin and then stabbed her repeatedly. The killer then attempted to rape her, despite the fact that she was menstruating (her sanitary belt and napkin had been removed and her shorts shoved into her crotch area). Just as shocking, Marianne's throat had been severely cut and there were signs of multiple stabs wounds and an obvious attempt to rape her. Her shorts had been cut down the side and rolled up around her breasts exposing the lower half of her body. Doctors later ascertained that the girls had died within half an hour of each other, but the hot sand had delayed rigor mortis setting in and it was difficult to determine the exact time of death. All police would say was they had died between 2 pm and midnight on 11 January.

Forensic pathologists later examined the bodies and found scratch marks on the inside thighs of each victim and male spermatozoa on Marianne's body. An examination of the contents of Christine's stomach detected some vegetable matter — but not what the other children had eaten for lunch. Interestingly, Christine had a blood alcohol level of 0.015 — enough to have consumed a 10 oz glass of beer. The professional opinion was that the alcohol had been consumed orally and was not just a case of the vegetable matter fermenting. Had Christine shared a meal and some beer with her killer? Why had the girls gone in a northerly direction away from the other children? Were they planning to meet someone? There were more questions than answers.

At 4.30 pm on 12 January, detectives from Cronulla Police Station travelled to Brush Road to obtain a more detailed description of what the girls were wearing when they disappeared. Marianne's black, one-piece swimming costume with white lace front and multicoloured sleeveless blouse; Christine's green and white patterned sleeveless blouse, white brassiere and white shorts, made the identification all that more sure. It was while one of the detectives questioned the Schmidt children about what Marianne and Christine were wearing when they disappeared that Wolfgang revealed that he had seen the teenage girls walking across the dunes with a 'fat boy'. The boy was described as being of high school age, about 14 and with fair hair, carrying a towel and wearing light grey trousers.

Wolfgang Schmidt's description of the main suspect has always bothered investigators — the young boy's recollections seemed to grow in exaggeration every time he was questioned. First there was his story of the boy walking with his sister and her friend; two days later he told detectives that it was the same boy they saw on the beach earlier in the day hunting for crabs with a homemade spear gun. A month later he added that the boy had a knife in a holster. When he saw the boy walking back along the sandhills just 10 minutes after the girls had disappeared, the knife was missing. The eight-year-old boy had even spoken to the youth as he walked back alone between the dunes.

'Where are the girls?' Wolfgang asked him. The youth walked straight past him.

On Wednesday, 13 January, as Sydneysiders woke to read details of the grisly find on a suburban beach, Mrs Schmidt returned home under doctor's supervision to break the news of her daughter's death to her younger children. The evening newspaper *The Sun* led its edition with:

> Detectives investigating the knife murder of two school girls whose bodies were found at Wanda Beach yesterday, are searching for a sixteen-year-old 'surfie' with long blond hair. The youth was seen talking

> to the girls shortly before the time they are believed to have been killed. His description has been circulated to all Sydney police.[4]

And so the blond teenage 'surfie' was cast in the community's mind as the chief suspect from the outset. Thousands of teenagers immediately became suspects and the public flooded the police with inquiries.

Police started the investigation by compiling a list of all people on the beach that day and slowly the final movements of the two victims became a little clearer. After leaving the younger Schmidt children, Christine and Marianne headed off in a northerly direction. The boys called out to them that they were going in the wrong direction but Christine and Marianne 'just laughed'.[5] According to Wolfgang, when the girls were about 36 metres away from the younger children they were joined by the 'fat boy'. However, no other member of the Schmidt family saw the youth. When the girls had been gone about 10 minutes, Peter Schmidt sent his younger brother Wolfgang to look for them. This is when he saw the 'fat boy' walking back alone towards Wanda Surf Club. Peter later asked Trixie to have a look for them, and she spotted two boys sliding down the dunes but there was no trace of the girls.

Dennis Dostine, a local fireman, was walking south towards Wanda Beach with his five-year-old son when he noticed two girls walking between the sandhills, about 200 metres inland from where he was walking at the water's edge. It was about 12.45 pm, 600 metres from the Wanda Surf Club and about 400 metres south of the eventual murder scene. The girls, who matched the general appearance of Christine and Marianne, were walking alone in a northerly direction. Dostine noted that one of the girls was looking behind her, as if being followed, and they were walking at a fast pace. This was the last official sighting of the girls.

Dostine also told police of several other people he had noticed on the beach that day: two separate groups of horseriders; a 19-year-old man — tall, wearing khaki shorts and white short-sleeved shirt; an older 'leathery' man — shorter, wearing black briefs; a man and a woman fishing; and a group of youths sliding in the sandhills. Although the girls riding horses were identified, the two men, who were heading in a northerly direction, never came forward. The horseriders told police that they too had seen several strangers on the beach as they rode back towards Wanda in the late afternoon — a man at Boat Harbour, wearing grey trousers, surveying the dunes — and a naked man, 35 to 40 years old, walking between the dunes 400 metres north of the murder scene at about 1 pm.

Frank Williams, a Cronulla local, was walking along Wanda Beach around midday when he saw a man lying partially buried in a sand dune, about 45 metres north of Wanda Surf Club. The man used a piece of corrugated iron, about 30 centimetres square, to hide his face from view but Williams could see that the man was wearing blue trousers rolled up to the knees, and described his feet as 'dirty, big and rough'.[6] Williams also saw a group of six children, obviously the Schmidts and Christine Sharrock, walking past the surf club. The man with the corrugated 'mask' was never questioned by police, so his motivations for hiding in the sand that day are unclear.

Detectives took Peter, Trixie and Wolfgang Schmidt back to Cronulla Beach and retraced the steps the children took on the fatal day. Police intended to build up an identikit sketch of the 'surfie' suspect, but when they tried to interview Wolfgang they found that the eight-year-old agreed with every suggestion they made. When Helmut Schmidt was asked to help his brother, Wolfgang merely agreed with everything Helmut suggested. The police were privately critical of the assistance they received from the older Schmidt children, especially Helmut, but this was particularly harsh. The Schmidts were young, traumatised 'New Australians' without parental role models and who knew nothing of police procedures. They had lost their sister Marianne ... how were they supposed to act?

Entries in the girls' diaries showed that they had met two boys at Cronulla Beach on New Year's Day and had parted with 'a kiss' and a promise to meet again, but investigations found that it was nothing more than an innocent encounter. Helmut informed police that Marianne had walked across the sandhills on their 2 January visit to Cronulla and had been missing from the family group for some time. Marianne's brothers had not seen her talk with anyone in particular (although they had swum with a young police cadet, and had hunted for crabs together, but again the identity of that young man was never established). Had she met someone with whom she promised to meet up with at a future date?

What the young girls didn't realise was that the Wanda sandhills were a well-known haunt for nudists, homosexuals and exhibitionists — 'a paradise for poofters and perverts' as one local put it.[7] The sandhills allowed anonymity for casual sex during the conservative 1960s when homosexuality was still a crime. Cars would park behind the dunes, allowing easy access and, in the case of this murder investigation, the possibility of a quick getaway. Careless speculation arose that Christine and Marianne deliberately wandered off into the sandhills looking for sex, but detectives publicly vindicated the girls' reputations and post-mortems revealed that they were still virgins when they died.

The problem remained that there were no eyewitnesses to the murder and very little physical evidence at the crime scene. Police used a front-end loader to sift through tonnes of sand around the crime scene but, by modern standards, the search lacked the necessary sophistication to find anything of importance. An old knife was discovered in the sand but despite some trumpeting in one local newspaper, the knife had no links to the murder. A slither of steel, possibly from a kitchen knife, was also found but it was never ascertained whether the metal had anything to do with the crimes.

On 15 January *The Sun* wrote, prematurely, that an 18-year-old boy 'with long, blond "surfie" hair' was being held by Brisbane CIB, but it was to be the first of many dead ends the Wanda investigation encountered.[8] During the initial investigation five men came forward and claimed to have committed the Wanda Beach murders, but because of their lack of knowledge of the crime scene detectives discounted their confessions. Detectives knew that these men, mostly mentally unstable, had read about the crime and merely applied what was reported to their own lives. It would have been easy for detectives to charge these people with the crime but they were committed to finding the real killer and would not risk revealing the intimate details of the case for a 'quick arrest'.[9] But the investigation needed a break — and quickly.

On 20 January, the two girls were buried in separate funeral services. The service for Marianne Schmidt was held in the West Chapel of the Metropolitan Funeral Home before her body was conveyed to Rookwood Crematorium. Christine Sharrock's service was conducted at St Michael's Catholic Church, Meadowbank, before her body was transported to Liverpool Cemetery, where she was buried alongside her natural father. Detectives mingled with the mourners, and all those present were photographed in the hope of securing the vital breakthrough.

By the end of the month, with the investigation stalling, public sentiment was running hot with many people calling for the reintroduction of the death penalty. In the early 1960s it was inconceivable to think that two teenage girls could be raped and murdered on a public beach — parents' worst fears had been realised. Their children were no longer safe. On Friday, 22 January, NSW Police Commissioner Norm Allen made a public appeal for help in solving the case. A record £10 000 reward was offered for information leading to the arrest of the person or persons responsible. That reward is still in existence.

When school resumed in February, detectives attended Christine's former school, St Therese's, Lakemba (she had left there the previous November to start work), and Marsden High School, Marianne's local high school, and interviewed their friends and teachers. They were still investigating the scenario that the girls had agreed to meet someone they knew at the beach that day and had wandered off into the sandhills to keep a secret rendezvous. The problem remained, however, that the girls had not intended to go to the beach on Monday — they were supposed to take the children on Sunday, 10 January, but the weather wasn't pleasant — and so the likelihood that someone had kept the appointment was remote.

On the 22 April 1966, a coronial inquest was held at the City Coroner's Court, Sydney, before Mr J.J. Loomes, the Stipendiary Magistrate and City Coroner. After hearing evidence from 28 witnesses, Mr Loomes found that Marianne Schmidt 'died from haemorrhage the result of a cut throat and four penetrating wounds of the chest' and that Christine Sharrock died from 'haemorrhage as the result of penetrating wounds of the chest associated with injuries, namely a fracture of the skull and injury to the brain'. Loomes also stated that he did not intend to canvass the evidence presented or to comment on it — 'to do so can serve no purpose and could perhaps hinder the inquiries'.[10]

In the eight years after the murders, until the final brief of the unsolved crime was concluded in 1974, over 14 000 people were interviewed and 5000 suspects questioned about the Wanda Beach murders. While some of the suspects had investigations suspended because of lack of evidence, most were deemed to have had nothing to do with the murders. The investigation produced over 10 000 typed pages which are contained in over 80 volumes of bound police reports. In the ensuing years several anonymous beach 'pests' and convicted murderers have been linked to the crime, ranging from the fantastic to the strangely familiar.

Police searched for a man, aged about 25 with light brown hair and medium build with ruddy complexion and missing teeth, who approached several women and offered them money for sex. A second man, slightly taller but heavier than the first, was dubbed 'the fat man' by investigators. Wearing grey trousers, with long hair and stubble, the man approached several woman on the day that Christine and Marianne died, saying that he was from 'South Australia'. He, too, approached women about having sex with him. Several other men seen on Wanda Beach that day were also sought: the 'leathery' man walking along the beach, the younger tall man, the naked man seen walking out of the dunes by the young horseriders, and a man masturbating on the beach some weeks later. But none came forward and they remain footnotes in the story of the Wanda Beach murders.

However, the murders of two other women the following year have been linked to the Wanda Beach investigation. On Saturday, 29 January 1966, the body of Wilhelmina Kruger was found in the basement of a Wollongong car park. The 57-year-old cleaning woman had started her shift at the Piccadilly Arcade in Crown Street in the early hours of the morning and was found bludgeoned and knifed to death at the bottom of a stairwell shortly before 6 am. Kruger had suffered multiple stab wounds, numerous other injuries, including a ruptured heart, and had been strangled with her own stockings. The ferocity of the attack sickened hardened

GATTON MURDERS

£1,000 REWARD

Home Secretary's Office,
Brisbane, 3rd January, 1899.

HIS Excellency the Governor, with the advice of the Executive Council, has been pleased to direct that a Reward of One Thousand Pounds (£1,000) be paid for such information as may lead to the apprehension and conviction of the person or persons who, at Gatton, on the night of Monday, the 26th December ultimo, murdered Michael Murphy, Norah Murphy, and Ellen Murphy, and that a Pardon be granted to any person concerned in the crime, not being the principal offender, who may give such information.

J. F. G. FOXTON.

Above: A rare photo of the Gatton outrage in 1898. On the night of the Boxing Day holiday, three members of the Murphy family were raped, shot and battered to death in the Queensland bush. The family's buggy, with broken right shaft, is clearly visible. Norah's body was under the tree (A) and the other victims were centre left (C). Collection: John Oxley Library, State Library of Queensland.

Left: The reward poster asking for information leading to the conviction for the murderer or murderers of the three Murphy siblings, January 1899. No-one was ever convicted for the crime. Collection: Queensland Police Museum.

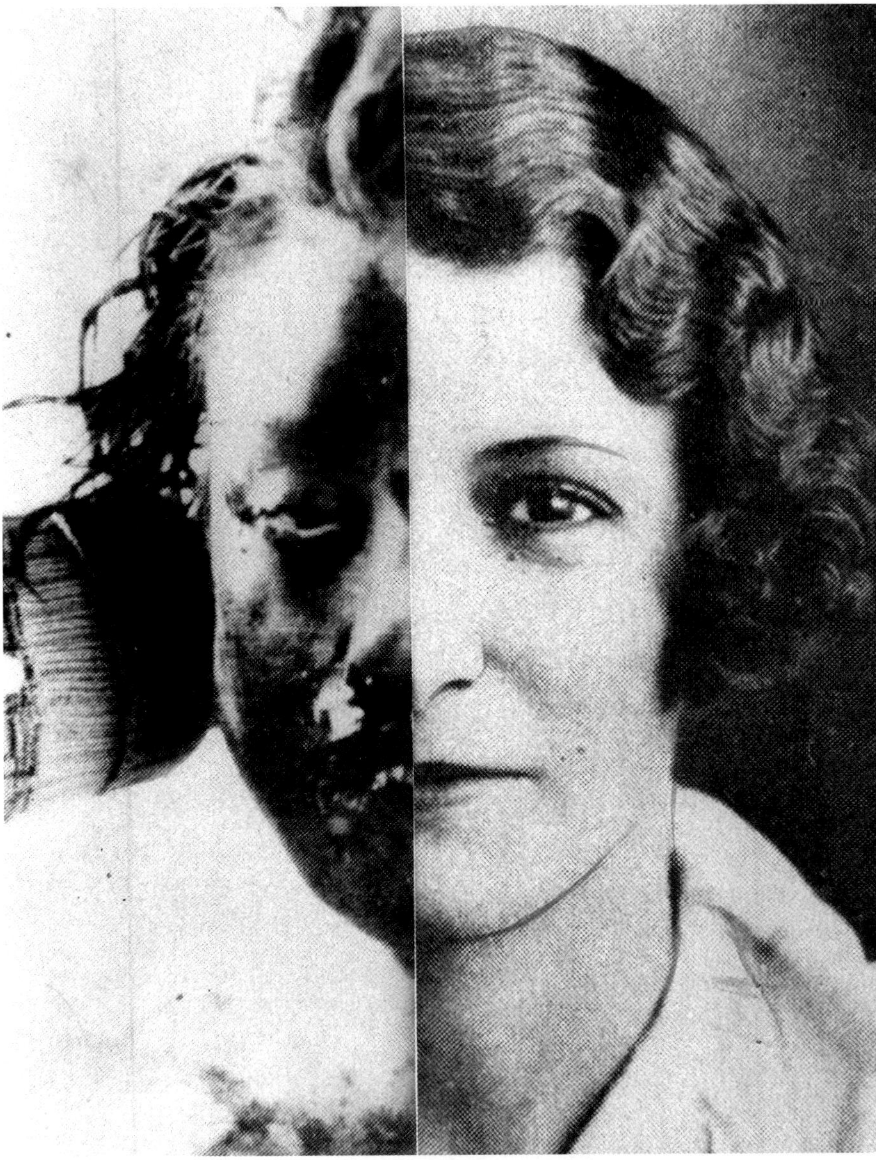

Above: A composite photo of the right side of the Pyjama Girl's face and that of Linda Agostini (nee Platt) after her true identity was proven in 1944. The only recognisable feature of the body when it was found in 1934 was the Chinese-style pyjamas the victim was wearing. Antonio Agostini killed his wife Linda in 1934 and left her battered and badly burned body in a culvert in Albury. It was not until a decade later that the victim's identity — and that of her murderer — was finally revealed.

Left: Sydney 'businessman' and waterfront smuggler Reginald Holmes, who was murdered in 1935 on the night before he was due to give evidence at the coronial inquest into the 'Shark Arm' murder.

Right: Small-time criminal James Smith who was murdered, his body cut up and whose arm was disgorged by a tiger shark on Anzac Day 1935 at Coogee Aquarium.

Left: American GI Private Eddie Leonski smiles as he awaits execution for the murder of three Melbourne women in 1942.

Below: The murder scene at Royal Park, Melbourne, as detectives and army personnel investigate the death of Leonski's third victim, Gladys Hosking, during the city's 'brown-out' regulations in 1942. A tent has been erected between the two trees over the victim's body.

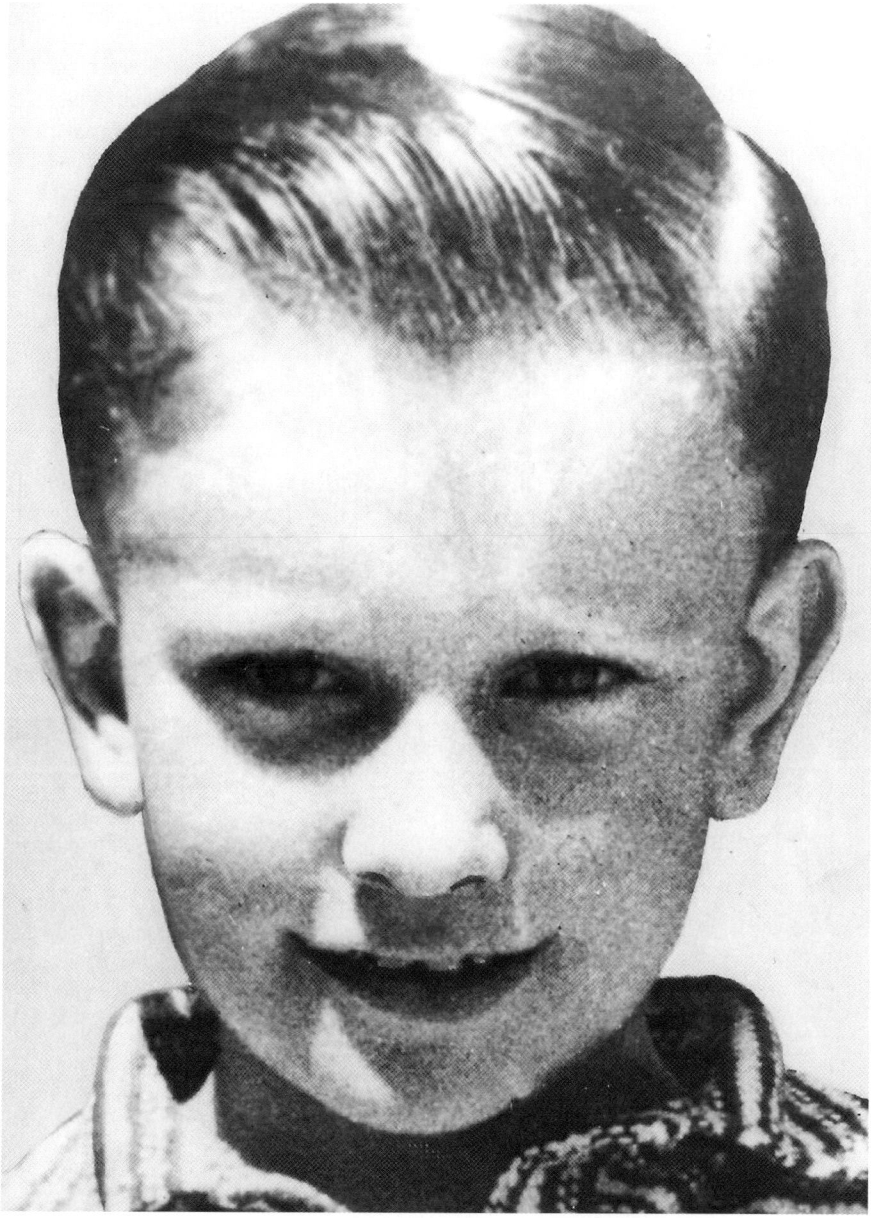

Above: Bondi schoolboy Graeme Thorne, aged 8, who was kidnapped and murdered after his parents won a £100,000 lottery prize in 1960.

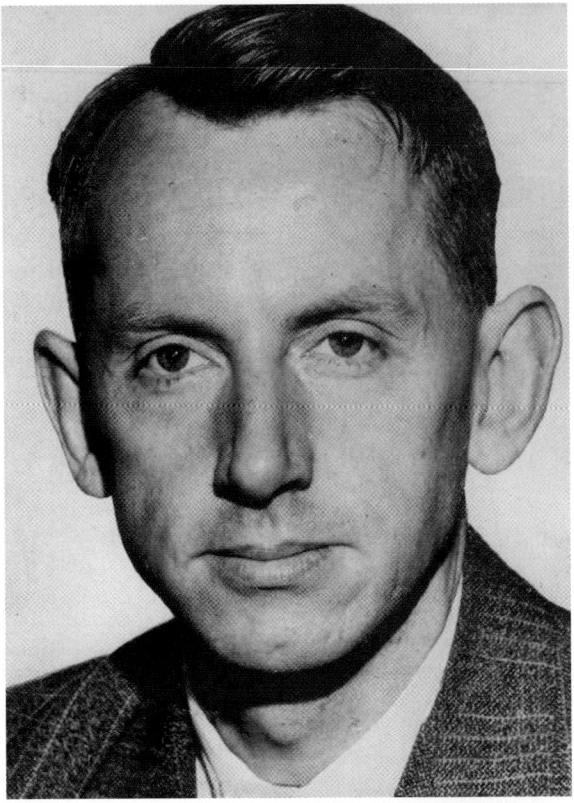

Left: Dr Gilbert Bogle, the New Zealand physicist whose body was found on New Year's Day 1963 at Lane Cove National Park in Sydney. Bogle, a brilliant scientist who was married with a young family, was found dead alongside the body of Margaret Chandler, a nurse.

Below: Margaret Chandler, whose husband was a work colleague of Dr Bogle's at the CSIRO, was also found dead in Lane Cove, her body covered with old beer cartons. Had the pair been accidentally poisoned or had they met with foul play?

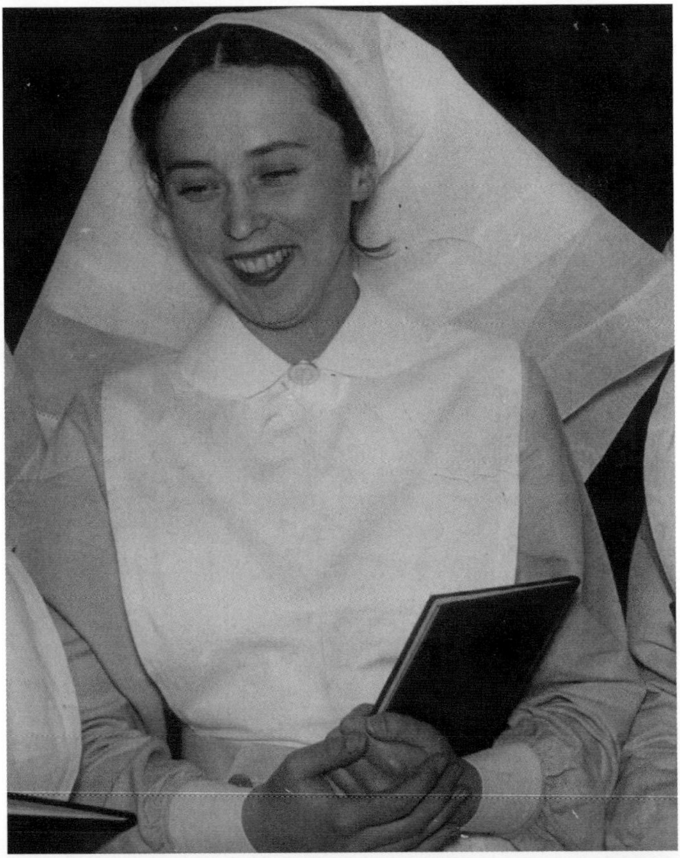

Above: West Ryde neighbours, teenagers Christine Sharrock and Marianne Schmidt, whose raped and mutilated bodies were found buried at Wanda Beach in southern Sydney on 12 January 1965.

Above: Sydney detectives, dressed in the distinctive suits and hats of the 1960s, inspect the murder scene at Wanda Beach, north of Cronulla. The partially buried bodies of the two victims are visible in the foreground.

Above: The three Beaumont children — Jane, Arnna and Grant (left to right) — who went missing at Glenelg Beach, South Australia, on 26 January 1966.

Above: An artist's impression of the man seen 'frolicking' with the Beaumont children at Glenelg Beach the day they disappeared. To date, the man has not been identified and remains the main suspect in the case.

Above: Anita Cobby (centre), pictured with former NSW Premier Neville Wran, was abducted, raped and murdered as she walked home from Blacktown Station on the night of 2 February 1986.

Above: The world of textbook psychopath John Raymond Travers collided with that of innocent victim Anita Cobby in February 1986. Eighteen-year-old Travers, easily identified by the tattoo of a teardrop under his left eye, was the ringleader of the group of five men responsible for the young nurse's death.

Above: Ivan Milat pictured at a family property at Wombeyan Caves, in the Southern Highlands, southwest of Sydney. Milat was convicted of the murder of seven backpackers, whose bodies were buried in the Belanglo State Forest between 1989 and 1992.

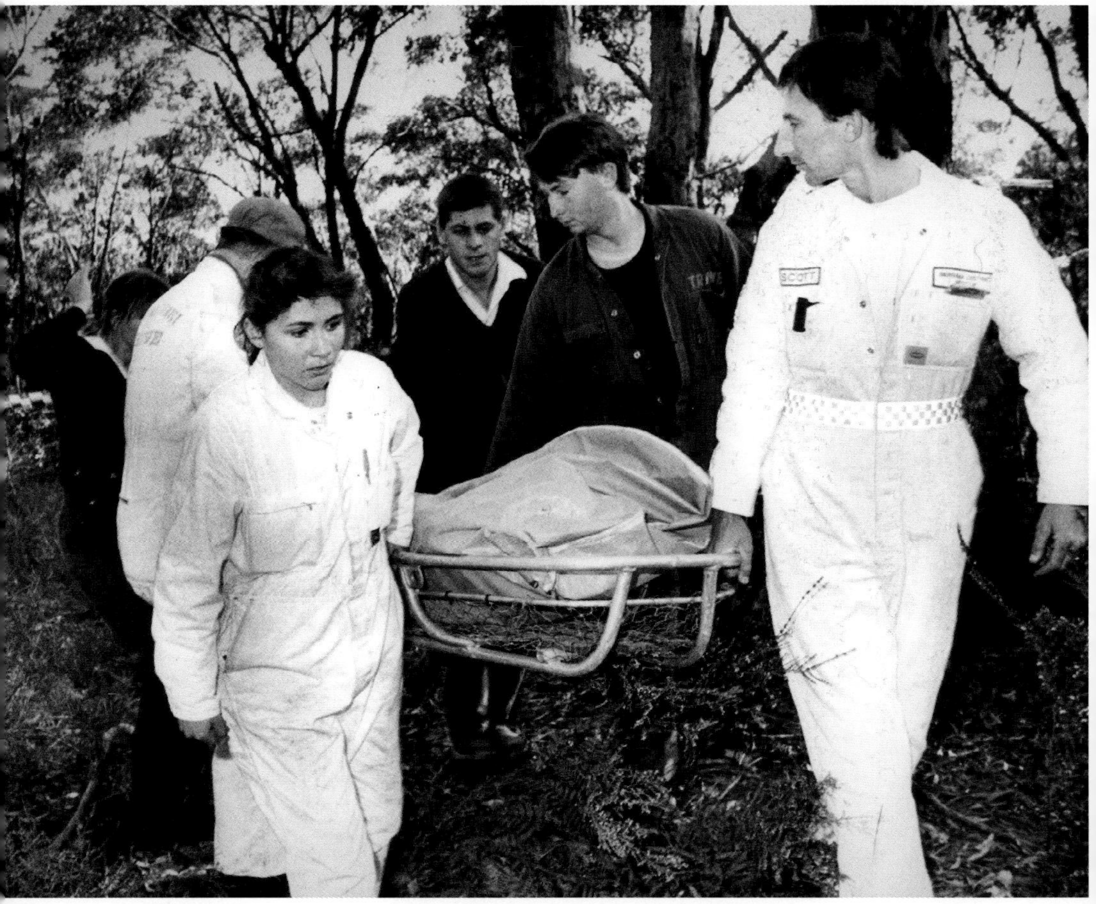

Above: The first of seven bodies is recovered from Belanglo State Forest in 1992. Two British backpackers travelling in Australia, Joanne Walters and Caroline Clarke, had gone missing the previous year while hitchhiking on the Hume Highway, south of Sydney.

THE AUSTRALIAN

NUMBER 9825 TUESDAY APRIL 30 1996 80 CENTS*

44 pages of COMPUTERS SPECIAL LIFTOUT: ATUG 96

The Port Arthur Massacre

FACE OF A KILLER

'He would go from a 25-year-old to a 12-year-old kid who was a delinquent just like that'

Howard call for guns crackdown

By BRUCE MONTGOMERY, LENORE TAYLOR and staff reporters

Violent loner spooked locals

Janet Fife-Yeomans

No sanctuary, no mercy for one little girl in flight

Cameron Forbes

Martin Bryant … neighbours locked their doors when he went on the prowl — Hobart Mercury picture

DIGITAL

MOTOROLA

$149

Strathfield

CALL 13 11 77 FROM ANYWHERE IN AUSTRALIA

HOME DELIVERY 1 800 022 552

THE DOLLAR — INDEX — LATE NEWS — TODAY'S WEATHER

Above: Face of a killer — Martin Bryant — who was responsible for the deaths of 35 people at Port Arthur, Tasmania, on 28 April 1996.

Above: Twenty-nine-year-old mainlander Janelle Patton, who was murdered on Norfolk Island on Easter Sunday 2002. It was the first such crime in the 148-year history of the island. Her body was found in the picturesque Cockpit Waterfall Reserve by a New Zealand tourist.

detectives, several of whom had worked on the investigation into the deaths of Christine Sharrock and Marianne Schmidt.

'On the information available to us we cannot discount the possibility Mrs Kruger ... met her death at the hands of the same person who is being sought for the murders at Wanda Beach,' stated Detective Dick Lendrum at a press conference in 1966.[11] The following month another murder heightened fears that police had a 'multiple' killer on their hands. On 26 February, the decomposed body of Sydney prostitute Anna Dowlingkoa (born Elizabeth Anne Dowling, in Perth) was found by the side of the Old Illawarra Highway at Menai, south of Sydney. The woman's body had remained hidden for several days before the killer returned and moved it closer to the highway so that it could be discovered.

South coast detectives thought they had made a vital breakthrough when a Unanderra man was charged with murder after a young woman's naked body was found on Mount Ousley (by-pass) Road, in Wollongong in June 1966. Nineteen-year-old Carolyn May Orphin had been raped, strangled and callously beaten to death with a large rock after leaving a Wollongong dance with a local man, Alan Raymond Bassett. The 21-year-old English immigrant was subsequently charged with Orphin's murder and sentenced to life imprisonment. He was later diagnosed as schizophrenic and was jailed in Morisset Psychiatric Hospital in Newcastle.

At the inquest into the unsolved murder of Wilhelmina Kruger in September 1966, government medical officer Dr J. Diment stated that there were 'very many similarities' between the murders of Wilhelmina Kruger and Carolyn Orphin.[12] However, while Alan Bassett denied any involvement in any murder other than the one that he was convicted of, several leading detectives were not as sure. Detective Inspector Cec Johnston was convinced that Bassett knew more about the Wanda Beach murders than what he was telling and for the next 10 years, until he retired as a policeman, he pursued a confession from the troubled young man.

Johnston and Bassett's relationship over the ensuing years became an important part of the mythology surrounding the unsolved Wanda Beach murders. Johnston would regularly travel to Morisset Hospital to talk with

Bassett, and developed a good relationship with Bassett's parents. On one such visit, Bassett gave Johnston a painting that he had done of a bush scene — 'a bloody awful thing', Johnston told his former work colleagues — but he hung the painting in his home.[13] The former Sydney detective, who left the police service because his obsession with the case had affected his health, voiced his suspicions about the painting to a willing media. Hidden in the bush landscape were the bodies of four women — Sharrock, Schmidt, Kruger and Dowlingkoa? Johnstone went to his grave in 1980 thinking so.

Bassett's father was so convinced of his son's guilt that he went on national television with his suspicions and actively fought his son's day release from prison in the 1980s. Bassett was finally released from prison in 1995 but has steadfastly maintained his innocence. Since then a number of other high-profile suspects have come to light. In 1984, Australian-born mass murderer Christopher Wilder was killed by Massachusetts police after a nation-wide manhunt. Wilder, who grew up in Australia before pursuing a car racing career in America, had a charge of rape against his name as a Sydney teenager. Incredibly, in 1982 while visiting Australia, Wilder allegedly kidnapped two teenage girls and forced them to pose for pornographic photos. Wilder escaped Australia after his family posted $350 000 bail and then conducted a murder spree that claimed the lives of at least eight young women. The blond and thickset Wilder was 20 years old in 1966 and living in Sydney. Was he the Wanda Beach murderer?

Recently, convicted murderer and paedophile Derek Ernest Percy was named as a 'person of interest' in not only the Wanda Beach murders, but also the 1966 disappearance of the Beaumont children, the murder of Canberra schoolboy Alan Redston the same year, the 1968 abduction and murder of four-year-old Sydney toddler Simon Brook, and the murder of Melbourne youngster Linda Stillwell. Percy, who was a naval rating during the 1960s and spent time in each of these cities, was jailed for life for the murder of Victorian schoolgirl Yvonne Elizabeth Toohey in 1970. He was described by a prison officer as Australia's 'Hannibal Lecter' and remains jailed in a psychiatric hospital.[14] The Adult Parole Board of Victoria has consistently refused to review his case.

Although my book *Wanda: The untold story of the Wanda Beach murders*, published in 2003, could not reveal definitively who was responsible for the crime — even advances in DNA technology could not unlock that secret — it did explore many of the myths and misunderstandings about the initial investigation. The publication of the full story of Christine Sharrock and Marianne Schmidt's fatal visit to Wanda Beach became a conduit for many readers' fears and misgivings of that long ago time. Several people contacted me via my publisher, offering their own recollections and hypotheses of the case.

There was the amateur detective who advocated the exhumation of Christine Sharrock's body (Marianne Schmidt's remains were cremated) in order to test it for DNA links to known suspects. I explained to him that as the case remained open it was the role of the police to advocate such a move on the evidence available to them. There was the woman holding steadfastly onto a family secret about a distant relative — pieced together from information given to her by her dying father. Discreet inquiries ruled out any involvement in the crime. A private detective contacted me about his investigations into the 40-year history of a western Sydney family — a story of incest and sadism — but his assertions that the two victims were taken from Wanda Beach in the afternoon and then returned there at night, murdered and buried, seemed fanciful. Another suspect came to light — a part-time lifesaver living in the Wollongong area during the 1960s.

Gradually an alternative scenario has begun to take shape. What if Wolfgang Schmidt's teenage 'surfie' really did exist but he wasn't the actual murderer? What if there were *two* murderers? Did the teenage boy lure the girls into the sandhills on the pretext of innocent 'boy-girl' talk for someone else to murder? Having delivered the girls to the murderer at some predesignated spot, did he immediately walk back along the beach, ignoring Wolfgang's questions? But what bond would make a teenage boy hold onto a secret for 40 years? Maybe the strongest bond imaginable — blood bonds. Was the Wanda Beach murderer the teenage boy's older brother, his uncle, or even father?

In my book I offered the unfulfilling reality that maybe we have been chasing a phantom all these years — someone who no longer exists and who took his secret with him to the grave. Part of my motivation for writing the book was to remember the victims, Christine Sharrock and Marianne Schmidt, who had hopes and dreams just like other teenagers and belonged to loving families who continue to grieve over their loss. Marianne's mother Elizabeth, now in her eighties, has waited 40 years for justice. Then there are the hundreds of police who earnestly investigated the case and worked tirelessly without that one, tangible piece of luck that would solve the case. Many of them were affected by the death of the two innocent teenagers for the rest of their careers, and the remainder of their lives.

For those reasons alone, the murders of Christine Sharrock and Marianne Schmidt deserve to be solved.

Chapter 8

The Disappearance of the Beaumont Children (1966)

More than any other crime, the disappearance of three siblings from a crowded Adelaide beach in January 1966 seems to have permanently damaged the Australian psyche. For the generation of baby boomers growing up in the mid-1960s, the subsequent investigation into the abduction and probable murder of the Beaumont children has both repelled and haunted us for almost 40 years. The case remains an open, ongoing investigation, and in many ways it has become one of the defining crimes in the history of this country.

On Tuesday, 25 January 1966, Robert Menzies resigned after a record 17 years as Australian Prime Minister. Replaced by his Liberal Party deputy, Harold Holt, it was the end of a conservative era in Australia. The following day, within hours of Holt's Australia Day speech, the worst fears of every Australian family were realised with the disappearance of three young children from Glenelg Beach.

On Wednesday, 26 January 1966, the three children of G.A. 'Jim' and Nancy Beaumont from the Adelaide suburb of Somerton Park — Jane, aged nine, Arnna, aged seven, and four-year-old Grant — asked their parents if they could go to nearby Glenelg Beach. Jim Beaumont, who was a linen goods salesman, had to travel to the Adelaide Hills township of Snowtown to see customers that day, but the temperature was expected to top 100 degrees on the old Fahrenheit scale and the children were persistent. The previous day the trio had caught the bus from their Harding Street home to Glenelg and had returned safely. Finally, their mother allowed them to make the short bus trip to Glenelg if they promised to return home on the midday bus. Nancy Beaumont gave the children eight shillings and sixpence (the equivalent of 85 cents) to buy some pasties for lunch, telling them to bring one home for her.

The children left their home at 10 am and caught a bus 10 minutes later from the corner of Diagonal Road and Peterson Street, just 100 metres from their home. The bus route took the children past Glenelg Oval on Brighton Street and left into Jetty Road. The bus driver remembered seeing the children get off the bus in Mosely Street, just a short walk to the beach — the eldest girl was carrying a paperback copy of *Little Women* under her arm. He did not remember seeing them on his afternoon bus, however.

When the children didn't arrive home on the midday bus Nancy Beaumont was not immediately concerned — she presumed they would be on the 2 pm bus. When that bus came and went, she felt she should go and look for them — perhaps they had missed the bus and were walking home. But the children could be walking several different ways back to Harding Street, so she decided to stay and wait for the 3 pm bus.

The day was a wasted one for Jim Beaumont as the customers he had to see in Snowtown had gone out for the day. He arrived home at 3.30 pm and when told that the children had not returned, he immediately took his wife to Glenelg Beach and frantically searched for them. The children were reported missing at 7.30 that night. 'Somebody must be holding them against their will. They would otherwise have come home,' the distraught father told the *Adelaide Advertiser* the following day.[1] Nancy Beaumont was sedated and comforted by friends.

Many calls were taken during the night of possible sightings of the children at other Adelaide landmarks — beaches, suburbs and in the city — but to no avail. Hundreds of citizens joined the search, as did members of the Suburban Taxi service, after it was discovered that Jim Beaumont was a former owner-driver, and members of the Girl Guides (Jane Beaumont had recently joined the Third Somerton Brownie pack).

By the end of the following day, a huge search of the Glenelg area had been completed but no trace of the children or their belongings was found. The Police Aqualung Squad searched the Glenelg boat haven, but the sediment in the water hampered any detailed search. At 5 am the police launch *William Fisk* had set out and searched close to the shore of the beach all the way to the coastal town of Aldinga and back to Henley Beach. Hollows and caves in seaside cliffs were thoroughly searched, as were stormwater drains opening out onto beaches.

The police investigated three possible scenarios: the children had run away, they had drowned, or they had been abducted. The first explanation defied logic — these were kids from a happy family heading off for a day at the beach. A note written by Jane to her parents two nights before they disappeared reflects the girl's responsible manner in babysitting her brother and sister, and the Beaumonts' tight-knit family relationships:

> Dear Mum and Dad
>
> I am just about to go to bed and the time is 9. I have put Grant's nappy on so there is no need to worry about his wetting the sheet. Grant wanted to sleep in his own bed so one of you will have to sleep with Arnna. Although you will not find the rooms in very good condition I hope you will find them as comfortable as we do. Good night to you both.
>
> Jane XXX
>
> PS I hope you had a nice time wherever you went.
>
> PPS I hope you don't mind me taking your radio into my room Daddy.

The second scenario was also quickly dismissed. It was highly unlikely that the three siblings could drown unnoticed on a crowded beach, and none of the children's belongings had been left behind. The third theory also had its detractors at the time — multiple abductions, especially three children from the same family, were almost unheard of.

Investigating detectives slowly started to piece together the movements of the children while at Glenelg Beach. At 11 am on the morning of their disappearance, a 74-year-old woman sitting in front of the Holdfast Sailing Club noticed the children playing under the sprinkler on the lawn on the adjoining Colley Reserve. Fifteen minutes later, a man wearing a blue swimming costume had joined them; 'the three children had gone over to him and he was laughing and encouraging them as they played,' she told the press. 'The boy was jumping over him, the younger girl too, and the older girl was flicking him with a towel.'[3]

At about 11.45 am, Jane, Arnna and Grant went into a milk bar on Jetty Street and bought some pasties and a pie. Although Nancy Beaumont had given her eldest daughter some coins to buy lunch, it was later reported that Jane paid for the food with a £1 note. Another woman, who was sitting on a park bench with her husband and 10-year-old granddaughter, noticed the man and three children return to the reserve area around midday. The man even approached them and asked if they had seen anyone going through his belongings, as some money was missing. They told him they had not, and he returned to the children. They all seemed friendly towards the man, the woman later told detectives. Soon after, the man started dressing the three children for their trip home. Mrs Beaumont later said that this in itself was unusual because Jane was a shy child and would never have let a stranger dress her.

Witnesses described the man as being in his late thirties or early forties, 178 to 185 centimetres tall, with a thin face and athletic build. His hair was light brown, parted on the side and long at the back. Although he had a fair complexion he was suntanned and generally described as a 'surfie type'. Another woman noticed the man pick up his towel and trousers and walk with the children to the Colley Reserve change rooms at about 12:15 pm, where the children waited on a seat for him while he dressed.

The group then walked behind the Glenelg Hotel. A tourist from Broken Hill later came forward and said that he too had seen the children with the stranger at 1.45 pm.

A local postman who knew the children later told police that he saw the three youngsters walking east along Jetty Road towards Mosely Street, 'holding hands and laughing'.[4] The postman could not remember if it was at the start of his round at 1.45 pm or at the end, at 2.55 pm, but there wasn't a man with them. This proved to be the final sighting of the children.

On Thursday, 27 January, police used the resources of ADS Channel 7 and radio station 5AD to appeal for public help and to gather information. Brian Taylor, an Adelaide newsreader, manned the station's outside broadcast unit for the entire day and into the night, providing interviews with police and locals who had been on the beach the previous day. 'Direct hourly progress reports were broadcast in the station's news services throughout the day from the search headquarters at Glenelg Beach,' wrote the *Adelaide Advertiser*, which was also conscripted into the search.[5]

The newspaper's sketch artist, Peter Czarnecki, drew the first preliminary drawing of the main suspect seen playing with the children at Colley Reserve. The image of the wanted man was broadcast Australia wide but it was merely a quick sketch, rather than a composite or 'identikit' drawing, based on the recollections of the elderly woman and the Broken Hill tourist. This image remains the only tangible description of the chief suspect.

By the following weekend, the disappearance of the Beaumont children had gained national press coverage. On 30 January, Jim Beaumont again went on national television to appeal to the public for any information that would lead to their return. 'Today is a world of prayer throughout Australia for Australia Day. I hope whoever is holding my children will return them,' Jim Beaumont said on ADS7's midday broadcast. He then broke down and said, 'My wife is not too good. She is still under sedation.'[6] While the nation collectively held its breath for the safe return of the children, Jim Beaumont visited the Glenelg Police Station twice daily, waiting for the news that would never come of his children's whereabouts.

Police were swamped with erroneous reports. People claimed they had seen the children in a car, or on a bus in the company of two men at nearby Semaphore Park, but the leads proved negative. While police described the public response as 'astounding', the unfolding drama also flushed out despicable opportunists.[7] A 33-year-old labourer telephoned police and said that a man driving a Holden came to his house in the Adelaide Hills and forced him to fill the Holden's radiator at gunpoint: inside the car were three children matching the description of the Beaumonts. The man signed a statement to this effect but was later charged with providing a false statement.

On Thursday, 3 February 1966, Nancy Beaumont held a press conference in the garden of her home. 'I can't be stupid and say they're going to come in with a skipping rope,' the 38-year-old mother told the press. 'I've got to feel the little things are huddled up somewhere and nobody has found them.' Jane Beaumont was a sensible, mature girl, her mother told the press. 'If the other two were keen to go with someone, Jane would go with them to look after them and wouldn't leave them alone.'[8]

The investigation stretched the limited resources of the South Australian Police to their fullest. The day of Nancy Beaumont's press conference, the 28 hectare Patawalonga Boat Haven was searched at low tide: the gates were secured, the lock drained and, while divers searched upstream, 50 police cadets waded waist-deep in the sludge. Later, the Adelaide Hills were searched along with the rubbish tip at Marion. Not a single piece of evidence relating to the children was ever found, and the only confirmed sighting of the children occurred at Glenelg on the day they disappeared.

When traditional police methods failed to solve the crime, the public turned to more unconventional means. Reckless gossip fuelled by national media exposure and hunches from well-intentioned people served only to distract police from their investigation. And then there were the psychics and charlatans.

In March 1966, a Dutchman named Jan Van Schie who was living in Adelaide recommended that Jim and Nancy Beaumont consult Gerard Croiset, a well-known psychic in The Netherlands. Fifty-seven-year-old Croiset, who was known as 'The Man with the X-Ray Mind' allegedly had some success in solving cases in Europe, especially those concerning missing children. Contacted in July 1966, Croiset stated that the Beaumont children were buried within a kilometre of where they were last sighted. 'I see an overhanging rock plateau under which there are stones of a nice colour and behind is a cave or hollow ...'[9]

News of Croiset's 'breakthrough' was seized upon by John Kroeger, the editor of the *Adelaide News*. Kroeger sent a reporter from the paper's London office to Holland with photographs of the Glenelg area. Croiset proclaimed through the paper that, 'There was no foul play, nor were they kidnapped. The children are dead. I am almost certain they suffocated; smothered alive. There was some sort of collapse.'[10]

When a local man, Dr Douglas Hendrickson, acting of his own volition, found some items while digging in dunes near an oval behind the Minda Home for disabled children, Croiset claimed that the children were buried metres from where a straw hat had been found. The Dutchman told the media to look for a 'kinderwagon' (pram) in the rubbish as a marker for the graves. In September 1966, the dunes were extensively searched and investigators were heartened when they found a pram among the rubbish, but it was later revealed that it was placed there by one of the patients who was just trying to be helpful. The dunes have since been leveled and covered with a sports field.

The problem of communicating with Croiset on the other side of the world was solved by Brighton car dealer Barry Blackwell, a family friend of the Beaumonts, and local businessman Con Polites who paid for Croiset to fly to Adelaide on 6 November 1966. Croiset declared that he would 'find the children in two days'[11] but on his arrival in Adelaide he quickly became engulfed in the growing media circus; he was pictured in the media as some sort of Svengali walking along Glenelg Beach and talking into a tape recorder while being followed by a trail of spectators.

When a woman contacted Croiset and told him that the floor of a food warehouse in Paringa Park, not far from where Jane and Arnna Beaumont attended primary school, had recently been concreted Croiset made a third claim that the bodies of the children were buried 'under concrete'.[12] Despite the fact that police had no evidence to substantiate Croiset's claim, this theory took on a life of its own. The South Australian state government even debated the merits of digging up the floor of the warehouse before abandoning the issue.

By 11 November, Croiset was 'baffled' and left for America without providing any new leads.[13] However, before he left the country Croiset backed a plan to excavate the concrete floor of the warehouse. This was despite the fact that he told the *Melbourne Truth* newspaper that the children had been accidentally buried under a concrete slab of a block of flats on the edge of Glenelg. A citizen's action committee raised $7000 for the specific purpose of ripping up the warehouse's concrete floor on the first anniversary of the children's disappearance Croiset claimed that he was '99.9 per cent sure' that a tunnel would be found under the concrete slab containing the children's bodies. On 8 March 1967, a partial excavation of the floor was completed but no trace of the children was found. A decade later Croiset was still convinced that the children were buried there. It was not until 1996, 30 years after the Beaumont children disappeared, that the warehouse floor was entirely ripped up, but nothing relating to the children was found.

The children's disappearance brought out the very worst in human nature. Anonymous callers abused Jim and Nancy Beaumont for allowing their children to go to the beach unsupervised. Then there were the blindly misinformed, the poison-pen writers and the pranksters. And, on 27 September 1966, Senior Constable Ron Grose of the small Victorian town of Kaniva was on the phone waiting to be connected to police headquarters in Russell Street, Melbourne, when he overheard two women discussing 'bringing back the Beaumont Children from Hobart'.[14]

Although Grose could not convince either the Victorian or South Australian police forces that the call was anything but a hoax, newsreader Brian Taylor drove Jim Beaumont the 380-kilometre trip to Kaniva to meet with Grose. The senior constable was genuine in what he had thought he had heard, but two local women came forward on 13 October and admitted that while they had been talking about the Beaumont children, they had quickly changed the subject and were actually talking about relatives in Hobart. Grose had made an unfortunate error. Taylor, a well-known news figure in Adelaide, would continue to investigate the case of the missing children long after his career ended.

In February 1968, Jim Beaumont received a letter postmarked Dandenong, Victoria, written in a child's handwriting and signed 'Jane'. The letter stated that if Jim went to the Dandenong Post Office at 8.50 am on Monday, 26 February, wearing a dark coat and white trousers, the children would be returned to him there. Although the writer of the letter threatened to cancel the arrangement if the police were contacted — and Arnna's name had been misspelled as 'Arna' — Jim Beaumont contacted Detective Sergeant Stanley 'Tonner' Swaine of the Adelaide Police and they decided to keep the appointment.

Jim Beaumont and the Adelaide Police Department conducted the trip to Dandenong in great secrecy and did not notify local Melbourne police of the meeting. The letter, however, was leaked to the press and the *Adelaide News* broke the story on the afternoon before the appointment. Local police learnt of the plan through the press when the publican who owned the Dandenong hotel where Jim Beaumont and Stan Swaine were staying became suspicious and contacted Melbourne police. A detective recognised Swaine's name and rang the Melbourne *Herald* to inquire if there had been any developments in the Beaumont case that the local police were not aware of. When Jim Beaumont kept his appointment outside the Dandenong Post Office the following morning, two reporters from the Melbourne *Herald* were watching as events unfolded.

At 9 am a postal worker delivered a message to Jim Beaumont; a man had phoned and said that the children would soon be there. Sometime later a telegram was delivered, saying that Grant Beaumont was sick and the children would not be able to come until after lunch. Beaumont waited until 3 pm but no-one showed up. When he and Swain returned to their hotel, they were confronted by journalists from the *Adelaide News*.

Three more letters were sent to the Beaumonts, two from 'Jane' and one signed from 'The Man'. One of the letters from 'Jane' read:

> Dear Mum and Dad,
>
> We had a really beautiful lunch today. We had some turky [sic] and a lot of vegetables. They tasted really nice. The man is feeding us really well. The man took us to see the Sound of Music yesterday. Little Grant

fell asleep in it though. He could not understand it. The man was very disappointed that you brought all those policemen with you. He knew all the time that they were there, he says that is why he sent the message to go across the street so that it would disturb the positions of the policemen. The man said that I had better stop now, so I will. Grant and Arnna send you their love.

Love Jane, Arnna and Grant. xxxxxxxxx[15]

A great deal of heartbreak resulted from these letters. The family identified the handwriting as belonging to Jane and there was a child-like manner in its construction. While police remained sceptical, Jim and Nancy Beaumont held on to a glimmer of hope that the letters were genuine. In May 1992, improvements in fingerprint technology allowed police to identify the man who wrote these letters to the Beaumonts. A Victorian man, who was 17 years old at the time he wrote the letters, told police it had all been 'a joke'. He was charged and jailed for creating a public mischief.

The disappearance of the three Beaumont children has some tenuous links to several other unsolved crimes. Sydney detectives investigating the murders of Christine Sharrock and Marianne Schmidt at Wanda Beach in 1965 could only have envisaged the remotest link between those murders and the disappearance of the Beaumont children 12 months later. But the timing and place of the two crimes was uncanny — in the January school holidays and on a public beach. The only connection Sydney police had with the Beaumont case was in March 1966 when retired Detective Inspector Ray 'Gunner' Kelly arrived in Adelaide. Sponsored by a Sydney newspaper, Kelly had been hired as a private detective, but although local police were polite the Sydney detective left Adelaide after only one day.

On 25 August 1973, two young girls were abducted from the Adelaide Oval during a South Australian National Football League match between North Adelaide and Norwood. Eleven-year-old Joanne Ratcliffe was at the match with her parents and was sitting next to four-year-old Kirste Gordon who was with her grandmother. Although the older girl did not know the toddler, the younger girl's grandmother asked Joanne to take

Kirste with her when she went to the toilet. The pair returned several minutes later. Just over 30 minutes later, however, Kirste again wanted to go to the toilet and Joanne volunteered to take her. This time they did not come back.

After 15 minutes, Mrs Ratcliffe went looking for the girls and was quickly joined by the other adults in the group when no trace could be found. Ken Wohling, the assistant curator of the Oval, saw the girls leaving the ground in the company of a man. In the hours immediately after the girls went missing, four different sightings of the man and the two young girls were recorded in Adelaide. A description of the man, who was wearing a wide-brimmed hat, was suspiciously similar to the suspect in the Beaumont case seven years before. Just as importantly, the circumstances were similar — two young girls (who could have been mistaken for siblings) abducted from a public place without a trace despite an extensive police investigation.

In the late 1970s and early 1980s, a series of crimes shed a faint light not only on the disappearance of the Beaumont children but also on the seedy underbelly of Adelaide, 'the city of churches'. The bizarre series of events started in 1972 when Dr George Duncan, a university law lecturer, was found drowned in the Torrens River. Duncan, who was openly homosexual, was bashed and thrown into the river by four men at a notorious 'pick-up' area for gay men on the banks of the Adelaide river. Another man, Roger James, was also bashed and thrown into the river but was saved by a passer-by, 25-year-old Bevan Spencer von Einem. (In 1987, two senior Vice Squad detectives later stood trial for allegedly throwing Duncan into the Torrens River but were found not guilty of manslaughter after a three-week trial.)

In 1979, the mutilated body of teenager Alan Barnes was discovered on the banks of the South Para Reservoir, northeast of Adelaide. Barnes, who had been missing for some weeks, had died only the day before his body was found. The post-mortem revealed that Barnes had died of massive blood loss from a wound to his anus. Two months later the neatly dismembered body of 25-year-old Neil Muir was found in the Port River in Port Adelaide. The body parts were sealed in plastic garbage bags and thrown into the river. In June 1982, the skeletal remains of 14-year-old Peter Stogneff, who had been missing for 10 months, were unearthed at Middle Beach, north of Adelaide. The boy's body had been neatly cut into three pieces.

Earlier that year, the body of 18-year-old Mark Langley was found in the Adelaide foothills nine days after going missing while walking on the banks of the Torrens River. Langley, like the other victims, had been surgically mutilated and had died from massive blood loss from a wound to the anus. In June 1983, 15-year-old Richard Kelvin was abducted from a bus stop near his North Adelaide home. On 23 July, the boy's body was found in the Adelaide foothills. A post-mortem revealed that although he had been missing for seven weeks, he had been kept alive for at least five weeks and his body contained traces of four different drugs.

The Adelaide press dubbed the killings 'The Family Murders' when detectives revealed the existence of a subculture of paedophilia and sexual sadism in the city's network of homosexual activity. One of the names in that network of relationships was Bevan Spencer von Einem, the man who had saved Roger James from drowning a decade before. Von Einem, now a tall, blond, immaculately groomed 37-year-old, was a known paedophile but denied any knowledge of the five unsolved murders. Police later searched von Einem's house and discovered three of the drugs found in Kelvin's body and matched von Einem's hairs to those left on the boy's clothing.

Von Einem was sentenced to life imprisonment for the murder of Richard Kelvin but when he stood trial for the murders of the other victims, sensational allegations were made against him by associates at his committal hearing. One of the prosecution's 22 witnesses, 'Mr B' (his identity was withheld for his own protection) implicated von Einem in the death of Alan Barnes. Mr B told a shocked courtroom that von Einem had allegedly told him that he had abducted the Beaumont children from Glenelg Beach in 1966 and had performed some 'brilliant surgery on them'.[16] Their bodies had been buried in Moana or Myponga, south of Adelaide. Although no names had been mentioned, von Einem also allegedly told Mr B that he had taken two young girls from Adelaide Oval — most likely Joanne Ratcliffe and Kirste Gordon.

On 11 May 1990, Bevan Spencer von Einem was committed to stand trial for the murder of Alan Barnes and Mark Langley, but the trial never went ahead. The following February the Crown's case collapsed when Mr Justice Duggan ruled that evidence tabled in the Kelvin trial would be inadmissible in any other proceedings. Mr B's assertions concerning von Einem's involvement in the Beaumont children's disappearance — and other murders — were never tested in court and Adelaide Police described them as being 'extremely fanciful' and not worth investigating.[17]

Over the years police received hundreds of leads about possible sightings of the children but each proved baseless: the children had been brainwashed by a cult, assumed new identities and taken interstate or even overseas. In 1985 a Western Australian couple told a local newspaper that they had lived next door to the three children in the Perth suburb of Reid. The children resembled the Beaumonts and often 'joked' that they were the missing children because they moved into the suburb the year the Adelaide children disappeared. The story was checked but the uncle of the 'Kilowski' children came forward and confirmed their identity.

The following year a suitcase full of press clippings about the children's disappearance was found on an Adelaide rubbish tip. Some clippings had handwritten comments in red ink down the side. Across one headline telling of a hunt in the Glenelg sandhills were the words, 'Not in sandhills, in sewerage drain'. This too was investigated, only to lead to another dead end; family members came forward saying that the clippings were the collection of an eccentric aunt who was obsessed with the case and had recently passed away.

In 1997, a retired Adelaide detective claimed that a Canberra woman was 'Jane Beaumont'. The matter went to court, where it was revealed the woman had been raised by a cult in Victoria and her childhood was but a vague memory but, no, she wasn't the eldest Beaumont child. Family and friends verified the woman's identity but the former detective remained unconvinced. A restraining order had to be taken out against him to stop him pursuing what was an obvious case of mistaken identity.

For years after the children's disappearance, detectives Ron Blight and Alec Palmer kept in contact with Jim and Nancy Beaumont, chatting with the distraught parents and keeping them informed of any developments. The Beaumonts were encouraged to leave Somerton Park and start again, but Nancy Beaumont at first refused. 'But I can't in case the kiddies come home,' she said. 'You see, I'm waiting for them to come back here. I never know. Perhaps someone could drop them at the front gate. Wouldn't it be dreadful if I wasn't here?'[18]

Not knowing the fate of their children ultimately took its toll on the Beaumonts' marriage, with the pair divorcing and retreating to the anonymity of private life. Computer-enhanced photographs of what the children might possibly look like as adults were circulated in the mid-1990s; Nancy Beaumont could not bear to look at them. Four decades later, the story of the Beaumont children continued to change and reinvent itself for a new generation.

In 2001, a Queensland man came forward and claimed that his father had been responsible for abducting the Beaumont children and had buried their bodies in an old well in the Queensland gem-fields near Sapphire. The man maintained that his father had abducted the children on a trip to Adelaide and although his father had recently died, he was simply 'trying to seek closure to get on with his life'.[19] The SA Major Crime Unit had previously investigated the man's claims but despite the fact that no part of his story could be substantiated, the Queensland man repeated the incredible scenario on the nationally syndicated *Today Tonight* current affairs program on Channel 7 in 2003.

The following year, news of the Beaumont children hit headlines on both sides of the Tasman Sea when a New Plymouth butcher made the extraordinary claim that a local man had told him that he had once lived next door to the Beaumont children in Dunedin, in the South Island of New Zealand, after their abduction. Although the story was relayed third hand, the news of this revelation brought a flood of telephone calls from Australia with several press and TV reporters quickly dispatched to New Zealand.

The disappearance of the Beaumont children remains a perpetual nightmare for parents who continue to warn their children of the dangers of walking away with strangers. Many people of that generation have not been able to move beyond the reality of what happened to the Beaumont children at Glenelg Beach that day. Some still cling to the hope that the children are alive and living somewhere under assumed names. Jane, Arnna and Grant would each be in their forties today, but the likelihood of them still being alive is remote to say the least. But for many people, the alternative is just too horrible to imagine.

In 1997, writer Beth Spencer best summed up the place the Beaumont children now hold in the Australian psyche:

> The Beaumonts are the lost children who never grow up: disappearing off the map one day, into a kind of Neverland. Still (presumably) within Australia but unable to be located by the usual means — by parents, police, journalists; even the clairvoyants couldn't find them. So now they are permanently locked in a kind of Louisa May Alcott world of notes left on kitchen tables, playing forever in the shadows at the back of old amusement park rides; trapped in a nation's memory vault and desire for an innocent past.[20]

Maybe we have been searching for something we lost on Glenelg Beach that summer's day 40 years ago ... our national innocence.

Chapter 9
The Anita Cobby Murder (1986)

The abduction, pack-rape and murder of Anita Lorraine Cobby in February 1986 has been described as one of Australia's most shocking murders. Almost two decades after the body of the 26-year-old Sydney nurse was found in a paddock in Prospect, in western Sydney, the appalling details of the young woman's final hours — and the subsequent capture of the five men who perpetrated the degrading acts of violence upon her — continues to resonate on the psyche of western Sydney. But where such crimes at first impact negatively on a community — with the fear and loathing generated invariably leading to the demonising of the perpetrators and calls for the return of the death penalty — the Anita Cobby case has continued to shape community attitudes and behaviours that reconcile, empower and inspire the families of murder victims.

Anita Lynch was born on 2 November 1959, the daughter of Garry Lynch, a graphic artist who had worked with the Royal Australian Navy, and his wife Grace, who was a nurse. Anita was raised in Blacktown, in western Sydney, with her younger sister Kathryn and attended a local high school. A popular student among her peers, Anita was persuaded to enter a local beauty pageant when she was aged 20 to raise money for the Spastic Centre. The attractive young woman won the Miss Western Suburbs title, and helping others was to become a recurring theme in Anita's short life.

Anita enrolled in a nursing degree and trained at Sydney Hospital, where she met John Cobby, a male nurse. The pair married in 1982 and spent the next two years travelling and working overseas before returning to Australia and settling for a time in Coffs Harbour on the north coast of New South Wales. John and Anita Cobby returned to Sydney in 1985, but soon afterwards their marriage broke down. Anita returned to her family home in Blacktown, although she and her husband remained on good terms. Anita also returned to Sydney Hospital, commuting to work by train. When she travelled home at night after a long shift, she would telephone her father to come and get her from Blacktown railway station.

Sunday, 2 February 1986 was one of those hot, sultry nights that occur late in the Sydney summer. Anita Cobby finished her shift at 5.30 pm and had dinner with two friends, fellow nurses Lyn Bradshaw and Elaine Bray, at a Lebanese restaurant in the inner-city suburb of Redfern. Although Anita had the opportunity to stay overnight with friends in the city, she had to work the following day and was keen to return home to Blacktown. Lyn Bradshaw dropped Anita off at Redfern railway station at 8.45 pm, although there was some conjecture about which train she caught that night.

Anita didn't phone her father from the station and when she didn't arrive home that night, Garry Lynch assumed that his daughter had stayed in the city with her friends. But the following day he received a phone call from Sydney Hospital inquiring why Anita had not started her 1.30 pm shift. Mr Lynch contacted several places where his daughter may have visited but when he learned that Anita's friends were at work and had not heard from her, he rang his wife Grace at her work. He then rang Anita's estranged husband John Cobby late that afternoon before contacting Blacktown Police to report that their daughter was missing.

On Tuesday, 4 February, Prospect farmer John Reen rang Blacktown Police. There was the naked body of a woman in one of his paddocks on the road that bore his family name, he told them, and they had better come and see. On Sunday night he recalled hearing a woman's screams but Reen Road was often used by young people as a 'lover's lane' and for drag racing so he didn't think too much of it. The following day, Reen noticed many of the cows crowded in one corner in his 'boiler' paddock, where he kept his older stock. When the cows were still in the same position on the Tuesday morning, Reen decided to investigate more closely. There, concealed in the long grass, was the naked body of a young woman. Although the cows had licked most of the blood from the victim's body, it was clear that she had been dragged through the barbed-wire fence, savagely beaten and murdered.

One of the many detectives and plainclothed officers called to the crime scene was Detective Constable Garry Heskett from the Homicide Squad. Heskett, who arrived at the murder scene with Detective Sergeant Ian Kennedy, had been an infantry soldier in the Australian army for six years and was later an ambulance officer with the NSW Ambulance Service before joining the police. Nothing in his previous experience prepared him for what he saw in the paddock on Reen Road.

> Once being briefed I saw the body of Anita Cobby lying naked on her stomach. She was positioned near a large tree. Her head was lying on her right arm and her legs were apart. There were a number of severe lacerations to her throat and other scratches and marks to her back and thighs. The deceased's body was rolled over and I saw more clearly the severity of the lacerations to her throat. Upon closer examination I could see quite clearly the lacerations to the inside of the deceased's left hand — the severity exposing the bone to two of her fingers, which was indicative of defensive wounds.[1]

The government medical officer, Dr Joe Malouf, conducted a detailed examination of the victim's body and the surrounding crime scene while a police scientific photographer took a visual record. Detective Sergeant

Kennedy, under the supervision of Dr Malouf, removed the gold Russian interlocking ring from the victim's right hand and secured it in a plastic bag. The police knew that the ring might be used to identify the victim but a conversation with a young policeman, Constable Murphy, from Blacktown Station was about to shed light on that matter. A missing person's report had been filed by Garry Lynch the previous day, and the constable had a photo of the man's missing daughter, Anita Cobby. In a bizarre coincidence, Constable Murphy had attended high school with Anita Cobby but did not recognise the victim as being the person he knew. But both Kennedy and Heskett knew instinctively that the body of the naked and brutalised young woman in front of them was the missing girl.

The two Homicide detectives visited the Lynch residence and found Garry Lynch and his wife Grace being comforted by their other married daughter, Kathryn. The detectives had the difficult task to perform of telling them that the body of the young woman resembled their daughter and to arrange a formal identification. Kennedy showed Grace and Garry Lynch the victim's wedding ring and they said that it looked like the one worn by their daughter. It was then that Garry Lynch made the statement that was to resonate with every parent in Australia: 'I could wish it was "someone else's daughter" but I can't, can I? They would have to go through what we're going through.'[2]

The detectives made brief inquiries about Anita's movements on the day she disappeared but did not stay any longer than was necessary. After obtaining a more recent photo of their daughter and a description of the clothing that she was wearing, the detectives left the Lynches with their grief. Later that afternoon Kennedy and Heskett returned to the Blacktown home, where they were joined by Anita's estranged husband, John Cobby. Earlier that day the distraught young man had travelled to Wollongong to see if Anita was visiting friends when he heard on the radio that the body of a woman had been found in Prospect. Cobby positively identified the interlocking wedding ring as the one he had given his wife when they married.

The detectives asked Garry Lynch to attend the mortuary with them to positively identify Anita's body, believing him to be the strongest of the family members. Kennedy and Heskett briefed the heart-broken father of the strategies the police would adopt to capture those responsible for his daughter's death but also warned of the inevitable intrusion of the media into their lives. However, watching Garry and Grace Lynch publicly handle their grief one couldn't help but gain an insight into the tenacity, determination and dignity shown by their daughter at the moment of her death: Garry, the family spokesperson — direct but emotional, stoically answering the media's questions; Grace, as always, in silent support by her husband's side.

A task force to investigate the murder of Anita Cobby was established at Blacktown Police Station. Twenty police were assigned to the task force, which was made up of 15 police from Blacktown under the direction of five Homicide detectives, including detective sergeants Graham Rosetta and Kevin Raue. A shocked Sydney media was also intent on playing its part in the investigation. Sydney newspapers found a photo of the NSW Premier Neville Wran awarding Anita Cobby her Miss Western Suburbs title in 1979. In posting a reward of $50 000 for information leading to the conviction of the woman's killers (this was quickly doubled) Premier Wran said, 'This is one of the foulest crimes of the century and the animals responsible must be brought to justice.'[3]

Public sentiment was running hot — community anger and outrage was almost palpable. 2UE radio broadcaster John Laws went one step further. At the end of a frantic week of reporting, Laws read out Anita Cobby's post-mortem results to his radio audience. Post-mortem results are never released to the public, out of respect for the victim's families and the fact that the report may reveal details that police need to catch those responsible for the victim's death, but Laws promised to reveal further details to his audience the following Monday. The leaking of the official post-mortem report drew a quick response from Sydney Coroner Derrick Hand, who contacted the Crown Solicitor, the head of the state government's Solicitor's Office, and stopped the rest of the report from being read. Hand kept this scathing comment about Laws' disclosure for his memoirs: 'Laws claimed he had been acting in the public interest — while it was probably interesting to the public that is not the definition of it being in the "public interest". In my view it was just sensationalism.'[4]

One of the first leads came from two Blacktown residents, teenage siblings John and Linda McGaughey. On Sunday, 2 February, 16-year-old Linda McGaughey and her older brother John were watching television in their Newton Road home at about 9.50 pm when they heard a woman screaming. When the pair went outside to investigate they saw a petite, dark-haired woman being bundled into a grey car they described as a Holden Kingswood. The incident so troubled the pair that when their older brother Paul returned home with his girlfriend, they recounted the story and gave a description of the car. Paul McGaughey decided to drive around the quiet Blacktown streets and check for the car, eventually driving into Reen Road. At the end of the street he saw a light-coloured HJ Holden, but did not investigate any further because it was not the car described to him. After two hours Paul and his girlfriend returned home, but the information the McGaugheys were able to provide police proved invaluable.

Police correctly suspected that Anita had been abducted in Newton Road on her way home from Blacktown station. Constable Debbie Wallace, then attached to the general duties branch at Blacktown station, was conscripted to re-enact Anita Cobby's movements on the night she died. Police not only needed to ascertain the approximate timing of the victim's movements but the re-enactment attracted heavy media coverage and this may have encouraged someone to come forward with more information. The re-enactment took place on Sunday, 9 February — one week after the murder — starting at Central railway station in front of a battery of TV cameras. Wallace caught the 9.12 train to Blacktown and on arrival at the station, walked towards the taxi rank. The journalists and TV cameras were left behind at this point as detectives wanted to gather as much information as they could about the victim's final journey in secrecy. Sergeant Ian Kennedy later recalled: 'At that stage we were despairing. There were no clues, no suspects. It looked like we were walking into a dead end.'[5]

On 21 February, police received a vital breakthrough when a western Sydney man informed them that three petty criminals — 18-year-olds John Travers and Michael Murdoch, and Les Murphy, aged 24 — had stolen a Holden sedan, sprayed it 'undercoat grey' and replaced the mag wheels with a standard set to avoid detection. All three were known to police; Travers had been under investigation for the alleged rape of a Toongabbie woman eight months earlier but had disappeared to Western Australia. Police were unaware Travers was back in Sydney but set about determining his exact whereabouts.

Despite being only a teenager, Travers was already a textbook psychopath — his adolescence was punctuated by episodes of truancy, vandalism, assault and stealing, with a complete disregard for authority and accepted boundaries of behaviour. Expelled from Doonside High School, he completed Year 10 at Newman High School at Wentworthville, where he lived with his grandmother. Travers was already drifting into petty crime — he was sent to Cobham Remand Centre for car theft and gun possession at age 16, but later found work at Riverstone Abattoir slaughtering animals. The teenage sadist was known to have engaged in acts of bestiality and cruelty — partygoers recalled him cutting the throat of a lamb at a barbecue at Mount Druitt in 1984. Travers also had two part bull-terrier dogs, which he named 'Slut' and 'Arse', and regularly beat them to turn them into vicious attack animals. He allegedly had sex with them to keep them 'faithful'.[6]

John Travers' home life was appalling. The eldest of seven children, Travers' mother bore him at the age of 15. Travers' father abandoned the family shortly after they arrived in their Housing Commission bungalow at Tich Place, Doonside, from nearby Mount Druitt. His mother Sharon suffered from Cushing's disease — an eating disorder that saw her weight balloon to almost 200 kilograms — and was confined to bed, trapped by her inability to care for herself. Community nursing staff refused to visit Mrs Travers at her home because of harassment by the Travers children.

Travers and Michael James Murdoch enjoyed an unnervingly close relationship — it was suggested by police that they were homosexual lovers but both men denied this. Murdoch lived in Doonside three doors away from the Travers family and hero-worshipped the young thug. At age 16, the pair used an amateur tattoo kit to cover themselves in homemade tattoos. Travers was tattooed on many parts of his body, including his penis, and had Murdoch tattoo a permanent blue teardrop under his left eye. Travers thought it made him stand out from the other career criminals in Sydney's west — and that it certainly did. It made him easily identifiable as the person responsible for a series of rapes and assaults and, finally, for the murder of Anita Cobby.

Detectives used their network of informants to determine the movements of the wanted trio. At the time of his arrest, Leslie Joseph Murphy was living in a caravan with Lisa Travers, the 17-year-old sister of John Travers, in the backyard of the Travers' family home in Doonside. Murphy had received his first conviction for car theft at the age of nine; a search of the Travers' property located the mag wheels and seat covers from a stolen 1970 HJ Holden fitted to Murphy's own car. Heavily armed policed simultaneously raided residences in the western Sydney suburbs of Wentworthville and Doonside. When police stormed the house in Wentworthville, they found Travers sharing a bed with Murdoch.

While the three men admitted that they had stolen the car, each denied involvement in the abduction and murder of Anita Cobby. The stolen car was an obvious key to the crime but, not surprisingly, the three offenders refused to provide any details of the car's whereabouts. Murphy and Murdoch were released on bail while Travers was kept in custody pending investigation into the rape charge. Travers then asked police to contact a female relative to bring him some cigarettes and to come and see him in jail. Police saw this as their best opportunity to gather incriminating evidence against Travers and to use it against Murphy and Murdoch.

When detectives questioned the woman, whom they codenamed 'Miss X', they discovered that she was in fear of her life. Despite being the de facto wife of a member of the extended Murphy family, she had been taken into Travers' trust and had been privy to the details of a succession of crimes committed by him. While in Western Australia, Travers had raped a young man and confided to the woman that he had threatened to cut the victim's throat. Having done this to animals in the past, Travers told her, he now wanted to know what it felt like to take a human life. Only when she was placed under witness protection did Miss X agree to help police with their investigations.

After briefly talking with Travers, Miss X was fitted with a recording device and taken to an interview room. Incredibly, through his own tears, Travers revealed in grim detail what happened that Sunday night. Travers, Michael Murdoch and the three Murphy brothers — Les and older brothers Gary (29) and Michael (33) — had decided to rob someone. Anita Cobby had simply been in the wrong place at the wrong time; they had taken her off the street, robbed her so they could fill up the stolen car with petrol, raped her in the car and then taken her to Reen Road. Travers had dragged her across the barbed-wire fence before each man raped and sodomised her. While she lay in the long grass under a tree, Michael Murphy had told Travers 'to do your thing'.[7] The 18-year-old returned to where the victim lay and, grabbing her from behind, had callously cut her throat.

Travers asked Miss X to go to his house and to get rid of the kitchen knife with the wooden handle as it was the one used to kill Anita Cobby. He also told her to tell Les Murphy to check if the stolen car was where they had left it — burnt out on the side of Plumpton Road in Blacktown. Again wearing a police 'wire', Miss X went to Doonside and talked to Les Murphy about the car. When they went together to check on the car in Plumpton Road, it was gone. The chance for police to check the stolen car for forensic evidence was lost. Later she returned to Blacktown Police Station and spoke to Travers again. At 11.30 pm that night, Miss X visited Michael Murdoch at his home in Westmead and tried to tape a conversation with the accused man. Murdoch drove around Parramatta with Miss X and her de facto husband and their child, but despite the fact that the recorded conversation was inaudible, police felt that they had enough evidence to rearrest Murdoch.

Armed with this extra information, the police also rearrested Les Murphy, who was found in a Granville home hiding under a blanket on a mattress between two young women. When questioned, Les Murphy and Michael Murdoch each blamed Travers for the murder of Anita Cobby, arguing that they had merely gone along for the ride. Travers, in turn, implicated all four men — including the two other Murphy brothers — in the crime.

On 24 February, police charged Travers, Murdoch and Les Murphy with the abduction, rape, robbery and murder of Anita Cobby. The trio was heavily guarded as an angry crowd gathered outside the Blacktown Local Court. Two days later, Michael and Gary Murphy were captured at a townhouse in the southern Sydney suburb of Glenside. Despite being told by a young woman at the scene that the Murphy brothers had already left, Michael Murphy was arrested as he watched television. Gary Murphy made a run for it but was tackled into a fence by police. Photos in the morning papers showed Gary Murphy handcuffed and bleeding, his pants soiled after he urinated on himself during his capture.

Despite the fact that the Murphys were considerably older than John Travers, the teenager had considerable control over them. There was no evidence that any of the men raised a finger to stop Travers on the night he killed Anita Cobby. Michael Patrick Murphy had spent most of his adult life in jail. Prior to Christmas 1985 Murphy had escaped from Sydney's Silverwater Prison where he was serving 25 years for a litany of crimes, including break and enter, car theft, being in the company of an armed person and escape from lawful custody. Linking with his two brothers, Les and Gary, he came into contact with their friends, Travers and Murdoch. Gary Murphy was not known to be a violent person and had been in a stable relationship for four years before fathering two children with another woman.

Both men indicated their involvement in the crime and were met by an even angrier mob when they faced Westmead Court on 27 February. 'We jumped in the car,' Michael Murphy told the police in a signed statement. 'John came running up with blood all over him. He said, "I cut her throat ... I think I cut a couple of her fingers off 'cause she put her hand up." He said, "It's me first one." Mick [Murdoch] asked him what it felt like. He said, "Like nothing."'[8]

In June 1986, all five men pleaded 'not guilty' when they faced committal hearings. After Miss X gave her evidence to the court, Travers lunged at her screaming, 'You bitch! You fuckin' bitch. I'll get you.'[9] (Miss X was later the major beneficiary of the NSW government's reward.) On 1 July, the five men were remanded in custody at Parklea Prison until their trial the following March for the kidnapping, sexual assault, robbery and murder of Anita Cobby. They were kept in Wing Five, the maximum security segregation section — not so they wouldn't escape, but so they wouldn't be killed by other prisoners.

On 16 March 1987, John Travers, Michael Murdoch and Les, Gary and Michael Murphy faced trial in the NSW Supreme Court. In a sensational start to proceedings, Mr Justice Maxwell was forced to abort the trial when Michael Murphy was identified in newspapers as an escaped prisoner. The jury was dismissed because Maxwell feared that Michael Murphy's identification would be prejudicial to his receiving a fair trial. A new trial started the following week, on 23 March. Murdoch and the three Murphy brothers maintained their 'not guilty' pleas but in another sensation, Travers changed his plea to 'guilty'.

At their trial, the full circumstances of Anita Cobby's death on that fateful Sunday night were revealed. Travers and the Murphys had been drinking at the Doonside Hotel when they ran out of money. Returning to Travers' Doonside home, they picked up Michael Murdoch who was also living there at the time. Driving off in the HJ Holden that Travers had stolen the previous week, the men headed towards Windsor, where they drank more beer and smoked some marijuana before returning to Doonside. It was then that the group decided to rob someone to get money for petrol. They saw Anita Cobby walking along Newton Road with her handbag slung over her shoulder. Travers and Murdoch bundled her into the car (although Murdoch denied his active role in her abduction at his trial), where she was repeatedly punched and her clothes torn from her body. After purchasing petrol, and holding the girl out of sight, Travers and Michael Murphy raped her at knifepoint before taking her to the paddock in Reen Road.

The group left the murder scene and returned to Travers' home. Travers was covered in blood, but his mother believed his story that he had been attacked by a dog and had killed it to protect himself. The men gathered Anita Cobby's clothing and belongings and burnt them in a drum in Travers' backyard, a scene later verified by their next-door neighbour. Several days later Travers and Murdoch took the stolen car to the side of Plumpton Road, Blacktown, and set fire to it.

Michael Murdoch and the Murphy brothers refused to be cross-examined during their trial, resorting to making unsworn statements from the dock. Michael Murdoch maintained that he did not take part in the rape or the murder of Anita Cobby, but remained in the car. Murdoch denied telling Detective Sergeant Ian Kennedy that he physically abducted Anita Cobby or had tried to have sex with her but couldn't. Les Murphy denied having sex with the victim, stating that his brother Michael had stopped him from taking part. Gary Murphy's defence was even more incredulous: he had drunk so much that day that he couldn't recall where he was on that night.

Although there was a host of forensic and circumstantial evidence to link the men to the murder (there was no DNA technology available in 1987), it was their own statements — and the confession of John Travers — that ultimately condemned them. The jury found that although Travers had been the murderer, each person present had entered into a common enterprise that had resulted in Anita Cobby's death. After nine hours' deliberation, the jury found all four men guilty.

On 10 June 1987, Mr Justice Maxwell remanded the guilty in custody for sentencing on 16 July. In handing down life sentences to each of the five men, Mr Justice Maxwell stated:

> This is one of, if not the most horrifying physical and sexual assaults I have encountered in my forty-odd years associated with the law. The crime is exacerbated by the fact that the victim almost certainly was made aware, in the end, of her pending death.
>
> Throughout the long trial, the prisoners, albeit to a lesser degree in the case of the prisoner Murdoch, show no signs of remorse or contrition. Instead they were observed to be laughing with one another and frequently were seen to be sniggering behind their hands ...
>
> The circumstances of the murder of Mrs Anita Lorraine Cobby prompt me to recommend that the official files of each prisoner should be marked 'never to be released'. If the Executive deems it proper in the future to consider their files, then I echo the advice proffered, by a former and distinguished Chief Judge at Common Law, that the

> Executive should grant to the prisoners the same degree of mercy that they bestowed on Anita Lorraine Cobby on the night of 2 February, 1986. I do not think the community would expect otherwise.[10]

Justice Maxwell was referring to the infamous judgment handed down to convicted murderers Allan Baker and Donald Crump in 1974 for the abduction, rape and murder of Mrs Virginia Morse in Collarenebri, New South Wales, the previous year.

In an aftermath to the trial, Raymond Patterson, Mavis Saunders and Debra McAskill were each charged with being accessories to murder after the fact. Despite going to police with vital information about the then unsolved crime, Patterson had allowed Michael and Gary Murphy to stay with him on the night after the murder, knowing that they had been involved in the crime. Les Murphy won the right for a re-trial through the High Court of Australia, but in July 1990 he was again found guilty in the Darlinghurst Supreme Court. By that time the Greiner government's 'truth in sentencing' legislation had been passed and 'never to be released' meant exactly that. John Travers resides in Goulburn's Maximum Security Prison, along with Australia's other most notorious murderers, including Ivan Milat.

The public tended to view the case in terms of 'black and white'. The murder of Anita Cobby was a needless crime perpetrated on a 'good' person from a happy, loving family by criminals from disadvantaged backgrounds. But the subsequent murder trial of the five men challenged and ultimately changed public perceptions, government policy on social justice and even the law.

Ultimately, the murder of Anita Cobby transcended geographic, economic, cultural and gender boundaries. The NSW government introduced the 'Charter of Victims' Rights' and the Victims Support Policy Statement. One of the mandatory lectures of the NSW Police Investigator's Course in the Detectives Education Program (DEP) looks at the Victims Support Policy Statement and the NSW government's 'Charter of Victims' Rights'. In 1996 this course was run by Detective Sergeant Garry Heskett, who worked on the original Anita Cobby murder investigation.

Garry Lynch took on a position on the Offender's Review Board and he and Grace have continued to help families coping with the murder of a loved one with their involvement in the Homicide Victims' Support Group. 'You go through a path that leads right into the centre of hell but ... there is a turning point,' Mr Lynch says. 'You don't know whenever it will happen. It will happen. When it does, go like hell to get to the other end ... to free yourself from this burden.'[11]

Anita Cobby's murder has taken on an almost mythic dimension in Australian culture. There is a memorial website at www.anitacobby.com where readers can leave messages and prayers on a bulletin board. Julia Sheppard's book *Someone Else's Daughter* has sold over 130 000 copies since its release in 1991. Some years later, Garry Lynch released his own memoir, *Struck By Lightning*. Anita's grave at Prospect's Pinegrove Memorial Park (in the same suburb in which she was murdered) is visited by members of the public who leave flowers, letters and even toys.

But the question remains: What social, cultural and economic factors led to such a heinous crime being committed? That question was not so easily answered. The victim and her attackers lived in adjoining suburbs, so it was almost impossible to attack the values of people living in western Sydney. Two years after the murder of Anita Cobby, 21-year-old Janine Balding was kidnapped from Sutherland railway station by a gang of 'street kids' who stole her car, raped her, bound her and then drowned her in a dam in the western Sydney suburb of Minchinbury. It seemed as though society had learned nothing from the events of February 1986.

But recently many people who lived through the Anita Cobby murder case — the Lynches, their family and friends, the investigating police and even the families of the perpetrators — began to ask a deeper question: How do you look beyond the factual aspects of a murder and come to terms with the rippling effect that such a crime has on the wider community? In March 2003, 17 years after her death, the Penrith Regional Gallery and the Lewers Bequest, in partnership with the Casula Powerhouse and Liverpool Museum presented the exhibition *Anita and Beyond*. Con Gouriotis, the curator or the Casula Powerhouse Arts Centre, had great success with the groundbreaking *Vietnam Voices* mixed-media exhibition in the early 1990s, which looked at the effects of the Vietnam War on the Australian public. Gouriotis first suggested the Anita Cobby murder as an important exhibition subject in 1999 but was not sure how to develop the idea. It took another three years, with the help of assistant director Lisa Havilah, before the exhibition started to take conceptual form.

The exhibition focused on 'developing synergies between contemporary visual arts practice, community cultural development and social history'.[12] *Anita and Beyond* included the Miss Western Suburbs sash Anita won in 1979, a Year 10 school uniform and a nurse's outfit that she wore, letters from patients whom she cared for, a painting completed by her in Year 12, and the watercolour she made two days before she died. There were examples of TV and print media coverage, and videos of the Homicide Victims Support Group meetings. The social history component of the exhibition consisted of oral histories, police archives, photographs, memorabilia and personal community mementos, while 12 artists were commissioned to present works to be exhibited.

The curatorial group overseeing the exhibition included a core of people close to the events surrounding Anita Cobby's death and her murder investigation. They included her parents, who approved of and guided the project; family friends Anne King and her son, Mike King; Detective Sergeant Garry Heskett and Detective Chief Inspector Debbie Wallace, who were both involved in the original investigation, as was retired court sheriff Allan Allsop; and writer Julia Sheppard. Contemporary experts included Sandy Goldstone, manager of the NSW Rape Crisis Centre, criminologist Russell Hogg, and Martha Jabour, executive director of the Homicide Victims' Support Group.

As Lisa Havilah, the curator of the exhibition, explained at the time, Anita Cobby's murder has 'become part of the identity of western Sydney. We hope that, when people come to the exhibition, they leave with a really deep understanding that when someone is murdered, that the pain doesn't go away. And it's not just two or three people; it's her family and her friends. It's actually hundreds of people impacted in a whole range of ways.'[13]

Maybe even a whole society.

Chapter 10

The Backpacker Murders (1996)

Australia had been seen as a safe haven for domestic and overseas travellers — especially young people journeying away from home for the first time — but the crimes of Ivan Robert Marko Milat changed that perception forever. The abduction and murder of seven backpackers in Australia in the early 1990s and the subsequent discovery of their bodies in the Belanglo State Forest, 140 kilometres southwest of Sydney, made international headlines for all the wrong reasons.

On the afternoon of Saturday, 21 September 1992, a body was found in the Belanglo State Forest, an area described as a 'rough and difficult area of thick natural bushland, steep gorges, pine plantations and twisting trails'.[1] Members of the Scrubrunners Orienteering Club in Campbelltown stumbled across a body covered in leaves and twigs near a large sandstone boulder. The murder site was about 100 metres off a dirt track, accessible only by four-wheel drive, 4 kilometres down the Long Acre fire trail after the turn-off from the main road.

When Detective Senior Constable Andrew Grosse, from the South West Region Major Crime Squad based in Goulburn, some 60 kilometres away, and Detective Senior Constable Bill Dowton, from nearby Bowral, arrived at the sealed-off crime scene they examined the body of a woman buried under a mound of bush refuge about 2 metres long and 60 centimetres high. Five months earlier the disappearance of two British backpackers travelling in Australia, Joanne Walters from Wales and Caroline Clarke from England, had been highly publicised. The parents of Joanne Walters had recently returned to Australia to search for their daughter and were staying in Sydney. When another body was located some 30 metres from the boulder — hidden under a huge tree trunk and covered in branches — the fate of the two girls was finally revealed.

It was over a year later, on Tuesday, 5 October 1993, that another body was found within kilometres of where the remains of Joanne Walters and Caroline Clarke were recovered. A fossicker searching for firewood found the body of a woman near the base of a tree, and when police arrived at the crime scene they quickly located another body. The bodies were later identified as Australians James Gibson and Deborah Everist, who had disappeared while hitchhiking together between Sydney and Albury on 30 December 1989. Unlike Walters and Clarke, the Australian pair had been stabbed and bludgeoned to death, not shot. Despite this, the fact that the bodies of four young travellers — two couples — had been found so close to each other meant that police had uncovered the burial ground of a serial killer.

Task Force Air was formed to investigate these murders (the name 'air' came from the fact that the four victims, and several other travellers, had seemingly vanished into 'thin air'). In the five weeks after the discovery of the bodies of Gibson and Everist, three hundred police, including trainees from the nearby Goulburn Police Academy, turned the Belanglo State Forest into a bustling tent community with the primary aim of ascertaining whether there were any more bodies buried there. On 1 November 1993, more human remains were located in another part of the forest. Superficial evidence at the crime scene identified the body as belonging to a young German backpacker, Simone Schmidl, who was last seen on

20 January 1991 while hitchhiking from Sydney to Melbourne. Again, no firearm-related evidence was found at this scene. A post-mortem examination revealed that Schmidl had been stabbed to death.

Days later, on 4 November, the sixth and seventh bodies were given up by the forest. The two bodies, which were buried about 60 metres apart, were a man and woman killed by a combination of gunshot and knife wounds. The skeletal remains of the woman, found in a shallow grave on the lee side of a fallen tree and covered with bush litter like the others, were missing the skull. The identified victims — Gabor Neugebauer and Anja Habschied — were, like Simone Schmidl, German nationals last seen backpacking on the outskirts of southwest Sydney on Boxing Day, 26 December 1991. While these were the last bodies to be found in the Belanglo State Forest, they did not exhaust the list of backpackers, hitchhikers, young couples and especially women missing in New South Wales stretching back to the 1970s.

Seven victims — each vulnerable in that they were many kilometres from home and travelling in an unfamiliar environment — had been snatched from the Hume Highway in southwestern Sydney between December 1989 and September 1992 and found murdered in the anonymity of the Australian bush. The search for more bodies was officially scaled down on 17 November 1993, with police satisfied that there were no more remains in the forest. While Belanglo State Forest returned to relative normality, the police started the immense task of piecing together the final movements of the victims and the identification of the person or persons responsible for these crimes from the available forensic evidence.

The respective autopsies of the seven victims, which were conducted by government forensic pathologist Dr Peter Bradhurst, provided macabre and sadistic evidence of the manner in which they died. Joanne Walters had suffered multiple stab wounds to the neck and chest with a large-bladed knife. The head of her friend, Caroline Clarke, was found wrapped in a maroon-coloured sweatshirt. When the skeletal remains were routinely X-rayed, her skull revealed 'numerous radio-opaque objects' — spent bullets.[2] When the decaying material was unwrapped from around the skull, 10 separate bullet entry holes made by a small calibre weapon were revealed. When the skull cap was removed, seven bullets were recovered; four from the skull cavity, with two more found in the material and another in the dirt covering the left shoulder. It was later determined that the bullets in Clarke's head were from a .22 calibre weapon fired from three different directions. She had also been stabbed in the chest.

Police had recovered two .22 Winchester fired cartridge cases from the first crime scene, but when they returned to the Belanglo Forest and used a metal detector they ultimately retrieved a further eight cartridge cases hidden in long grass. Three other bullets were retrieved from the soil on which Caroline Clarke's head lay. Each bullet entry was carefully marked with numbered flags so that it could be recorded using terrestrial photogrammetry (which gives a three-dimensional photograph of the relative positions of the killer when the gun was fired). However, the victims' parents were visiting the murder scene the following day and a well-meaning constable left to guard the site thought the flags had mistakenly been left behind and removed them from sight. Luckily, measurements had already been taken and no damage was done.

On Sunday, 29 September 1992, Father Gray conducted a memorial service for Caroline Clarke and Joanne Walters in the presence of Walters' parents and a small choir. He said, 'We have come here today, where something wicked happened, so that this place can be peaceful again and its memories put to rest. Where evil is very strong, and in this place, it does not have the last word ...'[3]

But Belanglo — which literally means 'beautiful angel' — had more secrets to reveal.

Budding conservationist James Gibson and his girlfriend Deborah Everist, both 19, had left the Melbourne seaside town of Moorooduc to hitchhike to Sydney in late December 1989. On 31 December 1989, a Ricoh camera later identified as belonging to the missing couple was found in the Sydney suburb of Hornsby. In March 1990, a red backpack belonging to Everist's brother Tim was found in Galston Gorge in north-west Sydney. Although they were found second, the advanced state of decomposition of the young Melbourne couple made it clear that they had been murdered long before the two British girls.

Near the body of Deborah Everist, police found knotted pantyhose that may have been used to tie up a victim and other scraps of clothing. Although Everist's remains had been disturbed by animals and the fossicker who found them (the excited young man took the skull with him to show police), it was clear that her jaw had been broken and her skull fractured. Forensic pathologist Dr Bradhurst found that she had most likely died of a single stab wound but evidence on her remains was consistent with having been slashed with a large knife, such as a machete or sword. There was also a 'sexual aspect to the young couple's murders'. Gibson had similar knife marks on his chest and the ribs under his right arm. The knife that had pierced his chest and back had 'been driven with such force that it chipped, cut and gouged his bones'.[4]

The body of victim five, Simone Schmidl, was found lying face down against the fallen branch of a tree about 40 metres from the Miners Despair fire trail. Although the advanced state of decomposition could not determine the sex or age of the victim where it lay, a closer inspection identified the clothing, hiking boots and purple bandanna as belonging to the missing German backpacker. Schmidl had failed to meet her mother, Erwine, at Melbourne Airport on 23 January 1991, where Mrs Schmidl had planned to join and then travel with her daughter. In May 1991, spectacles and a sleeping bag were found in Bright, 75 kilometres southeast of the Hume Highway as it crossed the New South Wales–Victoria border. When photographs were shown to Mrs Schmidl, who had returned to her native Germany, she was adamant they had belonged to her daughter 'Simi'.

Of the last couple to be found, Gabor Neugebauer had been shot six times in the head while his girlfriend had been decapitated. Neugebauer had a piece of cloth in his mouth that had been used to gag him while Habshied's pink jeans were found some distance away from her body. Inside the jeans was a knotted cloth, in the shape of a blindfold, while a leather leash was found nearby. Four bullets were recovered from inside Neugebauer's skull, with one of the exit bullets becoming the fifth bullet recovered from bones in the upper body.

Police were keen to ascertain whether the bullets recovered from Neugebauer's body matched those found in Clarke's remains, but they were to be disappointed. All bullets recovered from this later victim were heavily corroded and devoid of any markings. However, a macroscopic examination of the bullets by Sergeant Gerrard Dutton determined that the pieces of lead were from a .22 calibre bullet and had an impressed 'dimple' on their base, which ballistic experts knew to mean that they had been manufactured by Winchester, Australia. (The dimple is placed on the bullet by staff of the Winchester plant in Geelong, Victoria, to identify the lesser antimony of lead, which makes the bullets softer and allows easier expansion when striking animal tissue.) No fired cartridge cases or spent bullets could be located in the area where Neugebauer's body was found, so it could not be established where the German backpacker had been murdered. If he had been shot there, a missing .22 calibre bullet should have been found in the soil beneath him but police removed the soil to a depth of 30 centimetres and nothing was found.

Anja Habshied's remains were found some 60 metres away. Although her skull was missing and therefore it could not be determined if she, too, had been shot, there were large knife marks on the bones of her spine. It was clear that she had been decapitated by a large blade, probably a sword, and possibly while she was still alive. Her head was never recovered and police were of the opinion that because an animal could not have carried it away, it must have been taken by the murderer or murderers as a trophy.

The fact that an excessive amount of bullets were fired into one of the victims, and the extreme number of headshots coupled with the multiple stab wounds, marked these murders as being in the 'most unusual' category. But the available ballistic evidence also provided detectives with the best opportunity to solve the case. Experts first tried to identify the gun that fired the recovered bullets and spent cartridge casings, and compared these with those found near the respective victims. Simply put, police did this by comparing the striated marks — a series of fine scratches caused by the scraping of the metal bullets on the metal barrel of a gun — on samples test-fired by particular guns.

By examining the crescent-shaped impression left on the bullet casings, investigating police were able to determine that a Ruger 10/22 rifle had been used in the Clarke murder. Coincidentally, a Ruger had been used in another high-profile murder, the killing of Australian Federal Police Commissioner Colin Winchester in 1986, and Canberra Federal Police were able to establish a database of hundreds of Ruger rifles that had been tracked back to their owners. The test-firings of over 550 rifles were made available to Task Force Air so that they could be ruled out of the Backpacker Murders, as the Belanglo crimes became known.

More evidence was located in an area 165 metres south from where the body of Gabor Neugebauer was discovered. Assorted items and rubbish were found at an old campsite, including a number of sherry bottles and a cardboard box labelled Winchester 'Winner'. The Winner bullets, which are made for target shooting, was a significant find in that only a few types of these cartridges could have been the one used in the Clarke murder. The bullets used on Clarke had a specific combination of characteristics — brass composition; the use of an 'H' head stamp; the presence of case knurling; the lead was not coated in a copper wash; and lastly, the specific number of cannelures (knurled marks around the bullets).

Over 100 similar fired cartridge cases were found near the Neugebauer crime scene, with about half being Winchester brand with the distinctive crescent-type firing pin impression left by a Ruger rifle. Forty-seven bullet cases were identified as being fired by the same gun that had discharged the 10 cases found near the body of Clarke. Although an 'inter-comparison' of the Clarke and Neugebauer cases was made difficult because of the relative corrosion of the bullets, police were able to determine that the Clarke murder gun was discharged in close proximity to where the remains of Gabor Neugebauer were found, thus linking the two crimes. The remainder of the bullets were Eley brand, with a hemispherical firing pin impression, which obviously meant that they were fired by a separate weapon. A .22 calibre cartridge box labelled 'Eley "Subsonic"' was also found nearby. Although it was in a poor condition, experts from the Document Examination Section were able to verify the batch number on the cardboard box. Police now started the task of determining what type of gun fired the Eley bullets.

Searchers recovered six spent .22 calibre bullets from trees south of this campsite — the result of some unknown person taking part in apparent target practice. Some of the bullets were marked by a 'crooked' silencer, as was the case in the Clarke murder, but a positive match could not be made. Although police could assume that the spent bullets were from the Winchester or Eley cartridges, they kept an open mind on which type of gun was used to fire them.

Criminal psychologists began to build a profile of the serial killer: rational, well organised and ruthless; a person familiar with guns and the bush; possibly in his forties but extremely confident as shown by the fact that he also kidnapped couples. The murders had a blatantly sexual overtone with the disposal of the bodies done in almost ritualistic manner. Detectives were also convinced that if and when they found the murderer, they would also find some of the victims' possessions. However, the case suffered a potential setback when the media reported that the police were searching for a Ruger 10/22 rifle. Investigating detectives were dismayed that this piece of vital information would alert the murderer to get rid of or even destroy the gun. From then Task Force Air was careful to keep information 'in house'.

Of the thousands of leads forwarded to police, a man working at the Boral Industrial depot in Parramatta stated that he was in the company of a workmate, 'Paul Miller', when driving past the Belanglo Forest. Miller allegedly remarked that 'there are more bodies out there' and 'they haven't found the Germans yet'. Miller was a drug user and gun enthusiast who lived with his mother in Guildford, Sydney, but owned a property in the Southern Highlands. On another occasion, Miller was alleged to have remarked to his workmates that 'stabbing a woman was like cutting a loaf of bread'. Another informant, a Basil Milat, volunteered unsolicited that he had seen a man driving the missing English girls in Queensland. An anonymous caller suggested police investigate the entire Milat family because, 'they're a pretty weird bunch ... they've got guns and they go shooting'.[5]

But the vital breakthrough came from Englishman Paul Onions, who had contacted police in 1992 after the discovery of the first two bodies but, because of an administrative bungle, police did not interview him until 1994. Onions, who was referred to as the 'eighth backpacker' by investigating detectives, was secretly flown to Australia to be interviewed.

The 24-year-old Englishman said that on 25 January 1990, while hitch-hiking to Mildura he had accepted a lift from a well-built man with a 'Merv Hughes-type' handlebar moustache who introduced himself as 'Bill'. Travelling in Bill's silver four-wheel drive south along the Hume Highway, Onions said the driver was friendly enough but his conversation became increasingly aggressive. Approaching the Belanglo State Forest, Bill stopped the car on the pretence of getting some music cassettes from behind the seat. When he returned to the front of the vehicle, he produced a revolver and told Onions that it was a robbery.

When Onions saw Bill produce ropes from a bag, he made a split-second decision that was to save his live. Flipping off his seat belt, he stumbled out of the passenger door and ran from the car back up the highway. Onions avoided a gunshot and crossed the road with the man in pursuit. The pair wrestled for a while before the young Englishman was able to break free and flag down a passing van driven by Joanne Berry, with her sister and their five children inside. Against her better judgment, Berry let the young man into her car and, as the other man came close, launched her car into reverse and drove across the medium strip and headed for Sydney. Onions reported the incident to local police in the nearby town of Bowral but had lost his backpack, his passport and belongings, including $500 in cash. Onions later continued his travels and returned to England.

As police were already investigating the Milats, a picture of Ivan Milat was included in photographs shown to Onions as a potential suspect. The Englishman identified Milat as his attacker after police were able to obtain a 1989 passport photo of the suspect with his trademark moustache. But while Milat no longer wore the moustache, it was his 'evil grin' — formed by his distinctively crooked mouth — that identified him to Onions.

One of 14 children born to Stipjan (Stephen) Milat and his wife Margaret, Ivan Milat (born in 1944) first came to the attention of the police when he was charged with stealing in July 1962. Milat was later jailed on two further occasions for breaking and entering. In April 1971 he was charged with the rape of a woman, but the victim refused to press charges. In the ensuing months Milat was charged with bank robbery and fled to New Zealand (his brother Michael and his accomplices were given jail sentences). By the time Ivan Milat was brought back before the courts, in 1974, he was found not guilty of the robbery charges.

During the 1970s and 1980s, Milat worked for the Road and Traffic Authority (RTA) repairing roads but he was also employed by Boral under the name 'Bill' Milat (he also registered his car in the name of his brother Bill and assumed his brother's date of birth, 9 July 1947). Milat's other brother Richard also worked at Boral, under the name 'Paul Miller'. Worksheets obtained by police showed that Ivan Milat was not at work on any of the dates that the seven backpackers went missing, as well as 25 January 1991 — the date of the failed abduction of Paul Onions.

Task Force Air carefully planned simultaneous raids on houses and properties belonging to the Milat family, but their primary focus was the Eagle Vale home of Ivan Milat in Cinnabar Street. In the early hours of Sunday, 22 May 1994, members of the State Protection Group (SPG) met at Campbelltown Police Station to be briefed on the raid on Milat's home that he co-owned with his sister Shirley Soiree. Milat lived there at the time with his girlfriend, Chalinder Hughes. Police decided that they would barricade the surrounding streets and contact Milat by telephone while he was still in bed. Operational procedures had been changed to reduce the risk of injury, even death, to suspects and police as had occurred in previous raids.

When members of the SPG contacted Milat by phone, he at first thought it was a joke and remained in bed with his girlfriend. Contacted a second time, SPG could hear Milat moving around inside the house on their listening devices. When he apparently went into the garage and opened a car door, police thought he might be making a bid for escape but minutes later, Milat walked out of the house and was arrested. It was just before 7 am.

While Milat was questioned in the living room of his house by Detective Sergeant Steve Leach and Senior Constable Paul Gordon of Task Force Air, four officers — Goulburn Crime Scene Examiner Andy Grosse, Constable First Class Steve Blackmore of Macquarie Fields,

Detective Senior Constable Peter O'Connor of Task Force Air and Detective Sergeant Gerard Sutton — began a search of the house. The building was a relatively new, single-storey, four-bedroom brick home. At 8.20 am, while crawling in the ceiling space, Detective O'Connor found parts of a Ruger rifle hidden in wall cavities. Removing an insulation batt, he retrieved a white plastic bag resting on a noggin. Inside the bag were the dismantled parts of a Ruger rifle, including the breech bolt assembly, a complete trigger assembly and a Ramline aftermarket magazine.

When Milat was questioned about the find he said that he didn't know anything about them. No fingerprints were found on any of the items or on the plastic bag. Over the next three days members of the Joint Technical Support Group used flexible cameras to explore every corner of the house. Police found more components of the Ruger 10/22 and, in the garage, the plastic butt-plate of the gun and a homemade silencer. In a spare bedroom they discovered a broken barrel band and a Ruger 10/22 owner's manual. Police also found a .22 calibre fired cartridge case — with a crescent-shaped impression made by the Ruger's firing pin. The barrel, stock and cocking lever assembly of the Ruger were never recovered.

Various calibre cartridges were also found inside the house, along with a 7.65 millimetre Browning pistol. This included five boxes of Eley 'Subsonic' cartridges, the same type as the empty box found in the Belanglo Forest. The cartridges from Milat's home were later found to have the same lot number (manufactured on 23 March 1979) as the box found at the crime scene. Winchester 'Winner' boxes matching the type found in the forest were also relocated from Milat's home.

However, the cartridge cases recovered from Milat's bedroom were not able to be matched with 100 per cent certainty to the same gun that had fired the cases in the Clarke murder (the passing of time, the presence of dirt or a build-up of grease in a weapon can distort the markings made on a cartridge case), and the silencer was definitely ruled out as being used on the murder weapon. But when the Ruger rifle parts were reassembled using a rifle from the Ballistics Unit firearms reference library, the fired cartridge cases and spent bullets from the samples found at Milat's house matched those recovered from the Clarke crime scene. Detective Sutton later wrote that 'of the millions and millions of Ruger 10/22 breech bolts that have ever been manufactured in the world, I now knew the breech bolt fitted to the rifle that was used to kill Caroline Clarke, was the one recovered from the wall cavity at [Milat's house] Eagle Vale.'[6] Although police could not positively identify the bolt assembly as the one used in the Neugebauer murder because of corrosion, chamber marks on the bullets linked the two crimes.

And there was a lot of other physical evidence found in Milat's home to link him to the murders. A 'Salewa' brand tent, the type reportedly owned by Simone Schmidl and one not sold in Australia, was found in Milat's garage. A plastic water bottle found in a spare bedroom was examined under infrared lighting and found to have had the name 'Simi' scratched out on it. A metal camping and eating kit similar to the one carried by Schmidl and a multicoloured backpack belonging to her were handed over to police by the wife of Ivan's brother, Alex. Police also found Indonesian currency in Milat's home (the German nationals Neugebauer and Habshied had arrived in Australia from Indonesia) and a 20 pence English coin was recovered from his current Jackaroo vehicle. Blood on a sash cord (similar to that discovered near Neugebauer's body) was found in Milat's garage and was later 'DNA linked' to 'a child of Mr and Mrs Clarke'.[7] A photo of Milat's girlfriend Chalinder Hughes wearing a Benetton top, similar to the one owned by Caroline Clarke, was also recovered.

When the other items of interest came in from properties belonging to Milat's brothers Richard and Walter, the evidence started to mount up. Tens of weapons, including an Anschutz breech bolt were retrieved from the properties where Ivan was known to camp and hunt. Ten large tins containing approximately 14 000 .22 cartridge cases and 41 kilograms of spent bullets were eventually examined. Sutton wrote, 'All the Winchester fired cases from the Clarke and Neugebauer scenes, the single case from Milat's house, the four cases from Buxton and the four cases from Barrallier, were all positively identified ... as having been discharged in the same rifle [and] ... two of the Eley fired cases from the Neugebauer scene as having been discharged from a weapon fitted with the Anschutz breech bolt.'[8]

On 24 October 1994, committal proceedings against Ivan Milat began at Campbelltown Local Court before Magistrate Price for the murders of the seven backpackers and the attempted abduction of Paul Onions. The committal hearing lasted seven weeks and heard evidence from over two hundred witnesses with over six hundred exhibits tendered. Halfway through the trial Milat sacked his barrister Cate Holmes (for the second time) and was later represented by Queensland barrister Terry Martin, QC. Milat was subsequently committed to trial on 25 March 1996.

Much of Milat's defence rested almost entirely on casting doubt that the police had got the right 'Milat' and the basic assertion that someone other than the police had planted the evidence in his Eagle Vale home to make him 'look bad'.[9] The Crown was able to place the victims near or on the Hume Highway when they disappeared and determined that Milat did in fact own a silver Nissan four-wheel drive and wore a large moustache, as Paul Onions described. While Milat continued to declare his innocence under oath, the presence of so much property belonging to the victims being found in his house, although circumstantial, carried a lot of weight with the jury.

After the guilty verdicts were handed down on Saturday morning, 27 July 1996 — some six and a half years after the disappearance of James Gibson and Deborah Everist — Justice David Hunt stated:

> The case against the prisoner at the conclusion of the evidence and the address was, in my view, an overwhelming one. Although his legal representatives displayed a tactical ability of a higher order and conducted his defence in a skilful and responsible manner, in my view the jury's verdicts were, in the end, inevitable. Any other, in my view, would have flown in the face of reality.
>
> Each of the victims was young, they were between nineteen and twenty-two years old. Each was travelling far from home, the inference being that they would not have been missed for some time if anything happened to them. I am satisfied that each set out along the Hume Highway from near Liverpool in order to hitch-hike to the south. The jury's verdict means that the prisoner was involved, either alone or in

> company, in a criminal enterprise to pick them up there and then to murder them all. In my view it is inevitable that the prisoner was not alone in that criminal enterprise ...
>
> It is sufficient here to record that each of the victims was attacked savagely and cruelly, with force that was unusual and vastly more than was necessary to cause death, and for some sort of psychological gratification. Two of the victims were shot a number of times in the head. A third was decapitated in circumstances which establish she would have been alive at the time. The stab wounds to each of the three others would have caused paralysis, two of them having had their spinal cords completely severed. The multiple stab wounds to three of the seven victims would have penetrated their hearts. There are signs that two of them appear to have been strangled. All but one of them appears to have been sexually interfered with either before or after death.
>
> These seven young persons were at the thresholds of their lives, with everything to look forward to — travel, career, happiness, love, family and even old age ... it is clear that they were subjected to behaviour which, for callous indifference to suffering and complete disregard to humanity, is almost beyond belief. They would have been absolutely terrified and death is unlikely to have been swiftly applied.[10]

Ivan Milat was jailed for the term of his natural life on seven counts of murder and one of attempted murder. Sent to Maitland Prison in northern New South Wales, Milat later conspired with convicted drug dealer George Savvas to escape from prison on 17 May 1997. Kept in solitary confinement (Savvas later committed suicide), Milat was later sent to Goulburn Jail's maximum security multipurpose unit following the dismissal of his appeal in February 1998.

While in prison Milat came under suspicion for a host of unsolved crimes stretching back to the early 1970s that had long baffled police: the disappearance of Leanne Goodall, aged 20, Robyne Hickie, 18, and Amanda Robinson, 14, from the Newcastle area in the late 1970s; of engaged couple Alan Fox and Anneke Adriaanson while hitchhiking on the NSW north coast in January 1979; and the disappearance of Dundas nurses Gillian Jamieson and Deborah Balkan. In 1987 the skeletal remains of an unidentified backpacker were found in bushland near Taree and in January 1988, the body of 18-year-old Peter Letcher was discovered in the Kanangra Boyd National Park near Oberon, west of Sydney. Letcher had been shot five times with a .22 rifle and his head wrapped in material in a similar fashion to that of Caroline Clarke. On 11 March 1991, 22-year-old Carmen Verheyden was last seen hitchhiking in Casula, south of Sydney. Her body has never been found.

On 6 July 2002, NSW state coroner John Abernathy conducted a coronial inquest into the disappearance of Leanne Goodall and Robyne Hickie, both of Belmont North, and Amanda Robinson, of Swansea, who disappeared between December 1978 and April 1979. Milat was a member of a road crew in the Newcastle area during this time, and because of his *modus operandi* during the Backpacker Murders trial, he was called to give evidence during the inquest but denied any knowledge of the crimes. The convicted murderer continued to declare his innocence of the Backpacker Murders.

On 20 February 2003, Milat informed jail authorities that he had ingested razor blades, staples and a small chain from a pair of nail clippers as part of his campaign to have his appeal heard by the High Court of Australia. However, jail authorities believed Milat had a different motive — to be moved to a medical facility or a less secure prison where he could launch another escape bid. (Milat confessed that he had wrapped the razor blades in adhesive tape to avoid internal damage.)

In December 2003, Milat came under suspicion from Parramatta detectives investigating the disappearance of Dundas flatmates Gillian Jamieson and Deborah Balkan. The two nurses were last seen leaving the Tollgate Hotel in Church Street, Parramatta, at 7.30 pm on 12 June 1980, in the company of a man 'dressed in dirty work clothes and wearing a floppy black cowboy-style hat'.[11] At that time Milat was living at his mother's home in Guildford and working for the Department of Main Roads in the Parramatta area. Photographs retrieved from Milat's home during the backpacker investigation pictured him in his lounge room wearing a black hat with a red bandanna and holding a rifle. (Milat often dressed as a cowboy, loved guns and referred to himself as 'Tex' or 'Bargo Bill'.)

The crimes of Ivan Milat horrified a nation and divided the loyalties of his own family. Another member of the Milat family once speculated that his younger brother Ivan could be responsible for as many as 28 murders. That would make Ivan Milat, the Backpacker Murderer, the most prodigious serial killer in Australian criminal history.

Chapter 11

The Port Arthur Massacre (1996)

Can an act of madness change how a nation thinks or what a nation values? Can it change an entire nation's attitude towards violence? The madness unleashed by a Tasmanian gunman, Martin Bryant, at the tourist attraction of Port Arthur on Sunday, 28 April 1996, was unprecedented in Australia's peacetime history. At the end of the day, 35 people lay dead with another 28 wounded — an atrocity that not only reverberated around Australia but also the world.

Port Arthur was established in 1830 under the authority of Lieutenant-Governor George Arthur, and for the next 40 years became the main penal settlement on the island of Van Dieman's Land, which later was renamed Tasmania. Situated at the southwestern corner of the island 160 kilometres from the main city of Hobart, the convict settlement was isolated from the rest of the island by a narrow isthmus named Eaglehawk Neck, which itself was heavily guarded by soldiers and attack dogs. Laid out in a beautiful bush setting and protected from the sea by a still harbour named Carnarvon Bay, very few convicts tried to escape from Port Arthur because there was nowhere to escape to. The only place to go to was the Ile de Morts (Island of the Dead), in the middle of the harbour, where all the convicts who died at the settlement were buried.

Port Arthur was a brutal prison, with eight categories of punishment for the convicts jailed there. Surprisingly, the most severe form of punishment was solitary confinement, which was seen as being worse than hanging or flogging. (Hanging was never carried out at the penal settlement; convicts were locked in the Round Tower Guardhouse and transported to Hobart for execution.) Port Arthur's system of 'solitary punishment' sentenced convicts to suffer in absolute silence rather than 'take a flogging'.[1] Convicts who broke the rule of silence were placed in the 'dumb' cell and locked away in total isolation. The punishment invariably induced madness.

Port Arthur was a prison town; the 'model prison'[2] included a penitentiary, a hospital, an asylum and a boys' reform school across the bay. A church built in gothic style was completed in 1836 but was never consecrated because it was used by several denominations and also, as legend holds, because a murder took place while the foundations were being laid. The convicts took part in a bustling timber industry, but the combination of shackles and chains did not mix with the felling of trees — the Isle of the Dead is dotted with gravestones of convicts killed by falling logs. During its lifetime, 12 500 convicts passed through Port Arthur before transportation of convicts ended in 1853. However, because there was no other use for the settlement, the buildings soon fell into disrepair. The complex was gutted by fire in 1877 while onlookers cheered. But since becoming a tourist attraction, millions of visitors have strolled through the grounds of the former penal settlement.

Sunday, 28 April 1996 was a sunny, autumn day in Tasmania. Over 500 visitors were drawn to Port Arthur, the island's main tourist attraction. At 1.30 pm a large crowd had gathered at the information centre to wait for their guided tour to begin, while others wandered the site at their own leisure. The Broad Arrow Café, at the northern end of the complex adjacent to the main car park, was filled with visitors enjoying their lunch. Brigid Cook was the catering supervisor and worked that day with three others behind the servery, while second cousins Elizabeth Howard and Nicole Burgess served customers in the adjoining souvenir and gift shop. Almost none of the tourists noticed the tall, blond-haired young man walk into the café carrying a large sports bag and video camera. The young man with the glassy stare ordered a large meal, a can of soft drink and a cup of fruit juice. He took his tray outside, and sat at one of the tables on the balcony at the front of the café.

Patrons at the café later said that the young man remarked on the number of 'wasps' about — 'wasps' being a well-known acronym for 'white Anglo-Saxon people' but most certainly a general reference to white people. A little later the man commented upon the lack of Japanese tourists at the settlement that day and, after quickly finishing his meal, went back inside the café. Standing at the back of the café in the northwestern corner, he placed his belongings on a spare dining table and took out an AR15 semi-automatic rifle from his sports bag and began to fire.

In the space of 15 seconds — the amount of time verified by amateur video footage taken outside the café by tourists 200 metres away — 17 shots were fired, killing 12 people and injuring 10 others. The identities and fates of the victims are detailed here not to sensationalise their deaths but because each person deserves to be remembered individually, not just as a victim of a massacre.

Malaysian visitors Moh Yee William Ng and Sou Leng Chung were shot dead as they ate lunch; the gunman then brought his rifle up to his shoulder and wounded Mick Sargent in the head with his third shot. The fourth shot fatally wounded Sargent's partner, Kate Scott — the Perth couple were visiting Hobart that weekend for a wedding.

Anthony Nightingale, a loans manager with the Commonwealth Bank in Keysborough, Victoria, was shot dead as he jumped to his feet and shouted, 'No, no! Not here!' At about the same time Kevin Sharp, his wife Marlene, and his younger brother Ray entered the café to lunch with friends, who were already seated. Kevin Sharp was shot in the head and arm as he turned to protect his wife. Walter Bennett was shot in the neck, with ballistic evidence later proving that the doubly fatal bullet went on to strike Ray Sharp in the head. Another trio, Gary Broome, John Fidler and his wife, Gaye, were each struck by shrapnel from the bullets that killed these people.

It was at this point that Mick Sargent called out, 'Keep down! Keep down!' One of his party, John Rivere, had gone to the counter to be served and was crouching behind the servery. Another friend, Caroline Villiers, sought refuge under the body of Kate Scott along with Sargent, who was bleeding from a wound to the scalp. Sydney tourists Tony Kistan, his wife Sarah and friend Andrew Mills were lunching in the middle of the room. When the shooting started the men jumped to their feet and had shielded Sarah Kistan towards the door. Both Tony Kistan and Andrew Mills were killed by single shots to the head when they tried to disarm the gunman.

Peter Croswell, a Hobart coordinator of the Camp Quality organisation that helps support children suffering from cancer, tried to protect Camp Quality workers Thelma Walker and Pamela Law, but the two elderly women were wounded by fragments of bullets that killed Tony Kistan and Andrew Mills. Pat Barker was also struck in the arm, hand and cheek by flying metal before she could take refuge under her table with her husband. Melbourne property developer Robert Elliot, who was also at the table, was seriously wounded in the arm and head as he bravely stood to his feet to distract the gunman away from his wife, Alyece.

When the gunman moved to the centre of the room he found Carolyn Loughton, her boyfriend Graham Colyer and Loughton's 15-year-old daughter Sarah sitting at the table. Graham Colyer was wounded in the neck before the gunman's attention was diverted to another couple, Mervyn and Mary Howard, who were sitting in a corner. The Dunnstown couple were killed where they sat; Mervyn Howard still had a cup of coffee in his hand when he was shot while his wife Mary died beside him. The gunman missed Joanne Winter, who was hiding under a table with her father and one-year-old son while her husband was at the service counter, when he turned his attention to the Loughtons. Carolyn Loughton was seriously wounded as she tried to protect her daughter but despite her efforts, Sarah Loughton was fatally shot as she lay on the ground.

Outside the café Ian Kingston, the site security officer and the manager of the Tasman Unit of the State Emergency Service, was standing in the upper car park when the sounds of shooting reverberated across the harbour. His immediate thought was that the electrical wiring of the café was 'arcing out in the walls or something in the ceiling' and he raced to the scene.[3] Kingston ran through the door and then saw the gunman raise his rifle. He yelled for the cashier behind the servery to get out, and shepherded as many people as he could out the café door. The problem was that 30 or 40 people were only metres away from the door and were about to come into the café. Kingston called, 'There's a gunman!' but this only confused the tourists. In the end he had to yell, 'Fire!' to get their attention because people thought the shooting was a re-enactment.

In the gift shop people were trying to escape the gunfire but they found the back door that led to the balcony locked. Two staff members, Nicole Burgess and Elizabeth Howard, were shot while still standing at their counter. Dennis Lever was killed as he sheltered his wife and another elderly woman behind a screen with jumpers pinned on it. Adelaide nurse Jennifer Moors pushed two elderly women behind a screen as the gunman approached. Ron Jary and his wife, the Levers' friends from Red Cliffs, Victoria, also took shelter behind a screen in the gift shop while Ron Neander and his wife Gwenda, of Adelaide, hid behind a postcard stand. Gwenda Neander was the next to attract the gunman's attention and was killed instantly when shot in the face.

While the gunman was in the gift shop, Jason Winter, who was a short distance from his wife and infant son, attempted to return to his family. The New Zealand winemaker made the fatal mistake of thinking that the gunman had left the building and called out to Dennis and Mary Olsen who were hiding nearby, 'He's gone!' Bryant wounded Peter Crosswell as his attention was drawn back to the café and killed Jason Winter with two shots as the young father darted in front of the servery. Dennis Olsen, who was crouching behind the servery with his wife, was injured in the hand, chest, eye and head by shrapnel from the bullets that killed Winter.

Bryant found Ron Jary, Peter and Carolyn Nash, an unidentified Asian tourist and Pauline Masters unable to exit the locked door of the gift shop. Ron Jary, Pauline Masters and Peter Nash were each killed, with Nash able to shield his wife from the gunman before he died. When the gunman took aim at the Asian tourist, the magazine of the gun was empty. The gunman changed the magazine of the gun and then, inexplicably, left the café.

Because the shootings happened in a matter of two minutes, the sequence of events tended to be confused by the survivors and had to be verified by the ballistic and forensic evidence available. Twenty people lost their lives in the Broad Arrow Café but this number would have been much greater if not for the selfless acts of bravery by many of the people trapped inside. Melbourne policeman Denis Gabbedy, who was on holiday in Tasmania, was one of the first to reach the café after the gunman left and render aid to the victims. Melbourne nurses Lynne Beavis and her sister, Jean Andrews, ran from the penitentiary to the café, while Brisbane doctors William Maguire and John Windsor also helped the wounded despite the fact that the gunman was still nearby.

Author Margaret Scott, in her definitive account of what happened at Port Arthur that day, detailed the absence of panic inside the café as the gunman fired. Of the people trapped inside the café Scott wrote:

> They were generous, loving and brave and although many of them died, they demonstrated that, when put to the ultimate test, altruism is alive and well in late twentieth-century Australia ... in a time when it often seems that selflessness is an outdated virtue, we owe them an immeasurable debt.[4]

Bricklayer Mark Kirby had been contracted to do repairs on the stonework at Port Arthur and was working in a cherry picker that Sunday, repairing the third and fourth storeys of the penitentiary opposite the Broad Arrow Café, when he heard the shooting. Earlier that day Kirby had visited the café for lunch but had returned to work and was 8 metres in the air when he saw Brigid Cook, whom he knew, come around the back of the café and wave her arms to warn people that there was a gunman inside. Cook did not see the gunman but had immediately left the kitchen with the three shop assistants via the back door when the shooting started.

As about 80 people turned and ran towards the upper car park, Kirby instinctively started the motor of the cherry picker — inadvertently attracting the attention of the gunman who had exited the café at about the same time. As the tourists were herded into the upper car park by the guides and scrambled for their lives up the hill towards the tollbooth on Jetty Road, the gunman came out onto the café balcony and fired a shot at them (Ashley Law, a guide, heard the bullet hit trees behind him) as well as two shots at the cherry picker.

Selflessly, Brigid Cook headed west towards the row of buses in the lower car park to warn visitors there. The gunman tracked her as she ran and also moved towards the lower car park where he had parked his yellow Volvo with a surfboard attached to the roof-racks in order to change guns. Royce Thompson, the driver of the Tigerline bus, was fatally shot in the back as he sought cover. Brigid Cook was then shot through both legs and slumped beside a rear wheel of a Trans Otway bus. Cook was taken to a vacant sentry box by bus driver Ian McElwee, who attended to her wounds the best he could.

Adelaide woman Winifred Aplin was killed as she took cover behind her coach, while her friend Yvonne Lockley was injured. Neville and Janette Quin, owners of a wildlife park on the other side of the island, had doubled back towards the car park from the jetty when they saw the gunman head towards them. Janette Quin, who was separated from her husband in the confusion, was shot and injured as was Trans Otway passenger Douglas Hutchinson. The gunman finally reached his car and changed the AR15 for a .308 SLR. On his way back towards the buses, he fatally shot Janette Quin as she lay wounded beside the body of Royce Thompson. He then fired through the window of the Trans Otway bus and killed Elva Gaylard as she sat in her seat. Another passenger, Gordon Francis, tried to lock the front door of the coach and was shot in the shoulder.

Neville Quin found his stricken wife lying behind the Tigerline coach. The gunman saw him there and chased Quin around the bus 'at least two or three times'. Quin attempted to trip the gunman[5] and then tried to take refuge on the bus but the gunman saw him, followed him onto the bus and shot him in the neck. Quin was able to stagger off the bus and return to his dying wife as the gunman drove off in his yellow Volvo towards the tollbooth at the entrance to the complex.

By this time Mark Kirby had reached the ground and was able to guide tourists inside the penitentiary — eventually convincing some of them that it was not a re-enactment. Having seen Brigid Cook injured, he raced down to the car park but could not find where she had fallen. He eventually found her being treated in the sentry box by Ian McElwee, who had tied a tourniquet around her injured leg and packed the wound to stop the bleeding. Kirby tried to assist the fatally injured Janette Quin, then ran up to the information centre to phone for help.

In his confusion Kirby dialled four zeroes rather than the 000 emergency number and could not make contact. However, guide Wendy Surr had already alerted police when she had taken the fleeing tourists past the information centre into the government gardens on the left of Jetty Road, while Peter Roche, the ferry master to the Isle of the Dead, and security manager Ian Kingston had also made the call. Mick Sargent showed enormous presence of mind after helping his friend Carolyn Villiers from the café by running back inside — after the gunman had left — to check on his dead girlfriend and then ring 000 from the café's payphone.

Of the approximately 80 people who had turned back up the hill when the shooting started, the lead group of seven carried on towards the tollbooth rather than taking refuge in the Government Gardens. John and Caroline Boskovic and their friends Peter and Pauline Grenfell had already finished lunch in the Broad Arrow Café, while Nubeena mother Nanette Mikac and her two daughters, six-year-old Alannah and three-year-old Madeline, had gone to Port Arthur for a picnic while her husband Walter, a local pharmacist, enjoyed an afternoon of golf. The seven people heard gunshots from the car park but felt they were safely out of harm's way as they approached the tollbooth at the entrance to the convict settlement.

Tollbooth attendant Aileen Kingston had also thought the gunshot sounds were part of a re-enactment. Just before the lead group of people came up Jetty Road, Kingston allowed two cars to enter the complex — a gold-coloured BMW carrying Ken and Mary Rose Nixon, of Crabtree, and their NSW friends Jim Pollard, Robert Salzmann and his wife Helene; and a red Holden Commodore belonging to the Buckleys, from New Zealand. The two cars had only travelled about 100 metres down the entrance road when they were warned by the lead group that there was a gunman on the loose. The Buckleys immediately turned around, parked on the side of the road and approached the tollbooth to ask Aileen Kingston what was happening. The gold BMW also turned around and pulled up just past the tollbooth, facing the Arthur Highway.

When the yellow Volvo approached the tollbooth on Jetty Road, the people there had no way of knowing that it was the gunman. Nanette Mikac, carrying her youngest daughter, instinctively approached the car as the gunman stopped and got out. The Boskovics and Grenfells, who had been joined by a third couple, the Duttons, noticed the gun the young man was carrying and ran for their lives. Nanette Mikac was told by the gunman to get down on her knees as she pleaded for the lives of her children. She and her daughter Madeline were killed by a single bullet, while six-year-old Alannah attempted to hide behind a nearby tree. The gunman callously stalked and killed the helpless child.

The Buckleys saw the gunman kill the Mikac family and abandoned their car and ran for the highway where they were picked up by a passing couple, Keith and June Edwards. Aileen Kingston hid in the tollbooth as the gunman drove past and parked alongside the gold BMW. The occupants of that car had not got out of their vehicle and did not see what had happened to the Mikac family. The tall, blond-haired driver of the Volvo approached the occupants and demanded their car. He shot and killed Robert Salzmann when he argued with him and then the driver, Jim Pollard, who got out of the car and confronted him. As another car, driven by Debra Rabe, turned off the Arthur Highway into the entrance to the tollbooth, the gunman killed Helene Salzmann and Mary Rose Nixon. Ken Nixon was injured but survived.

Debra Rabe quickly reversed out onto the highway as another car, a maroon Magna driven by Graham Sutherland, came towards the toll-booth. Sutherland, his wife and two children saw the bodies of the victims and the gunman transferring his weapons into the BMW. As they reversed back onto the highway, the gunman shot out the Magna's windscreen. Keith Edwards was trying to stop anyone from entering the Port Arthur site as the Sutherlands drove to the service station and shop immediately north of the tollbooth entrance. Debra Rabe also arrived to alert people of the impending danger — a gunman was coming. Glenn Pears, a Tasmanian lawyer living in Sydney, drove into the service station with girlfriend Zoe Hall. At that moment, the gunman drove into the service station and blocked Pears' car. The gunman confronted Glenn Pears, who tried to placate him and spare the life of his girlfriend. Pears was made to get into the boot of the gold BMW and then the gunman returned to Pears' car and shot Zoe Hall through the heart.

The gunman then drove towards the Seascape guesthouse north of Port Arthur. Police later learned that the gunman had already killed the owners of the guesthouse, David and Sally Martin, on his way to Port Arthur earlier that day. The gunman swung the gold-coloured BMW off the Arthur Highway and stopped in the entrance to the Seascape guesthouse. He took aim at John Rooke, who was driving a Datsun, but nothing happened. But the next car, a Holden Frontera driven by Linda White from Melbourne, was struck by bullets that shattered White's forearm. Her passenger, Michael Wanders, attempted to drive the car but it was disabled by the gunshot damage. Doug Horne, who was driving with Neville Shilkin and their wives in a maroon Ford Falcon sedan, was wounded in the chest, shoulder and right arm with the gunman's next shots. Linda White and Michael Wanders were rescued from the scene by Neville Shilkin, who drove the two groups to safety in Horne's sedan.

Anne Wardle, who was travelling down the Arthur Highway in her Magna, saw the gunman fire at Doug Horne's group and quickly reversed her car and swung onto the wrong side of the road. Simon Williams, a Canadian Embassy official on holiday with his wife Susan from Canberra, saw Wardle reversing on the wrong side of the road but did not understand the significance of what was happening and continued on to Port Arthur. Before he had a chance to stop, two bullets smashed into the front window of his red Falcon. Susan Williams was wounded in the head, and both she and her husband suffered serious injuries to their hands.

The gunman then drove into the entrance to the Seascape guesthouse and took Glenn Pears inside the house and handcuffed him to the stairs. After taking the AR15 and FN rifles out of the gold BMW, he doused the car with a can of petrol he had carried in his Volvo and set the car alight. Some time during the next few hours, as police closed in on the guesthouse, he shot Glenn Pears, his final victim, in cold blood.

Local constables Paul Hyland and Garry Whittle answered the call to go to Port Arthur, driving in separate cars from Tasmania's northwest peninsula. When they reached Nubeena they were alerted to look for a yellow Volvo with a surfboard on the roof-rack, so the pair decided to split up and arrive at Port Arthur from separate directions. On the long way around to Port Arthur, Hyland was told to now look for a gold-coloured BMW. Just past the entrance to Seascape, Hyland noticed an abandoned Frontera and, after speaking to several witnesses, drove to the entrance into Seascape. At the same time Constable Whittle, who had been notified of shots being fired on the Arthur Highway, drove up behind him. The constable could see black smoke from the burnt-out BMW and a man running between the guesthouse buildings, but wasn't sure if it was the gunman or an accomplice. Hyland and Whittle decided to set up a roadblock into the complex and wait for reinforcements.

Constables Pat Allen and Perry Caulfield from the Hobart Accident Investigation Squad arrived soon after. After leaving his colleague at the entrance to the road, Constable Allen almost immediately came under fire and was forced to abandon his car and hide in a ditch at the side of his car. The gunman, who also had access to a collection of guns owned by David Martin and his sons, fired at the police and pinned down constables Allen and Whittle in the ditch. It was now becoming dark and it was not until two officers from the Special Operations Group joined them later that night that the two constables were led to safety. By that time the rest of Australia had caught up with the details of the massacre and the biggest police operation in the state's history was under way.

Unforeseen problems compounded the situation. Craig Coombs, the general manager of the site and other members of his management team, were attending a seminar at Swansea on the east coast and there was a lack of coordination of resources at Port Arthur. Poor radio reception in that part of the island hampered communication between police at Port Arthur and those at Seascape; adding to the confusion, tourists at Port Arthur who had witnessed the gunman's escape in a yellow Volvo were horrified to find the car abandoned at the tollbooth entrance. Had the gunman doubled back on foot? No-one was sure. The Arthur Highway was inaccessible because the gunman was shooting across the highway; there was little cover around the Seascape guesthouse for the police to launch a direct attack and they still did not have a positive identification of the accused gunman. Frustratingly, no-one knew if the Martins or the man taken hostage at the service station were still alive.

However, there were also unknown elements working in the victims' favour. Royal Hobart Hospital had recently implemented a new disaster plan and the hospital's emergency response strategy was widely praised. A Royal Australian College of Surgeons course was being conducted there that weekend and three rescue helicopters — instead of just the one usually rostered on a weekend — were available for use. A training session for volunteer ambulance officers was also in progress at the headquarters of the Tasmanian Ambulance Service. Grant Lennox, the director of Tasmanian Ambulance, was able to coordinate assistance from the radio room while members helped to transport the injured to the hospital when they started to arrive by helicopter shortly after 3 pm.

Steve and Pam Ireland, who had taken over the sole medical practice on the northwest peninsula, arrived at the Port Arthur site having been told that four people had been injured in a shooting incident. They were faced by an unimaginable situation and yet continued to work into the night providing medical assistance and helping to coordinate the evacuation of the injured by helicopter. On the fourth Sunday of each month — that day being the fourth Sunday in April — members of the Anglican Church conduct a service at Port Arthur. Felicity and Michael Langley arrived just after the gunman killed seven people at the tollbooth. Together with church members Alan Imber and David Coombs, the group immediately began diverting traffic away from the site and helped search for blankets to keep warm those survivors who were in shock and to cover the bodies of the dead. Many people used their first aid training — a mandatory skill in many parts of remote Tasmania — to good effect that day and due to the prompt action of medical staff and volunteers, none of the injured died before they could be evacuated.

During that long night, local people gathered to help the wounded at Port Arthur, to support the Tasmanian Ambulance Service and the volunteer members of the State Emergency Service as they tended the victims and assisted police investigating what had happened that Sunday afternoon. Steve Ireland and volunteers like Mark Kirby checked the bush for survivors and for more victims. Nanette Mikac was well known to workers at Port Arthur — she worked part-time there as a guide — and the discovery of her body and that of her two children was particularly distressing. Later that afternoon, Walter Mikac arrived at Port Arthur and was frantically searching for his family among survivors at the information centre when he was informed of their deaths. That night an unofficial report swept the Port Arthur site that the gunman had escaped from Seascape and returned; when a car door slammed outside the information centre, the building was blacked out and survivors hid for a second time.

Under the supervision of Sergeant Terry McCarthy, police spoke to the gunman inside the Seascape guesthouse over the next six hours until the cordless telephone went dead. During the night the gunman rang the local police station and taunted the police and their relatives. Then, at about 8 am on Monday morning, 29 April 1996, smoke was seen billowing from the Seascape guesthouse. Shortly after, a man rushed out of the house, his clothes on fire, and stripped his shirt from his body. It was the gunman. At 8.25 am he fell to the ground and, after offering little resistance, was arrested. His name was Martin Bryant.

Martin Bryant was born in 1969 and was described as an 'intellectually stunted child' with poor social skills.[6] The pressures of coping with

Bryant's developmental problems indirectly led to his father, Maurice, committing suicide at the family farm in Copping, Tasmania, in 1993. In 1987 Bryant met an elderly, eccentric New Town lady, Helen Mary Harvey, and started doing odd jobs around her house. Bryant became her 'companion' and when she died in 1992 — the victim of a car accident in which Bryant was driving — the 23-year-old became the beneficiary of the woman's estate. Ms Harvey owned a property and a 1/1400th stake in the George Adams Tattersalls' fortune. When the Tasmanian state government seized Bryant's assets to pay his victims compensation following his trial, the estate was valued at $1.3 million.

Martin Bryant's troubled upbringing gave only a shadowy insight into the reasons why he committed the massacre at Port Arthur. According to an examining psychiatrist, Bryant 'took life and gained excitement from tormenting others and "revels" in the memory of his acts and the notoriety they have bought him'.[7] Prison service psychiatrists described Bryant as 'simple and attention seeking ... he has the emotional level of a two year old. His IQ has been estimated at 11 years, which is the low to normal range.'[8] Bryant is a man of limited intelligence who suffered from a significant personality disorder. The Martins, who were his first victims, had allegedly refused to sell part of the property to the gunman's father some years earlier. (Bryant was also stopped from selling homemade trinkets there as a nine-year-old but it is unclear whether this played a part in his plan.) Bryant used the money from his inheritance to travel interstate and overseas, ostensively to meet people to talk to. He previously had a girlfriend but had become increasingly alienated from society in the year before his outrage. He continues to show no remorse for the killings — most likely because he has no insight into the impact of his actions.

The healing process for the Tasmanian community was slow and painful. The massacre immediately attracted blanket coverage as all forms of media descended on Port Arthur. Services were held all over the country, with prayer vigils on the island highlighted by burning 35 candles symbolising the victims. An ecumenical service in Hobart was attended by newly elected Prime Minister John Howard, the Opposition leader Kim Beazley and Tasmanian Premier Jim Bacon. Flags were flown at half-mast throughout

Australia and the funerals of the victims were held all over the country and, in the case of the Malaysian couple, also overseas. The Broad Arrow Café was razed to the ground and replaced by a modest memorial to the victims. But still Australia could not forget. By November of that year $3.5 million had been donated to the Port Arthur Victims' Appeal Fund.

The Port Arthur massacre came at the end of a decade — following the Hoddle Street, Queen Street and Strathfield massacres — that focused intense scrutiny on gun control in Australia.[9] National gun laws had been piecemeal to say the least: the federal government had placed restrictions on what guns could be imported into the country but the fragmentary nature of how the states checked licences, granted permits and monitored the use of prohibited weapons somehow made it possible for someone like Martin Bryant — who never owned a gun licence — to purchase five semi-automatic weapons. The week after the Port Arthur massacre, the newly elected federal government was to sit for the first time. Gun control had not been an election issue but it certainly was one now.

In the months after the events of 28 April, a nation's disbelief turned to anger and transformed into action. On 10 May, John Howard achieved a consensus from each of the state and territory police ministers (with some concessions to farmers) to ban the use of semi-automatic weapons. It was, as Margaret Scott commented, 'an enormous shift in Australian culture [away from] the possession, use and ownership of guns'.[10] Provisions were made for the recording of gun sales between states and a national buy-back scheme was established to compensate the owners of surrendered weapons. There was still some ongoing dispute, especially in Queensland, but arguments for tighter gun control laws were just too compelling. Just three months after the death of his family, Walter Mikac addressed an anti-gun rally in Sydney.

On 30 September, Martin Bryant pleaded 'not guilty' to 35 counts of murder and 37 counts of attempted murder, aggravated assault, wounding, causing grievous bodily harm and unlawfully setting fire to property. On the day before his trial was to begin, on 8 November 1996, Bryant changed his plea to 'guilty'. When the 72 charges were read out, on the fiftieth charge — and the twenty-seventh count of murder — Bryant began to laugh out loud in the courtroom. Supreme Court Justice William Cox stated that Bryant's 'limited capacity for empathy or imagining the feelings and responses of others left a terrible gap in his sensibilities, which enabled him not only to contemplate mass destruction, but to carry it through'.[11] Bryant was sentenced to imprisonment for the term of his natural life on the 35 counts of murder and on the remaining 37 charges, 21 years on each count to be served sequentially — effectively, 777 years.

As for Martin Bryant, who survived his injuries from his murder spree to mock his victims and their families from the dock of the Hobart Courthouse, he now languishes in Tasmania's Risdon Maximum Security Prison without any prospect of parole. Perhaps it is best to paraphrase the sentiments expressed long ago in another time and place: '... let us remember his name no more'.[12]

Chapter 12
The Norfolk Island Murder (2002)

The history of Norfolk Island, 1500 kilometres northeast of Sydney and 1060 kilometres northwest of Auckland, is intertwined with the history of convict settlement of New South Wales, the story of HMS *Bounty* mutineers and the tragic legacy of South Pacific's Pitcairn Island. First discovered by Lieutenant James Cook on his 1774 voyage, Norfolk Island became home to Australia's second penal settlement in March 1788. In 1856, the picturesque island was settled by descendants of the 1789 *Bounty* mutineers who originally found refuge on Pitcairn Island. Many of the 'Pitcairners' later vacated the island when murder, sexual assault and a lack of natural resources corrupted the future they had planned for themselves. Names such as Adams, Buffet, Christian, Evans, McCoy, Nobbs and Quintal still form the nucleus of the Norfolk Island community, who are called 'Islanders' as opposed to 'Mainlanders'.

Despite its violent beginnings and turbulent history, Norfolk Island had not experienced a murder in 148 years as a self-administered territory of New South Wales. The relative serenity of the popular tourist destination was shattered forever on 31 March 2002, when the body of a young woman was found at a tourist spot on the island. Twenty-nine-year-old 'Mainlander' Janelle Patton had been stabbed and bludgeoned to death, and her body wrapped in black plastic. The investigation into her murder, and the immediate failure to name the person or persons responsible, acted like a prism that magnified deep-seated prejudices and hatreds within the tightly knit island community.

Over the Easter long weekend in 2002, Norfolk Island's population of just over two thousand permanent residents and general and temporary permit holders swelled to 2771 with the arrival of visitors and tourists on the island. Easter Sunday, 31 March 2002, was a blustery autumn day that reached a high 26°C, with the wind blowing from the north. But in the afternoon the wind picked up from the west, as much as 30 knots, and 12 millimetres of rain fell on the island between 3 and 4 pm.

At 6.33 pm on that Sunday night, Senior Constable Michael Julius was 'on call' when he received a telephone call at his home from New Zealand tourist Helen Opie. Opie reported that she and her partner had been walking in the Cockpit Waterfall Reserve about 15 minutes earlier when they discovered what appeared to be the body of a female wrapped in black plastic. Opie, who said that the body appeared to have dark hair and was wearing white joggers, had immediately returned to her apartment with her partner and contacted police.

Senior Constable Julius travelled by police vehicle to the Cockpit Waterfall Reserve, arriving at 6.43 pm. He found the unsealed track which leads into the reserve from Prince Phillip Drive muddy and slippery as a result of the heavy rain that fell that afternoon. Entering the reserve, Julius found the body of a woman, partially covered in black plastic sheeting, on the grass area next to a concrete slab and three rubbish bins. The woman's lower legs, her buttocks and upper thighs and one arm were partially visible against the black plastic. When Julius attempted to find a pulse on her wrist he noted a significant amount of blood on the plastic sheeting and observed that the plastic also had pools of water on it from the storm earlier that afternoon.

The dead woman was wearing a black singlet top with a red trim; light, multicoloured drawstring shorts; black underpants; white sports shoes; white sports socks; a hair elastic and a black 'scrunchie' hair band. The amount of jewellery on the body — three gold neck chains, two gold rings, gold bracelets on both wrists, a gold anklet chain and one pearl and one gold ear-ring in each earlobe — seemed to rule out robbery as a motive.

Julius saw that the woman's shorts and underpants were torn or cut on the right side and were pulled down as far as her upper thighs, exposing her buttocks. She was lying face down with her right arm outstretched and her left arm bent under her body. There were deep wounds on her right shin and a number of other wounds, including grazes and bruises, were also easily visible.

A quick inspection of the area in the failing twilight did not reveal any other items associated with the body, possible weapons, footprints or tyre tracks. Julius returned to his vehicle and contacted Detective Sergeant Brendan Lindsay, the officer in charge of Norfolk Island Police. Lindsay arrived at the reserve shortly after 7 pm and Julius briefed him on the situation. While looking at the body, Lindsay saw a watch lying between the woman's upper left arm and the front of her neck. The watch, which was showing the correct time, was not secured and had part of the gold-coloured buckle missing.

Senior Constable Julius then set up a barricade to the area and returned to the police station to organise support personnel while Lindsay secured the scene. Julius collected Dr Lloyd Fletcher at his home and took him to the reserve to examine the body. While the Norfolk Island Volunteer Rescue Association set up a generator and lights, Special Constable Michael Johnston took up a position at the barricade with instructions not to allow any unauthorised vehicle or person to enter the area and to log the entry and exit times of all persons and vehicles trying to do so.

At 7.50 pm, Special Constable Brendan Anderson was manning the police station when Ronald Patton reported that his adult daughter Janelle was missing. Ronald Patton and his wife Carol, from Sydney, had arrived the previous day to visit their 29-year-old daughter, who had been living and working on Norfolk Island since October 1999. Janelle Patton had last been seen at about 11 am that morning as she set out on a daily walk on the Rooty Hill Road.

At the time of her death Janelle Patton was living in a self-contained flat adjacent to the Allendale Drive home of Baker 'Foxy' McCoy and his wife Ruth. A short time later Ronald and Carolyn Patton, accompanied by the McCoys, attended the police station and had a conversation with Detective Sergeant Lindsay. It was Ruth McCoy who accompanied Lindsay to the Cockpit Waterfall Reserve, arriving there at about 9 pm, and positively identified the body as Janelle Patton. Lindsay and Ruth McCoy then returned to the police station and broke the news of their daughter's death to the Pattons.

At 9.20 pm that night, Senior Constable Julius and Special Constable Tom Greening entered the secured area and filmed the crime scene on video. At 10.22 pm Detective Sergeant Lindsay returned to the scene in the company of Ross Reynolds, the Norfolk Island coroner, and removed the victim's body to Norfolk hospital by ambulance. Later that night Lindsay and Julius inspected Janelle Patton's flat but did not find any signs of disturbance that could suggest the young woman had been murdered there.

During that long night Lindsay contacted Australian Federal Police (AFP) headquarters in Canberra to arrange support for the investigation and forensic examination. Arrangements were made for two crime scene examiners from the AFP Forensic Services, and a forensic pathologist from Sydney to travel to Norfolk Island to assist with investigations. Robert Walter Peters, a detective sergeant in the AFP, was contacted at his home in Canberra and was directed to travel to Norfolk Island with Detective Senior Constable Anthony Edmondson at the earliest available opportunity. His initial role was to provide assistance and support to Detective Sergeant Lindsay but by 3 May 2002 the AFP promoted him to case officer.

Peters later wrote that, 'It quickly became obvious that the usual Australian Federal Police methods of recording and managing information, inquiries, and the progress of investigations were not suitable for use on Norfolk Island. As a result it was necessary to develop and implement a localised database for this purpose.'[1]

The investigation into the death of Janelle Patton was allocated the name of 'Operation Dunedin'. As with any crime, the methodology employed in this investigation focused on answering the following questions:

- What happened?
- Where did it happen?
- When did it happen?
- Why did it happen?
- Who was involved?

The answers to those questions would hopefully be found through the collection of forensic evidence; the testimony of witnesses; clues gleaned from the personal background of the victim; the identification of motive and opportunity, including those who had exclusive access to the murder scene; the testimonies of accessories or confidants of the offender; or the principal offender's admission of his involvement. There was also a strong possibility that the person or persons responsible for Janelle Patton's murder may have known her and had some form of relationship with her prior to her death.

Janelle Louise Patton was born on 30 June 1972 in Sydney, New South Wales. She attended Pennant Hills High School from 1984 until 1989 when she completed her Higher School Certificate. On leaving high school she began a university course in orthoptics but she did not complete the first year of the course. (Janelle's parents believed she enrolled in this course mainly because of her good results in chemistry and biology rather than a specific interest in orthoptics.) She began her working career at Westpac Banking Corporation as a settlements clerk in 1990 and spent much of the next decade working in the banking industry with Banker's Trust, Citibank and Bank of Tokyo before moving to IMB, where she worked as a leasing administrator.

Janelle's failed relationships with several men, one who assaulted her and left her with a broken jaw, saw her eventually leave Sydney. In his official report Peters wrote that, 'In each of these relationships Janelle displayed an inability to accept that they were finished. This inability to accept the end of a relationship was to carry over to her life on Norfolk Island. She had developed a very low level of self esteem and had begun drinking heavily and taking anti-depressant medication and her physical health was suffering.' Janelle's parents had honeymooned on Norfolk Island and spoke fondly of the idyllic setting. When Janelle decided to move away from Sydney and make a fresh start, she did so by applying for a job at the South Pacific Hotel on Norfolk Island via the internet.

Janelle Patton arrived on Norfolk Island on 23 October 1999 and started work the following day as a room attendant with the South Pacific Hotel. She left the hotel on 16 December and started work as a general supermarket assistant with Norfolk Island Supermarkets Pty Ltd (Foodlands) two days later. While on Norfolk Island Janelle became involved in a complicated combination of personal relationships that reflected the previous turmoil in her life.

Peters again wrote that although 'Janelle continued to drink alcohol to excess on occasions and to smoke cigarettes heavily she had ceased taking anti-depressant medication and her general health and outlook on life had improved considerably from the time she first arrived on the Island ... she had strong personal opinions on a variety of subjects and was not afraid to express these views, albeit sometimes with a lack of diplomacy or tact. She has been frequently described as a woman who was fastidious about her grooming and appearance and who liked to carefully plan her life and her activities.'

Janelle was known to make regular entries in diaries. On Monday, 8 April 2002, Carolyn Patton returned to Janelle's flat and located her daughter's 2002 diary. Janelle's last entry was on 9 February 2002, and police could not speculate why there were no further entries beyond this date. Janelle's parents described her as a 'hoarder' of personal documents but although her diaries from 1992 up until 1999 were recovered, as well the various cards and letters she had received and saved, her 1999 and 2000 diaries were missing. It was left for Janelle's 2001 and 2002 diaries to provide the investigation team with valuable background information concerning her relationships and casual contact with a number of people.

After arriving on Norfolk Island in 1999, Janelle Patton formed a relationship with Canadian Larry Perrett. Following a trip to Sydney in March 2000 she confided in Foodlands co-worker Susan Fields that, despite living with him, her relationship with Perrett was over. Fields arranged for her to live with a neighbour, Charles 'Spindles' Menghetti. However, Patton had a falling out with Fields and Menghetti asked her to leave the address. Patton found accommodation with Menghetti's brother Paul, who was known as 'Jap', and the pair formed an intimate relationship. Patton's relationship with Jap Menghetti caused problems for his children, especially his oldest daughter, Dana. After another brief trip home to Sydney, Janelle and Susan Fields had a 'physical confrontation' at the Norfolk Island Sports and Workers Club, which was reported to police.

Janelle left Foodlands and was employed by H. Martin Estate and World Trades but her relationship with Jap Menghetti deteriorated and she moved out. Patton later moved into the flat owned by 'Foxy' McCoy and his wife, where she lived until her death, but still visited Menghetti — even after the pair had formed new relationships — and her diaries revealed that she still hoped to rekindle their affair. Patton did not live with her new partner, Laurence 'Bucket' Quintal, but the relationship was intense and ultimately broke down. Janelle was retrenched on 18 January 2002 and started a new job at the Castaway Hotel the following month in charge of food and beverages in the hotel's dining room. Although she was involved in a number of other platonic friendships, she was not effectively involved in a relationship when she was murdered.

On Saturday, 30 March 2002, Janelle worked at the Castaway Hotel during the breakfast shift from approximately 7 to 10.30 am. She met her parents Ronald and Carolyn when they arrived at Norfolk Island airport at approximately 11.10 am. When her parents arrived they noticed how well she looked and that she appeared in good spirits and was excited about their visit. After they checked into their apartment, Janelle took them for a tour around the island. The tour took longer than expected and Janelle mentioned that she had planned to go for a walk before work but decided to postpone it until the following day. She drove her parents back to the

Panorama Apartments at about 3.30 pm and they arranged to meet at Christian's Restaurant at the Castaway Hotel at 7.00 pm that night.

At about 9 pm Janelle's parents were starting to feel tired and told her they were going to their accommodation. Janelle told them that she would have to stay working until 11 pm or later, as the crowd there was quite large. The Pattons arranged to meet her the following day and her timesheet indicated that she finished work at 11.15 pm that night. Janelle told them she was working the next morning on the breakfast shift and would then go for her walk, so her parents arranged to look after themselves during the morning. Janelle offered to pick them up from Panorama Apartments sometime between 1 and 2 pm on Sunday afternoon.

Telephone records showed that Janelle received a phone call from her friend Brent Wilson in New Zealand at 11.32 pm (Norfolk Island time) and that the call lasted approximately 50 minutes. Brent Wilson later told police that during this conversation Janelle expressed excitement about her parents arrival on Norfolk Island, and talked about her plans to visit him in New Zealand in the coming weeks. She did not mention any person or incident that was worrying her at the time. At 2.20 am on Sunday, 31 March 2002, a further telephone call was made to Janelle's flat from outside Norfolk Island. This call lasted one minute and 47 seconds. To date the source of this call has not been identified.

Janelle worked her shift at the Castaway Hotel during the morning of Sunday, 31 March 2002, and then went for the walk she had postponed from the previous afternoon. She had planned to show her parents around the island and then prepare dinner for them at her flat on Allendale Drive. Janelle's work colleagues and several guests stated that she was in 'good spirits' and was looking forward to seeing her parents later that day. However, Janelle's employer, Hamish Martin, told police that he later heard of Janelle complaining to co-workers that she had been involved in 'a heated argument' on the telephone overnight. Martin was not present at the Castaway Hotel that morning and could not identify the source of this information (inquiries with Janelle's co-workers also failed to corroborate this claim).

Janelle was seen driving by herself from the hotel to Foodlands supermarket, where security camera footage showed her moving around the aisles of the shop before exiting via a checkout aisle. Ruth McCoy told police that between 11 and 11.30 am that morning she was at the Foodlands shopping mall and was approached by Janelle, who handed her a small plastic basket containing four Easter eggs and wished her a happy Easter. She stated that Janelle appeared to be in hurry and she did not get the opportunity to reply before Janelle left the area. Foxy McCoy later saw Janelle driving her car into the property towards her flat at approximately 11.30 am. Approximately 10 minutes later Janelle was observed walking from Allendale Drive into Collins Head Road in the direction of the intersection with Rooty Hill Road. Janelle had quickly changed into shorts and a singlet top and was walking briskly. A number of people saw Janelle out on her morning walk but at about midday she all but vanished into thin air before her body was found later that evening.

Several cars were spotted in the vicinity of the Queen Elizabeth Lookout tourist spot, including a small white Toyota starlet and a blue or black tourist car, while some people heard sustained adult screams between 11.40 am and 12.00 pm. A number of people were identified as having driven past the Cockpit Waterfall Reserve area between 11.30 am and 4.30 pm that day. No-one reported seeing any person, vehicle or incident that may be connected with Janelle's death or the disposal of her body in the reserve. While Janelle's body was not discovered until shortly after 6 pm, it was established that her body was at the location sometime before 4 pm because of the pools of water on the black plastic from the rain that fell between 3.15 and 3.50 pm.

A local group building a garden near the Cockpit Waterfall Reserve between 1 and 3 pm was unable to see vehicles entering the reserve but told police that they heard 'two or four vehicles, one of which was possibly a four-wheel drive or small tourist bus', cross the wooden bridge on Prince Philip Drive near the entrance to the reserve. When the storm began shortly after 3 pm they packed up and left the area. At about the same time the son of a Queensland tourist who was visiting the reserve with his family saw what he thought to be a homeless person sleeping under some black plastic. Some young boys riding boogie boards down the wet grass slopes of the reserve that afternoon were also identified. Although they did not recall seeing any black plastic, they had filmed their antics with a small, hand-held video camera. When police replayed the tape, the enhanced background revealed the black plastic. The video's automatic timer read 15:57 (3.57 pm).

News of Janelle Patton's death swept the Norfolk Island community. Investigating police appealed for community assistance through the local media but the murder inquiry quickly attracted the attention of media outlets in mainland Australia, New Zealand, the United Kingdom, Europe, Asia and the United States. Police recorded information at face value and assessed its potential but Bob Peters noted that, 'whilst by far the majority of information received has been provided with a genuine desire to assist the investigation, unfortunately some people took the opportunity to malign others for their own purposes. In many instances the potential value of information received has been debased by rumour and innuendo.'

Peters made the decision to prepare and send to each person over 10 years of age who was on the island that weekend a survey in which they were asked to record details of their movements on the day of the murder, to indicate if they knew Janelle personally, if they had seen her that day and if they had any additional information that they wished to provide. While Peters was aware that any person involved in Janelle's death (or the disposal of her body) was unlikely to complete the survey, let alone complete it honestly, in his own words the local response was nevertheless 'generally disappointing'. Approximately 56 per cent of the targeted group who were living and working on Norfolk Island on that day returned completed surveys. Identical surveys were sent to tourists or visitors who were on Norfolk Island that Sunday, 31 March 2002, and 84 per cent were returned.

On Wednesday, 3 April 2002, forensic pathologist Dr Allan Cala conducted a post-mortem examination of Janelle Patton's body at the Norfolk Island hospital. The full extent of the victim's injuries was not revealed until the inquest into her death two years later. In summary, Dr Cala found a litany of injuries:

> A laceration to top of head (25 x 10 mm); 35 mm long incised wound to top of forehead; a 40 mm incised wound above left eye; fractured skull above left eye under location of incised wound (fracture had no effect on brain beneath); a 100 mm incised wound from under the chin towards right side of face; further superficial incised wounds and lacerations to face and a number of superficial incised wounds ...
>
> ...a 'V'-shaped stab wound in the chest region (which was the main injury) consisting of two wounds measuring 12 mm and 15 mm in width with the overall external width dimension of wound being approximately 25 mm. The depth of the stab wound was 150 mm with a large amount of blood located to left chest area on cavity dissection. The wound penetrated anterior of left second rib and into left upper lobe; three stab wounds visible on inner rear of the left chest cavity wall (6th rib) suggesting the offender may have thrust the knife at least three times once it had entered the chest.
>
> ... a gaping incised wound to right thumb (80 mm in length) and a jagged incised wound to interior of right middle finger; superficial incised wounds to back of index and middle fingers; red bruising to interior left wrist; purple/red bruising to right thigh, knee and upper lower leg; a lateral abrasion to right thigh; five almost parallel incised wounds to right lower leg — two of the wounds are major, ranging from 50–80 mm in length; dislocation and red bruising to left ankle 70 mm diameter.
>
> ... superficial incised wounds to the back of the neck; large area of abrasion to the right rear shoulder; a number of other abrasions and bruising which was linear approx 15 mm wide; a fractured pelvis; fractured ribs (10, 9 and 8 on the left side of body); and a fracture to the skull above left eye.

It was clear that Janelle Patton had died after a sustained attack — the number of defensive wounds meant that she fought for her life where she stood, before being knocked to the ground, dislocating her ankle and breaking her pelvis. She even grabbed the knife at one stage, before being set upon and stabbed to death.

Forensic scientist David John Royds investigated particles of a green-coloured paint recovered from the victim's hair, shorts and underneath a fingernail. The paint particles were most likely transferred onto Janelle's body and clothing from either the sheet of black plastic that was wrapped around her body, the vehicle in which her body was transported, or from the site where she was killed. On 11 April 2002, crime scene investigators examined a utility motor vehicle belonging to local man Ray 'Tugger' Yager. Although the available paint evidence supported the general proposition that the vehicle and Janelle Patton were somehow associated, a number of other green paint particles were collected from other vehicles, residences and public areas on Norfolk Island. However, in all other instances, these green paint particles were not found to have the same properties as those located on the victim's body and clothing.

A large number of glass fragments were also recovered from Janelle's hair. The glass was examined under the microscope and the larger fragments appeared to have 'a yellow hue' similar to wine bottle glass. This suggested to police that some of the lacerations found on the victim's head may have resulted from her being struck by a wine bottle which was used as a weapon. However, no match was found to this type of glass on the island.

Janelle wore non-prescription sunglasses when walking and a number of witnesses who saw her on Sunday, 31 March 2002, recalled that she was wearing them at the time. When her body was found at Cockpit Waterfall Reserve later that day her sunglasses were missing. On Monday, 1 April 2002, while supervising a line search along Rooty Hill Road, Detective Sergeant Lindsay recovered a pair of non-prescription sunglasses between two driveways, near where Janelle had last been seen. The sunglasses, which had a black metal frame and no brand name, were damaged and the left lens was missing (the missing lens has never been found). A number of people who knew Janelle personally later told police that they believed the sunglasses to be either Janelle's or a pair very similar to those often worn by Janelle, and despite a public appeal no other person came forward claiming to own the sunglasses. Peters later wrote, 'If the sunglasses were in fact Janelle's, their location and condition is a possible indication that she was involved in some form of physical confrontation at a point on Rooty Hill Road ...'

The sheet of black plastic found partially covering Janelle's body was obviously of considerable importance to this investigation. The piece of 'builder's plastic' is of a fairly common type on Norfolk Island. The condition of the plastic suggested that it had been previously used and was not taken from a fresh roll. A piece of the plastic measuring 185 centimetres by 130 centimetres — the edges torn rather than cut — was missing from one corner. Three pieces of silver duct tape were affixed to one edge, suggesting that the plastic may have been attached to some other object such as concrete formwork.

On 10 April 2002, the Legislative Assembly of Norfolk Island passed the Norfolk Island Crimes (Forensic Procedures) Act 2002. The provisions of this Act allowed the obtaining and analysis of a number of forensic samples including fingerprints, DNA profiles and dental impressions from members of the community under specified conditions. The Act only allowed the collection of forensic samples on a voluntary basis, however, and placed limitations on how those samples could be obtained. Unfortunately, the only DNA evidence identified on any of the exhibits belonged to Janelle Patton.

Later that month, AFP Forensic Services treated and examined the sheet of black plastic and located ten areas of latent fingerprint and palm print impressions. However, it could not be forensically determined whether any or all of the prints on the plastic had been left on the day of Janelle's murder or had been deposited prior to the day of her murder. Furthermore, it could not even be determined whether the prints were from one or more persons.

In an attempt to identify the sources of the latent prints detected on the sheet of black plastic, Bob Peters initiated a program on 12 August to collect fingerprint samples from as many volunteers as possible. In all, 1632 people fitted into the 15 to 70 age category and the Voluntary Fingerprint Collection Program operated seven days a week for the following four weeks to gather samples. When the program concluded in September, some 1285 people had volunteered their fingerprints (this figure later grew to 1311). Peters wrote, 'To date there has been one positive comparison between the right palm print supplied by one volunteer and two of the ten latent prints located on the black plastic exhibit.' However, the identified man denied knowing Janelle Patton and the prints may have been on the plastic for some time. A further 342 people who did not live on the island — 265 from Australia and 77 from New Zealand — also fell into this category. A total of 262 sets of fingerprints were received and compared with the unidentified prints found on the black plastic exhibit, but no matches have been found.

In March 2003, the Norfolk Island Legislative Assembly announced a reward of $50 000 for information which leads to the arrest and conviction of the person or persons responsible for the death of Janelle Louise Patton. That offer also included the possibility of indemnity, under certain conditions, from prosecution for any accomplice who had not actually taken part in killing Janelle. In August 2003, the Australian government joined the Norfolk Island government and increased the reward to $100 000. On 19 March 2004, the Australian and Norfolk Island governments jointly increased the reward offer to $300 000.

The motive of the murder still remains unclear. Although Janelle's singlet top, shorts and underpants were cut, there was no evidence of sexual assault having taken place. Janelle's shorts and underpants were cut through at the right thigh area but there was no injury to Janelle's right thigh, suggesting that Janelle's clothing was cut after she was killed in an effort to make it appear as though the attack was sexually motivated. Police considered the following possibilities: the murder was a premeditated attack 'with the intent of committing an offence of a sexual nature'; it was a premeditated attack with the intent of causing bodily harm as a result of some past grievance; an opportunistic attack with the intent of committing a sexual offence or bodily harm; or lastly, Janelle Patton's murder occurred to conceal a separate offence or incident.

The site where Janelle Patton suffered her injuries, and most probably lost her life, was not established although there is a strong probability that she was initially confronted by her attacker on Rooty Hill Road close to where the broken sunglasses were found. It was assumed that a vehicle was used to transport her from the Rooty Hill Road area, possibly to some other site and then to Cockpit Waterfall Reserve where her body was found. However, to date that vehicle has not been found. What is known is that Janelle Patton was killed and her body transported and disposed of in daylight hours. Because the murderer did not wait for night and ignored the inherent risks of transporting a body during the day, police assumed that the murderer was operating under a time constraint. Did the murderer, or murderers, have to work that night? Were other people expected at the place where the murder took place?

Peters wrote, 'There has been considerable speculation as to why Janelle's body was left in the open in a public area such as the Cockpit Waterfall Reserve rather than, for example, throwing her off a cliff into the ocean or burying her in bushland. It has been speculated that to choose the Cockpit site suggests the person responsible had little knowledge of the Island.' Maybe the person or persons responsible panicked, or were there potential witnesses about? Or perhaps the 'public display' of the body was deliberate?

The four-day inquest into the death of Janelle Louise Patton opened on 31 May 2003, with ACT coroner Ron Cahill returning an open finding. Mr Cahill named 16 'persons of interest' to the police investigation but police publicly stated that there was not enough evidence to charge anyone with the crime, and made it clear none of the people named was considered a suspect. It was revealed in the report that Islander Raymond 'Tugger' Yager, whose advances were also rejected by Janelle Patton, steamcleaned his utility van for several hours on the day of her murder. The police found green paint fragments in this vehicle that were identical to those found on Janelle's body. On 2 April, two days after the discovery of her body, Yager left Norfolk Island to visit his four-year-old son in Western Australia. Yager did not return to Norfolk Island and currently lives in Cambodia, where he pursues his business interests.

In an interview with the Nine Network's *Sunday* program in July 2004, federal Liberal senator Ross Lightfoot said police 'knew who killed her but had insufficient evidence' to charge anyone. Senator Lightfoot, the chair of a parliamentary committee that oversees Norfolk Island, said the evidence clearly pointed to the murderer but residents were so afraid of reprisals they refused to come forward with information. Senator Lightfoot told the *Sunday* program, 'The evidence we've been given, without names, clearly points to a male and clearly points to an Islander. I'm told by one of the police officers that they're aware of the killer but they have insufficient evidence to arrest him and I think that's very sad.'[2]

This public speculation concerning the death of Janelle Patton, by no less than a federal government senator, is fairly symptomatic of the Australian 'experience'. Trialled in the media, her private life publicly exposed and the details of her death laid bare for all to read, Janelle's parents lamented that their daughter's best qualities — her love of her family, her loyalty to her friends, her smiling face — had not been highlighted in the papers. Only her failures and shortcomings.

For the time being at least, this case exists in a cultural 'twilight zone' between historical fact and reckless conjecture. As a nation we need to ensure that the Norfolk Island murder of Janelle Patton does not suffer the same fate as 'Gatton', 'Bogle and Chandler', 'Wanda' and 'The Beaumonts' and become an Australian byword for unsolved crime.

Endnotes

Chapter 1: The Gatton Murders (1898)

1. *Sydney Morning Herald*, 28 December 1898.
2. Official police statement, January 1899.
3. Sergeant Arrell's original statement, 27 December 1898.
4. Dr W. Stury von Lossbergher's post-mortem report, 28 December 1898.
5. *Darling Downs Gazette*, 9 January 1899.
6. Thomas Drew's statement, Magisterial Inquest, 1898.
7. Margaret Carroll's statement, Magisterial Inquest, 1898.
8. Sub-Inspector Fred Urquhart's letter to the Queensland Police Commissioner, 5 January 1899.
9. Merv Lilley, *Gatton Man*, McPhee Gribble, Victoria, 1994.
10. William Arrell's statement, Magisterial Inquest.
11. Stephanie Bennett, *The Gatton Murders*, McMillan, Sydney, 2004.
12. Merv Lilley.
13. John Pinkney, *Great Australian Mysteries*, Five Mile Press, Victoria, 2003.
14. Merv Lilley.
15. Merv Lilley.

Chapter 2: The Pyjama Girl Murder (1934)

1. *The Sun*, 2 September 1934.
2. *The Border Morning Mail*, 3 September 1934.
3. Robert Coleman, *The Pyjama Girl*, Hawthorn Press, Melbourne, 1978, p. 28.
4. Robert Coleman, p. 30.
5. Robert Coleman, p. 30.
6. Robert Coleman, p. 32.
7. Robert Coleman, p. 32.
8. Robert Coleman, p. 40.
9. Robert Coleman, p. 56.
10. Robert Coleman, p. 58.
11. Robert Coleman, p. 62.
12. Robert Coleman, p. 67.
13. Robert Coleman, p. 214.

Chapter 3: The Shark Arm Murder (1935)

1. Alex Castles, *The Shark Arm Murders*, Wakefield Press, Adelaide, 1995.
2. Vince Kelly, *The Shark Arm Case*, Horwitz Publications, Sydney, 1963.
3. Vince Kelly.
4. Alex Castles, ABC Radio broadcast, 29 April 2002.
5. Vince Kelly.
6. Alex Castles, *The Shark Arm Murders*.
7. Alex Castles, *The Shark Arm Murders*.
8. Alex Castles, *The Shark Arm Murders*.
9. Vince Kelly.
10. Noel Sanders, 'Crimes of Passion', *Australian Journal of Cultural Studies*, May 1983.

Chapter 4: The Brown-Out Murders (1942)

1. Ivan Chapman, *Private Leonski: The brownout strangler*, Hale & Iremonger, Sydney, 1982.
2. Andrew Mallon, *Leonksi: The brown-out murders*, Outback Press, Victoria, 1979.
3. Henry McGowan, official police statement, 10 May 1942.
4. Andrew Mallon.
5. Andrew Mallon.
6. The conversation between Ledena and Leonski is from Andrew Mallon.
7. Andrew Mallon.
8. Testimony of US Private Spencer Neil Smith, Leonski's court martial, 17 August 1942.
9. *Melbourne Truth*, 18 August 1942.
10. Colonel Drumwarring's address, Leonski's court martial, 18 August 1942.
11. All quotes from transcripts of Leonski's court martial, August 1942.
12. Andrew Mallon.
13. Colonel Drumwarring's address, Leonski's court martial, 20 August 1942.
14. All quotes from transcripts of Leonski's court martial.
15. Andrew Mallon.
16. *Melbourne Truth*, 21 August 1942.
17. Peter Dunn, *Australia@War*, www.ozatwar.com (2003).

18. Melbourne *Herald*, 10 November 1942.
19. Peter A. Thompson and Robert Macklin, *The Battle of Brisbane*, ABC Books, Sydney, 2001.
20. Peter Dunn.

Chapter 5: The Graeme Thorne Murder (1960)

1. Noel Sanders, 'Crimes of Passion', *Australian Journal of Cultural Studies*, May 1983.
2. Noel Sanders.
3. *Daily Mirror*, 8 July 1960.
4. *Sydney Morning Herald*, 8 July 1960.
5. *The Sun*, 8 July 1960.
6. Bill Archibald, *The Bradley Case*, Horowitz, Sydney, 1961, p 8.
7. *Daily Mirror*, 13 July 1960.
8. A.F. Clarke, 'Scientific Aspects of the Thorne Kidnapping and Murder', *Australian Police Journal*, July 1962.
9. *Daily Mirror*, 8 July 1960.
10. Peter Hoysted and Paul B. Kidd, *Shallow Graves*, Five Mile Press, Victoria, 2002.
11. A.F. Clarke.
12. Peter Hoysted and Paul B. Kidd.
13. *Sydney Morning Herald*, 25 March 1961.
14. A.F. Clarke.

Chapter 6: The Bogle and Chandler Mystery (1963)

1. *Melbourne Sun*, 2 January 1963.
2. www.dictionary.com.
3. James Franklin, *The Push and Critical Drinkers*, www.unsw.edu.au (October 2004).
4. Philip Cornfield, 'Bogle and Chandler: Death by LSD', *Sydney Morning Herald*, 20 January 1996.
5. Malcolm Brown, 'LSD Suspected in Riverside Deaths', *Sydney Morning Herald*, 21 May 1989.
6. Philip Cornfield.
7. Philip Cornfield.
8. Evan Whitton, 'Countdown to Death', *Sun Herald*, 28 May 1994.
9. John Pinkney, *Great Australian Mysteries*, Five Mile Press, Victoria, 2003.

10. Evan Whitton.
11. Evan Whitton.
12. Evan Whitton.
13. John Pinkney.
14. Philip Cornfield.
15. Malcolm Brown.
16. Malcolm Brown.
17. Philip Cornfield.
18. William Collinge, 'Yohimbine Problems Rising', Healtheon/WebMD.com, 2000.
19. Evan Whitton.
20. John Pinkney.
21. John Pinkney.
22. Malcolm Brown.
23. Malcolm Brown.
24. Leigh Dayton, 'How LSD Can Kill: The scientist's view', *Sydney Morning Herald*, 27 January 1996.
25. Philip Cornfield.
26. Leigh Dayton.

Chapter 7: The Wanda Beach Murders (1965)

1. Official police statement, 14 January 1965.
2. Official police statement, 14 January 1965.
3. Official police statement, 14 January 1965.
4. *The Sun*, 13 January 1965.
5. Official police statement, 16 January 1965.
6. Official police statement, 14 January 1965.
7. Alan J. Whiticker, *Wanda: The untold story of the Wanda Beach murders*, New Holland, Sydney, 2003.
8. *The Sun*, 15 January 1965.
9. Alan J. Whiticker.
10. Stipendiary Magistrate and City Coroner J.J. Loomes, at the Coronial Inquest at the City Coroner's Court, Sydney, 22 April 1966.
11. Alan J. Whiticker.
12. *Illawarra Mercury*, 30 September 1966.
13. Alan J. Whiticker.
14. *Sydney Morning Herald*, 14 June 1998.

Chapter 8: The Disappearance of the Beaumont Children (1966)

1. *Adelaide Advertiser*, 27 January 1966.
2. Russell Brown, 'The Beaumont Children', www.beaumontchildren.com (1999).
3. *Adelaide Advertiser*, 30 January 1966.
4. *Adelaide Advertiser*, 28 January 1966.
5. *Adelaide Advertiser*, 29 January 1966.
6. *Adelaide Advertiser*, 30 January 1966.
7. *Adelaide Advertiser*, 28 January 1966.
8. *Adelaide Advertiser*, 3 February 1966.
9. Russell Brown.
10. *Where Were You When ... The news that stopped a nation*, News Custom Publishing, Victoria, 2003.
11. *Adelaide News*, 7 November 1966.
12. Russell Brown.
13. *Adelaide News*, 11 November 1966.
14. Russell Brown.
15. Russell Brown.
16. *Where Were You When...*
17. Peter Hoysted and Paul B. Kidd, *Shallow Graves*, Five Mile Press, Victoria, 2002.
18. John Pinkney, *Great Australian Mysteries*, Five Mile Press, Victoria, 2003.
19. Ruth Miles, Australian Associated Press report, 11 March 2003.
20. Beth Spencer, '101 Degrees', ABC Radio National's Radio Eye, 1997.

Chapter 9: The Anita Cobby Murder (1986)

1. Detective Sergeant Garry Heskett, 'Remembering the Anita Cobby Investigation', *Australian Police Journal*, March 2003.
2. Julia Sheppard, *Someone Else's Daughter: The life and death of Anita Cobby*, Ironbark Press, Sydney, 1991.
3. Detective Sergeant Garry Heskett.
4. Derrick Hand and Janet Fife-Yeomans, *The Coroner: Investigating sudden death*, ABC Books, Sydney, 2004.
5. Jenny Cooke, *Sydney Morning Herald*, 10 June 1987.
6. Michael Cordell, *Sydney Morning Herald*, 12 June 1987.
7. Derrick Hand and Janet Fife-Yeomans.

8. Michael Cordell.
9. Derrick Hand and Janet Fife-Yeomans.
10. Detective Sergeant Garry Heskett.
11. Anne Loxley, *Sydney Morning Herald*, 8 November 2002.
12. 'Anita & Beyond: The exhibition', *Australian Police Journal*, March 2003.
13. Anne Loxley.

Chapter 10: The Backpacker Murders (1996)

1. Sergeant Gerard Dutton, 'Belanglo Forest "Backpacker" Murders: forensic firearms evidence', *Australian Police Journal*, September 1999.
2. Sergeant Gerard Dutton.
3. *Telegraph Mirror*, 30 September 1992.
4. Sergeant Gerard Dutton.
5. Richard Shears, *Highway to Nowhere*, Harper Collins, Sydney, 1996.
6. Sergeant Gerard Dutton.
7. Richard Shears.
8. Sergeant Gerard Dutton.
9. Richard Shears.
10. Richard Shears.
11. *Sydney Morning Herald*, 15 December 2003.

Chapter 11: The Port Arthur Massacre (1996)

1. Peter Luck, *A Time to Remember*, William Heinemann, Victoria, 1988.
2. Peter Luck.
3. Margaret Scott, *A Story of Strength and Courage*, Random House, Sydney, 1997.
4. Margaret Scott.
5. *Where Were You When … The news that stopped a nation*, New Custom Publishing, Victoria, 2003.
6. *Where Were You When …*
7. *Where Were You When …*
8. Noel Eastwood, *Jung Meets Martin Bryant*, Federation of Australian Astrologers, Vol. 30/3, September 2000.
9. On Sunday night, 9 August 1987, Melbourne teenager Julian Knight killed seven people and injured another 19 in a sniping rampage in suburban Hoddle Street in North Fitzroy. The troubled 19-year-old, a Duntroon army reject, was jailed for 27 years to life. Four months later, former Melbourne law student Frank Vitkovic killed eight peo-

ple and wounded 17 others in the Australia Post building in Queens Street, Melbourne, before jumping to his death. The disturbed student, described as 'paranoid, psychotic and insane' was allegedly seeking revenge for a perceived betrayal by a former friend who worked at the offices. In August 1991, Sydney man Wade Frankum used a Chinese assault rifle and a large hunting knife to kill seven people at a Strathfield shopping centre before turning the gun on himself.

10. Margaret Scott.
11. Justice William Cox, *Comments on Passing Sentence on Martin Bryant*, David Syme & Co Ltd, Tasmania, 1997.
12. General Winfield Scott Hancock's remark concerned the fate of the four Civil War conspirators — Lewis Powell, George A. Atzerodt, David E. Herold and Mary Surratt — who were hanged for helping John Wilkes Booth plan the assassination of President Abraham Lincoln in 1865: '... let us remember their names no more'.

Chapter 12: The Norfolk Island Murder (2002)

1. All quotes, unless otherwise stated, are from Robert Peters' Statement in the Matter of the Death of Janelle Louise Patton, Norfolk Island Police, 5 May 2004.
2. Australian Associated Press report, 5 July 2004.

Index

Index

About the Author

Born in Penrith, New South Wales, in 1958, Alan J. Whiticker is the author of 14 books including *Say It Loud: Jimmy Barnes* (2002), *Wanda: The Untold Story of the Wanda Beach Murders* (2003), *A History of Rugby League Clubs* (2004, with Ian Collis) and *The Battle for Troy: An Adaptation of Homer's Iliad* (2004). Alan, who has pursued the dual careers of teacher and freelance writer since 1986, lives with his wife Karen and two children in Western Sydney.